Programmed Learning and

Computer-Based Instruction

PROGRAMMED LEARNING AND COMPUTER=BASED INSTRUCTION

Proceedings of the Conference on
*Application of Digital Computers
to Automated Instruction*

October 10–12, 1961

JOHN E. COULSON, EDITOR

System Development Corporation

Co-sponsored by Personnel and Training Branch and
Information Systems Branch of the Office of Naval Research,
and System Development Corporation

John Wiley and Sons, Inc.
New York   London

Library of Congress Catalog Number: 62-14648
Printed in the United States of America

FOREWORD

by Conference Co-Chairmen:

Glenn L. Bryan; Vance R. Wanner, *Office of Naval Research*

Launor F. Carter, *System Development Corporation*

It was inevitable that the areas of programmed learning and digital-computer utilization would overlap. The same onrush of technology which produced rapid and astonishing computer developments also created an insatiable requirement for new training. More and more people needed to learn technical information and to develop new skills. Interestingly enough, the popularity of digital computers themselves engendered tremendous training needs.

The men involved in the early developments of programmed instruction and those involved in the development of new computer uses were alike in many ways. They were innovators, eager to try out new things. They were revolutionaries, militantly attacking traditional procedures and established ways of doing things. And, as a result, both groups of innovators had to grow in the face of subtle (but real) opposition from established professions. Perhaps because of this opposition, and emboldened by early successes, both groups acquired tendencies toward self-reliance which sometimes led them to pursue independent developments in areas in which collaboration might have been possible. Meanwhile, many trainers and educators watched with interest to see whether they should open the door or bar it, whether to join the movement or oppose it. Although an improved instructional technology was desperately needed, serious doubts existed regarding the actual utility of educational notions spawned in the laboratories of the experimental psychologist and the engineer.

Undoubtedly this situation was apparent to all observers. But it was

v

nowhere more apparent than in ONR. Engineers were seeking support through the Information Sciences Branch on studies of how to teach. Psychologists were submitting proposals to the Personnel and Training Branch covering investigations of automated instructional systems controlled by digital computers. In spite of almost complete overlap of interest, neither the psychologist nor the computer specialist was well acquainted with the other's work. Both were intent upon independent development. It was fair to say that interest, sympathy, and understanding were often lacking.

Cross-pollination efforts were made by the two ONR branches involved, but additional efforts seemed indicated. Numerous informal discussions led to the idea of holding a large open meeting. Interested scientists and scholars from the three areas—programmed learning, computer use and development, and education—would be invited.

Several organizations indicated an interest in holding such a meeting. Ultimately the present three-way sponsorship agreement was reached, and a conference was held which sought to bring together scientists and educators interested in exploiting the potentialities of the digital computer for instructional purposes. It was hoped that it would promote understanding and useful collaborations which would, in turn, lead to a more orderly development of automated instruction.

The material in this volume is a direct outgrowth of that meeting.

GLENN L. BRYAN, Psychology Division, ONR
VANCE R. WANNER, Information Processing Division, ONR

AS INDICATED IN THE EARLIER PORTION OF THIS FOREWORD, there is a tendency for educators, psychologists, and information-processing experts to travel separate paths in their approach to education and training. However, it was only natural that when research in automated education was undertaken at the System Development Corporation the psychologists and educators involved turned to computer-based teaching machines.

The System Development Corporation had its beginnings in experimentation with, and the development of, a complex system training program based on materials developed through computer simulation. Since we had been deeply involved in developing both a training program and a computer programming system for the SAGE air defense systems, our training specialists had become intimately familiar with high-speed digital computers. Three years ago we decided to initiate a research program in automated education. After some preliminary experimentation with "branching" teaching materials, our psychologists and information processors devised an instructional system based on a digital computer. With this system they undertook additional research, some of which is reported in the journal literature and some in this book.

As Dr. Bryan and Commander Wanner indicate, ONR also saw the possibilities of combining the specialized skills of educators, psychologists, and information processors. As a result of our mutual perception of the advances that could result from combining the knowledge and efforts of these diverse groups, the System Development Corporation felt itself particularly fortunate to be able to join with the Office of Naval Research in sponsoring a Symposium on the Application of Digital Computers to Education.

LAUNOR F. CARTER, System Development Corporation

PREFACE

This book is based on the proceedings of the *Conference on Application of Digital Computers to Automated Instruction,* held in Washington, D. C., on October 10–12, 1961. Sponsoring agencies for the conference were the Personnel and Training Branch and the Information Systems Branch of the Office of Naval Research and System Development Corporation.

In early meetings of the sponsoring agencies it was decided that the conference proceedings should have three major parts. The first part was intended to provide a foundation of empirical data and theoretical structure concerning automated teaching and programmed learning. Speakers in this section summarized experimental findings obtained with a variety of research instruments ranging from specially organized textbooks to highly complex electromechanical systems. Other presentations included theoretical models of the underlying processes in automated teaching and programmed learning. Conclusions were drawn by some speakers concerning future directions for progress in these fields.

Whereas Part I represented a state-of-the-art summary of knowledge regarding the basic variables and methods of autoinstruction, Part II described current attempts to apply computing machinery to automated instruction. Although some experimental data were reported here, this section consisted largely of discussions of the factors leading to the development of computer-based instructional systems, of descriptions of the equipment and various methods used in the application of the equipment to specific learning situations, and of preliminary observations regarding the effectiveness of such equipment and procedures. A number of the speakers drew upon their knowledge of computer capabilities, and upon their experiences with computer-based instructional systems, to predict important roles for such systems in future schools.

Still further extrapolations were made by speakers in Part III, whose backgrounds were largely in the area of computer design and computer programming. These speakers based their predictions upon their intimate knowledge of computers, of developments already foreshadowing the coming improvement of computer hardware, and the simplification of communication between computers and humans. Problems as well as opportunities in the application of computers to instruction were discussed.

General conference chairmen were Glenn L. Bryan and Commander Vance R. Wanner (USN), representing the Office of Naval Research, and Launor F. Carter, representing System Development Corporation. The welcome was presented by F. J. Weyl, ONR. Session chairmen for the five sessions were G. L. Bryan, D. Madden, D. G. Ryans, R. Trumbull, and Commander V. R. Wanner (USN).

The organization of this book corresponds closely to that of the conference. Some changes have been made in the order of papers to allow a tighter structure of the three major parts. Three papers have been omitted from the book. Heinz Von Foerster of the University of Illinois was originally scheduled to speak but was unable to attend the conference for reasons of health. A. J. Perlis of the Carnegie Institute of Technology and S. N. Alexander of the National Bureau of Standards presented papers at the conference, but these papers were not available for inclusion in the book.

The paper authored by R. E. Dear and R. C. Atkinson was delivered at the conference by Dr. Atkinson.

Panel discussions, which were held after each of the three major conference sessions, are not reproduced in this book. A number of the authors, however, have added sections to their original papers to clarify points raised during these discussions.

As may be expected in any interdisciplinary consideration of a complex problem, the level of specificity and technicality varies widely among these papers. Some authors have restricted themselves largely to their own area of particular professional competence; these papers generally contain considerable technical detail, couched in the specialized language of the author's own skill area. Other authors have viewed the problems of automated instruction from a more eclectic position and have attempted to bridge the gap among the various skill areas. These papers are stated at a more general level and are addressed to a broader audience. Those that discuss concepts outside the author's primary skill area may in some cases appear elementary to the specialist in the field concerned.

Some editorial changes have been made in the papers, particularly to increase uniformity of format. In most cases their basic content and the individual writing styles of the authors have been retained without serious modification. Nevertheless, some slight shifts of interpretation or emphasis may have occurred within the papers. The full responsibility for such unintentional alterations must rest with the editor.

Where differences exist in practice regarding hyphenation of words, a fairly arbitrary editorial choice has been made to bring consistency among the various papers. In one or two specific instances, however, the author has indicated a particularly strong preference for a spelling or hyphenation that is not consistent with the rest of the papers; such preferences have been respected in the reproduction of these chapters.

I am particularly grateful for the assistance of Mr. Lorimer McConnell, Head of the Editorial Liaison Office at SDC, whose editorial experience played a large role in guiding the many coordinative activities required in the preparation of this book. Thanks are also due to Mr. Claude Baum and Mrs. Ruth Keane for their help in the proofreading; to Mr. Thomas Steel, for his assistance in editing one of the more technical papers; to Miss Christine Marcy and Mrs. Eva Kansor for their patient and expert typing help; and to my wife Anne for her assistance in preparation of the materials.

JOHN E. COULSON

Santa Monica, California
March 1962

CONTENTS

PART II   Computer-Based Instructional Systems

PART III   Computer Technology in Automated Teaching

PART I

Theory and

Experimentation

in Programmed

Learning

The challenge of automation in education

LAUNOR F. CARTER

System Development Corporation

Other chapters of this book contain technical information on the progress of automated education, in its research and developmental aspects. In contrast, this chapter presents the challenge of automation in education; it is a philosophical and speculative consideration.

The Image of the School

To see what this challenge is, let us look first at the popular idea of the educational system. Our image of "the school" is usually a large square room with about 40 pupils seated at rows of desks; some books are open and a teacher is lecturing. This popular picture is probably the same today as it was two or three hundred years ago. Since the time of Socrates there have certainly been the teacher and pupils; for the last three or four hundred years there have been books. These three ingredients—pupils, the teacher, and books—have constituted the important parts of all educational systems.

Is it not surprising that today's picture of the education process is so similar to the picture that was held hundreds of years ago? There are few other areas in modern life in which this is still true. The great impact of technology has been felt in almost all other fields. Farming, transportation, and homemaking, the basic occupations of mankind over the centuries, are all viewed today in terms of a highly complex technology; in terms of tractors and mechanized farm equipment; in terms of airplanes, trains, and cars; in terms of electric stoves, refrigerators, vacuum cleaners, and frozen food. Most of this change has come about within the last hundred years, and great changes are still taking place with dramatic rapidity. Yet in education the impact of technology has had only a nominal effect.

Some time ago a Sunday comic strip pictured education in the classroom of tomorrow. It showed many ingredients of the technological change which is discussed in this book. In the picture the pupil was seen at an individual console which allowed him to receive instruction over television or to have individual instructional material presented by a teaching machine. He could be asked questions and respond to them and immediately be shown how well he did. There were motivational devices such as lights and bells.

This may, indeed, be the way in which much of our education will be presented 20 years from now. But what forces are going to bring this about? What are today's developments which may make this science-fiction comic strip the classroom of tomorrow?

In thinking about these questions, I asked myself, "What are the goals of education?" "What are we trying to achieve?" In giving you my answers, my frame of reference is the child from the age of 5 or 6 up to 16 or 17; thus I am going to consider the situation in what we commonly refer to as the public schools (although I think my statements—particularly the system of analysis I am going to illustrate—can be applied equally well to training in industry or in the military). I suggest that we attempt to understand the impact of automation on education by engaging in armchair analysis of the educational situation as it concerns children in this age group. A really thorough system analysis would demand a great deal of careful data collection, study, and analysis. By contrast, what I present here are personal, rather carefully thought out but idiosyncratic ideas about the educational system.

The Goals of an Educational System

Initially we should ask, "What are the goals of a modern system of education?" Table 1 lists some of the goals. Most people think these are important in the development of the child as he progresses toward adulthood; many would agree that these goals to a large extent fall outside the immediate, primary responsibility shouldered by the parents.

The first goal shown in Table 1 is to impart subject matter. Most of us forget how much content matter the young child must learn and

TABLE 1   PARTIAL LIST OF
EDUCATIONAL SYSTEM GOALS

1. Imparting subject matter
2. Training in thinking and creativity
3. Developing skills and techniques
4. Developing attitudes
5. Socializing
6. Physical development
7. "Child care"

how rapidly the bulk of it is increasing. So we have a great need to increase the efficiency with which pure content is transmitted to the learner.

The second goal of the educational system is to develop within the individual an ability to reason and to think, to be creative in attacking life's problems. Some will say that the schools are not giving adequate training in this area, yet a great deal of school time is actually devoted to this subject. When we compare the naïve first grader with the high school senior, it is apparent that the school or some like experiences must have trained the individual or developed in him certain capacities to reason and think.

The third goal of any educational system is to develop skills and techniques. For example, the student must be taught to write, to manipulate equipment, to drive a car, and so on. Particularly among those who will enter the skilled or semiskilled occupations, the development of skills such as welding or metal working or the development of the agricultural skills is of tremendous importance.

The educational system also has a great responsibility for developing desirable attitudes. Of course, other sectors of the child's environment (the home, for example) also have a responsibility in this area. It is in the educational system, however, that much of the common and uniform attitude development takes place.

Another goal, particularly for younger children, is the development of a certain degree of socialization. Training children to live in reasonable peace with other children and later, in teen age, meeting the need for a certain amount of heterosexual experience is an important aim of child development.

Still another goal is physical training. As our culture continues its trend toward urbanization, physical development and training away from the home become more and more important.

Finally, the child-care function is a goal of many educational systems. In many cases it is desirable to get the child out of the home for extended periods of time. This helps to develop socialization and to give broadening experiences. In many families it frees the mother to work and to take part in activities which need to be carried out away from the home. In this way the school serves a very real purpose in our general scheme of urban life.

Some will disagree with this analysis of the particular goals of the educational systems. They will want to change the emphasis, delete some goals, or add others. This is not critical to the general argument, which leads us next to consider various implications of the goals with regard to the context through which they can be achieved.

Achieving the Goals in an Educational System

Certain techniques are needed to achieve a system of education which will lead to the goals I have described. Table 2 shows an analysis of various considerations. On the left the seven goals are listed again. The columns permit us to consider the goals from particular points of view, emphasizing the appropriateness of a particular set of questions toward the achievement of each of the goals. Table 2 uses a five-point scale: capital "YES" indicates that the question can be answered very strongly; small "yes" indicates a little uncertainty; a question mark indicates neutrality or real uncertainty whether the particular goal can be achieved through this agency; small "no" and capital "NO" are self-explanatory.

TABLE 2   CONSIDERATIONS IN ACHIEVING EDUCATIONAL-SYSTEM GOALS

	Individual Activity?	Adult Required?	Home Adequate?	Books Adequate?	Teaching Machine Adequate?
1. Subject-matter training	yes	NO	yes	yes	yes
2. Thinking and creativity	yes	?	yes	?	?
3. Skill development	yes	yes	NO	NO	NO
4. Attitude development	yes	yes	yes	yes	?
5. Socialization	NO	yes	NO	NO	NO
6. Physical development	yes	NO	yes	NO	NO
7. "Child care"	YES	yes	NO	NO	NO

Let us consider the column headed "Individual Activity?." Here we ask whether the particular goal can be accomplished by the learner as an individual (i.e., without interaction with teachers or other students). The table indicates that some goals could be achieved without interaction with others, the "yes's." However, Socialization seems to require other people with whom to socialize; almost by definition, Socialization cannot be accomplished through individual effort. The answers to this question thus suggest that most of our educational goals could be achieved without interaction between individuals. We could put a child into a cubicle or leave him in the home and still accomplish most of the goals.

The second column asks, "Is an adult essential to the achievement of this particular goal?" In subject-matter training, for instance, an adult is not required. Subject matter can be taught through means other than personal transmission by an adult. Could thinking also be trained without an adult? Here we are not so sure. Certainly books or other techniques are useful, but thinking and creativity which are acceptable to our culture probably demand interaction with adults. You will note that skill and attitude development, socialization, and child-care also probably require the presence of an adult. Of course, the answer to these questions will vary somewhat, depending on the age of the particular learner.

In the third column we ask whether or not the home is an adequate environment in which to fulfill the educational aim. With adequate automation techniques and television, the home might well become the center for training; yet this question is answered with three strong "NO's." In the area of skill development, many homes are not likely to be equipped for, let us say, instruction in welding or in metal working; presumably the home could be so equipped, but it would be expensive and uneconomical to do so. As for socializing, it requires the child to interact with other children; in many homes there is no opportunity for this process. Finally, the home is not adequate for child care—that is, for getting the child out of the home to release the parents for other activities. The question "Home Adequate?" leads to the conclusion that some kind of an educational setting outside the home is required for achieving many of our educational goals. This conclusion leads to the further conclusion that we need centralized buildings and grounds in which education can take place.

In the next column we ask whether books by themselves are adequate to achieve the particular educational goals. One is rather surprised in looking at the results to see how many of the goals do not seem to be dependent on books. Only subject-matter training and attitude development place a clear dependence on books, with a less sure note regarding thinking and creativity; skill development, socialization, physical development, and child care seem to be independent of books. This is surprising when we recall that the popular stereotype of education is so often associated with "book learning."

Finally, we consider whether the teaching machine is an adequate instrument for achieving the various goals; again, it is surprising to see only one "yes" for all of the goals listed. The teaching machine can be used to transmit subject matter. There is more debate about whether thinking and creativity or attitude development are effectively fostered by teaching machines. It is surprising that so few of the goals seem to be adequately met by them.

After analyzing Table 2, we can conclude that a well-rounded education which attempts to achieve the goals listed requires that adults be involved—that is, teachers participating in the educational process. Second, it is probably necessary to have this process take place in a special setting—that is, separate from the home. We can also conclude that other children must be involved, that the learner cannot achieve all of the goals listed by himself. Finally, we can conclude that books are required but do not play the dominant role usually supposed and that teaching machines will probably play an equally restricted role.

Technology in the Educational System

Having concluded that we need school systems in much the same setting as we now know them, it is interesting to look more closely at the way in which various new techniques might be applied in the educational system to assist in some of the functions which are essential to achieving the goals we have discussed. Table 3 shows educational-system functions broken into a number of the detailed activities necessary to achieve the goals we have considered. Grouped together at the top of Table 3 are activities dealing with instruction (the transmission of information, attitudes, etc.); in the middle of the table are the functions connected with guidance; administrative activities are at the bottom of the table. How can these activities be served by simple punch-card equipment, by digital computers, by teaching machines, and by other special aids?

Let us look at the column headed "Punch-Card Equipment." Inter-

TABLE 3   EDUCATIONAL-SYSTEM ACTIVITIES AND TECHNOLOGY

System Activity	Punch-Card Equipment	Computers	Teaching Machines	Special Aids
Instruction				
1. Classroom instruction	NO	yes	YES	YES
2. Homeroom period	NO	yes	YES	YES
3. Laboratory work	NO	yes	YES	YES
4. Physical training	NO	yes	yes	YES
5. Driver education	NO	yes	yes	YES
6. Library work	yes	yes	yes	yes
Guidance				
7. Student guidance	YES	YES	NO	NO
8. Testing for guidance and content	YES	YES	YES	YES
9. Registration	YES	YES	NO	NO
10. Room assignment and scheduling	YES	YES	NO	NO
Administration				
11. Cumulative record keeping	YES	YES	NO	NO
12. Report-card preparation	YES	YES	NO	NO
13. School personnel records	YES	yes	NO	NO
14. Fiscal records and control	YES	YES	NO	NO
15. School logistics	YES	YES	NO	NO
16. Administrative planning	YES	YES	NO	NO

estingly, punch-card equipment does not seem to contribute at all to the immediate goal of transmitting information to the students or in helping to achieve the more traditional educational goals. However, when we come down to the necessary but less training-oriented activities such as registration and room assignment, we see that punch-card equipment can make a contribution; it certainly can be used in such areas as personnel records, property records, and control of school logistics.

Turning to the column headed "Computers," it is surprising to see all "yes's"; the computer could be used in all these activities. It clearly could be used in those places where it is indicated that punch-card equipment could be used, but it could also be used in classroom instruction, laboratory work, and the like if we recognize that a computer could be an integral part of a teaching-machine installation in a school.

The next column asks whether teaching machines could be useful in all these school activities. (It is assumed here that we are talking about teaching machines which are not computer-based. If we were talking about a computer-based teaching machine, we would combine the two columns "Teaching Machine" and "Computer.") In this "Teaching Machines" column we notice that the teaching machine can be used for all of the instructional activities, including physical training. A certain amount of physical training is the transmission of information about the body and its control, about posture, etc.; this information can be given on a teaching machine. Certain aspects of the strategy and tactics of field games can also be taught by teaching machines. Going beyond the instructional and library areas, a "YES" has been noted for the use of teaching machines in testing for guidance and content. Obviously, a teaching machine can indicate very satisfactorily the progress a student is making; it can also be of great assistance in guidance. In registration, assignment, record keeping, etc., the teaching machine does not seem particularly useful.

The fourth column, "Special Aids," includes all the many audio-visual and training aids which can be produced by our advanced technology. Television, films, devices for driver education, and micro-film readers for the library (to mention only a few) can be very useful in the educational system. We should not lose sight of the fact that many aids besides teaching machines can perform functions better than teaching machines. (Some might object to the "NO" for record keeping and the functions which follow it, but we do not include standard bookkeeping-type equipment under the heading of training aids.)

A surprising conclusion can be drawn from Table 3: computers (and teaching machines which have a computer base) can serve all of the different educational-system activities that we have considered. From Table 2 we concluded that teaching machines have a relatively limited role in achieving a number of educational goals. From Table 3, however, we conclude that teaching machines, particularly those based on a computer, can be used very widely throughout a school system to achieve various system activities. Superficially, these two conclusions seem incongruous. They can be reconciled if we note that Table 3 asks a somewhat more limited question than the one that was asked in Table 2. In Table 2 we asked if the particular goal could be achieved almost exclusively through the teaching machine or the book; in Table 3 we ask if a teaching machine could be useful in a significant way in particular activities. (We are not considering the more stringent question—whether the teaching machine could completely fulfill the requirements in any particular category.)

Table 3 appears to validate the germaneness of our conference. It seems to indicate that, indeed, it would be useful—perhaps extremely useful—if computer-based teaching machines and computers themselves were introduced into the educational system. They would help to fulfill an important function in all of the many different activities listed. The question is often raised whether school systems can possibly afford large general-purpose computers. Perhaps not now, but with the new developments in computer technology just over the horizon, we would be foolish not to start thinking and experimenting now. Other chapters in this volume have more to say on this point, but I for one am convinced that in the long run economics never stands in the way of technology.

Automation and School Personnel

Finally, we should consider the impact of automation on school personnel. Let us start by assuming that automation has been rather completely introduced into the school system; that teaching machines are used for the rapid transmission of information; and that computers and punch-card equipment are in use in the other areas of school activity.

First a word about automation and the teacher. In a brochure produced by one of the more aggressive organizations selling self-tutoring equipment we find the question, "Will the teaching machine ever replace the classroom teachers?" The brochure's answer is, "This is not its purpose nor its function. The teaching machine simply presents the student with information about a subject in step-by-step fashion. The teacher is free to spend more time on planning, discussion, and the problems of the individual child." This answer really begs the question. We should face up to the fact that the teaching machine will some day absorb many of the teacher's present activities, particularly in transmitting content and information. The teaching machine will largely change the role of the teacher, so that the teacher will have the opportunity to take on different activities, such as those having to do with the socialization of the child and with the transmission of attitudes rather than with content transmission. It seems that this will be a more difficult and demanding role for the teacher. It seems that this role will be one that true professionals will welcome.

Similarly, the role of guidance personnel will change. Hopefully, the present rigidly compartmentalized class-year system will be broken down in many areas, and the student will be allowed to progress at a speed which corresponds to his particular abilities. Children of quite different chronological ages will study material appropriate to their individual abilities, not their age classification. This will require much more careful guidance and planning of the student's progress, paying close attention to the student's ability and to his long-range goals. The introduction of better data-handling systems will permit much more intensive guidance. It may be that a new profession will grow up which might be named "Program Planner." The Program Planner could be given responsibility for planning a student's educational career over a long period of time; he would remain the major consultant to the student for five or six chronological years. Through the increased information available and through more adequate checks on progress, we would be able to administer a much more coherent educational program than is currently the case.

These rather visionary and speculative thoughts provide a framework around which the more technical presentation can be organized. If imaginatively applied, many of the new developments presented in later chapters will be at the heart of our educational system of tomorrow.

Characteristics of some recent studies of instructional methods

HARRY F. SILBERMAN

System Development Corporation

Automated teaching seems to be one of those topics on which almost everyone has an opinion. In the last three years the frequency of articles on this subject has increased at an exponential rate. It is becoming increasingly difficult to distinguish between published statements that are based on experimental data and those that are based on faith, enthusiasm, and overgeneralization from anecdotal observation. In order to gain perspective and to clarify some of the issues, we have conducted a review of the literature.[1]

Articles on programmed instruction cluster into three groups: popular surveys, programming experiments, and field studies. Like the three blind men, each of these clusters tells a different story. The popular literature is optimistic, the experiments on programming are pessimistic, and the field studies hover between these poles. One thesis of this paper is that this apparent conflict is resolved by distinguishing between a science of programming and a technology of education.

The General Literature

The first, and by far the largest, group of articles consists of general essays that have appeared in the popular literature. Such articles

[1] Mr. Melvin Croner abstracted the articles summarized in this chapter. The bibliography is filed as Document No. 7126 with the ADI Auxiliary Service, Library of Congress, Washington, D. C. A copy may be secured by citing the document number and by remitting $3.75 for photoprints or $2.00 for 35-mm microfilm. Make checks or money orders payable to: Chief, Photoduplication Service, Library of Congress.

optimistically describe programmed learning as a highly profitable, though somewhat controversial, technological revolution in the application of learning laws in the classroom. In general, this literature has made a promise of dramatic improvement in education; this promise has excited the public imagination and paved the way for educational innovation. Whether we are ready to deliver on this promise depends on the science of programming and the development of a technology of education.

Programming Experiments

A second cluster of articles centers on the science of programming. More than a hundred studies in the last three years report the results of experimental variation of programs. Yet the research evidence on the science of programming has barely scratched the surface. Beyond demonstrating that a carefully written set of materials will teach if a student will spend enough time studying them, we have little unequivocal evidence for principles of programmed instruction. Ideally, it would be desirable to identify specific structural features of programs which invariably contribute to their effectiveness. This would greatly simplify the evaluation of programs; unfortunately, such relationships have not been established.

The studies on programming explore problems that are primarily extensions of laboratory studies of learning. They have concentrated on three problem areas. The first problem area concerns the definition of the responses the student makes to the items. This includes comparisons of different response modes. A second problem area centers on the methods of eliciting the desired responses from the student. This includes the problems of step size and sequencing and the comparisons of different prompting and confirmation methods. The third problem area centers on the adaptation of programs to individual differences. This includes the problems of branching, pacing, and repetition.

Table 1 shows some of the characteristics of experiments on programmed instruction. Most of the studies were conducted in the last three years, using adults who were required to serve as subjects.

Short linear constructed-response programs in mathematics, science, or languages were generally used. More than half the studies were conducted without the benefit of a machine. Only one of the studies reported used a computer.

TABLE 1   CHARACTERISTICS OF 80 STUDIES ON PROGRAMMED INSTRUCTION

Machine	45%	Constructed response	70%
No machine	55%	Multiple choice	30%
100 items or less	60%	Studies prior to 1959	30%
More than 100 items	40%	1959 or later	70%
Adults or college students	80%	Student volunteers	20%
Public school students	20%	Required participation	80%
Math-science-language	60%	Linear items	85%
All other subjects	40%	Branching items	15%

Table 2 summarizes the results of experiments on the step size, sequencing, and confirmation variables. Of five studies comparing small-step with large-step programs, four favored the small-step program with respect to learning score on a posttest. With respect to training time, all five studies favored the large-step programs, which took less time than the longer small-step programs. Of three studies comparing logically sequenced with randomly sequenced programs, two showed no difference between them in learning or in time, and the third favored an ordered sequence. Twelve studies made some form of comparison between a prompting and a confirmation procedure. In the conventional confirmation procedure the stimulus term is presented, followed by a student response, and then the response term is

TABLE 2   STUDIES ON METHODS OF ELICITING THE CORRECT RESPONSE

	Score	Time		Score	Time
Small step	4	0	Prompting	7	10
Large step	0	5	Confirmation	2	0
No difference	1	0	No difference	3	2
Ordered sequence	1	1			
Random sequence	0	0			
No difference	2	2			

Note. Entries in Tables 2 to 5 designate the number of studies yielding superiority in criterion score or training time for the indicated experimental conditions.

giving one group extra information or added training time, may disappear on transfer tests given after short retention intervals, but such measures are seldom reported. In short, we find that the experimental literature does not agree with the overly optimistic picture conveyed in the popular literature.

Field Studies

Articles in the third cluster generally report the results of field tests, featuring global comparisons of programmed and conventional instruction. These studies are summarized in Table 5.

Of 15 studies comparing programmed instruction with conventional instruction, nine favored the programmed methods on learning scores and six showed no differences between them. In all 15 studies the programmed groups took less time than the conventional groups.

Seven studies compared the effectiveness of programmed instruction with and without the use of a machine. Six studies showed no difference and one favored the programmed instruction without the machine. Of these seven studies, four favored the programmed text or programmed lecture with respect to time.

The results of field studies generally favor programmed over conventional instruction. There is some indication, however, that the students in many of the conventional classes that have fixed training intervals may not be receiving the same material or may not be using their time as efficiently as they could, because comparisons of programmed lectures, programmed textbooks, and programmed machines yield no significant differences.

TABLE 5   GLOBAL COMPARISON FIELD STUDIES

	Score	Time
Programming methods	9	15
Conventional instruction	0	0
No difference	6	0
	Score	Time
Teaching machine	0	0
Programmed text or lecture	1	4
No difference	6	3

In studies comparing conventional and programmed instruction the programmed groups usually take less training time. Perhaps the experimental groups work only on test-relevant material, whereas control groups cover a wider range of topics. Conditions of conventional instruction are seldom described in such reports. The "Hawthorne" or novelty effect may also be operating here.

Although the global-comparison field studies have not contributed much to the science of instructional programming, they have served to lend perspective to the different factors that can make a technology of education. They have shown that programming is just a part of the problem.

Field tests have uncovered at least six practical problems that must be considered if the technology of programmed learning on a broad scale is to be realized.

1. Teacher and student motivation is a part of the problem. The field tests have indicated that teacher attitude is a major variable; some classes taught with programmed materials alone, without the help of a teacher, proved superior to classes using the same material with the help of a teacher with a negative attitude.

2. Obtaining agreement on, and complete specification of, behavioral goals is a major issue. Questions have been raised by teachers who think that the range of behavioral objectives and the depth of the repertoire being shaped by hastily prepared programs are too limited and circumscribed.

3. The logistics for the production of quality programs for the total school sequence is still unsolved. If educators are forced to choose between an insufficient supply of quality programs and a plentiful supply of programs of inferior quality, they may choose the inferior programs with subsequent disenchantment.

4. Methods of using programs in the schools are still to be specified. Are they to be used in a fashion more analogous to the teacher or to the textbook? What is their period of use and who revises and improves them? Some of the radical changes predicted earlier for grading, testing, and grouping practices appear less imminent now.

5. Some reports indicate that the introduction of programs may accentuate the problems of individual differences in schools, particularly when half the students either have trouble reading or simply do not want to learn.

6. Maintenance problems have also been observed. If teachers, the

majority of whom are women, fail at machine repair and find the machines to be more trouble than textbooks, we can expect strong resistance to the revolution.

In short, the field studies have been both optimistic and pessimistic.

A Distinction between the Science of Programming and the Technology of Education

Perhaps we need to adopt a dual strategy for implementing the technological revolution. On the one hand, we have a science of programming, concerned with explanation and prediction, which should never be in a position of mustering evidence to justify practical commitments. Doubt and critical attitudes are required in this venture. Although field realities must be considered as a major source of hypotheses, they must not be permitted to distort the controls that are necessary to develop a valid theory of programming. Long-term studies and model building are required for a science of programming.

On the other hand, attitudes of doubt and suspended judgment may be inappropriate strategy for educational innovation in which social change and control are the objectives. A different stance is required for effective implementation of those procedures that, on the basis of current evidence, offer the greatest promise. Such procedures, whether they be programmed textbooks or computer-controlled teaching machines, should be advanced with faith, conviction, and careful attention to the practical economic and political problems of instituting a change within a school system.

Because these research and implementation strategies are quite different, I suggest that a clear distinction be made between the science of programming and the technology of education. The apparent inconsistencies in the literature are, at least in part, a result of not making this distinction. The scientist who attempts a field study with the dual purpose of building a science of programming, and at the same time innovating a technology of education, may achieve neither goal. As Hilgard [2] has indicated, we should maintain a division of labor between science and technology with free flow of two-way communication and an equitable distribution of prestige between those who

[2] Hilgard, E. R. Learning theory and its application. *New teaching aids for the American classroom.* Stanford, California: Institute for Communications Research, 1960.

work in science and those in the fields of application. If this division of labor is obtained, we may expect to realize many of the potential advantages of programmed learning.

Significance of the New Technology

The most significant advantage of programmed learning may well be its stimulation of a sense of cause or mission in education. This renewed excitement, which has been dormant since the 1930's, will probably result in improvement in at least five areas by 1965:

1. More carefully written textbooks will be published.
2. Instruction will be directly contingent on frequent testing.
3. There will be a greater relative emphasis on development of instructional materials in contrast to the presentation of those materials.
4. A greater effort will be devoted to the maintenance or retention of learning in contrast to its acquisition.
5. A greater emphasis will be placed on specifying the behavioral goals of education.

The Role of Computers in the Future of Programmed Instruction

With respect to the role of hardware in the developing technology of programmed instruction, it is evident that simplified teaching machines are already taking their place in the arsenal of teaching aids along with films, language laboratories, and television. By 1965 there may be some experimental projects using computers in the classroom, but, in general practice, the role of computers will still be limited to noninstructional purposes such as school-data processing, record retrieval, administrative studies, and research.

If we extrapolate from current research on computers, however, we obtain a more encouraging estimate of the role that computers might play in educational practice a few decades from now. Rapid developments in the areas of automatic programming, artificial intelligence, language translation, and information retrieval suggest several possibilities for the future of programmed instruction.

With the application of some of these methods, computers might well be used in the *preparation* of instructional programs as well as in their presentation. Computer programmers have written compilers to save themselves the laborious task of coding problems in machine language. The compiler will accept from the programmer powerful instructions representing operations that involve many machine instructions. It will translate the macroinstructions of the programmer into a computer program, recorded in machine language, that consists of a larger number of machine instructions.

Instead of programming computer behavior, the educator is programming human behavior. The preparation of a set of teaching items is now comparable to writing computer instructions in machine language. A separate item is written by the instructional programmer for each student response. We may expect in the future that compilers will be written for the preparation of instructional programs in much the same way that they have been written for computer programs. The instructional compiler might include verbs such as REVIEW or TEST, which involve a large number of item-sequencing operations.

Inputs to the instructional compiler would consist of molar statements, in a problem-oriented language, about the existing response repertoire of the learner, the educational objectives of the program, and prestored items in a fact-retrieval system. Items would be indexed by teaching function, sequential rules, and other taxonomic labels. The output would be a detailed instructional program ready to be presented and adapted to the individual student by a self-organizing teaching machine.

The self-organizing teaching machine may represent an advanced stage in computer design. In these machines methods that prove to be most effective might be weighted so that their teaching will improve with time. Precise learning models might also be incorporated in their circuitry. Discrepancies between predictions of student behavior and their actual behavior would be used to modify these models to fit the students better.

Special-purpose teaching systems will probably be designed for different types of learning. One system may be concerned with reading or arithmetic skills. Another may be designed as a special diagnostic and remedial tool for improving decision making or inductive reasoning. A speculative example of a diagnostic-remedial system is provided in Fig. 1.

The right-hand portion of Fig. 1 represents the student, with a number of mental processing stages. I have included three cognitive stages here for the purpose of illustration only. Many different models

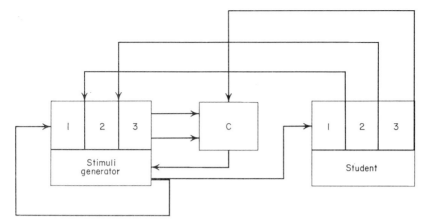

Fig. 1. Diagnostic-remedial teaching system.

of cognitive function would be equally appropriate. There could, of course, be more than three stages involved. Let us assume that stage 1 represents some form of perceptual coding of external stimuli. Whether the encoding process is a random storage operation, or occurs according to some hierarchical list structure, is not relevant to this example. The purpose here is to illustrate a possible remedial-diagnostic design for some future teaching system. Let stage 2 represent an association process, whereby connective relationships are established among the encoded elements in storage. Stage 3 can represent a response formation process. The left side of the figure represents a machine that contains an *ideal* set of mental processing stages; these stages constitute the educational objectives of the system. A stimuli generator, also included in this machine, operates under control of a comparator mechanism for presentation of stimuli to the student. The comparator is labeled C in the figure.

Stimuli are presented to the student and responses are output at different stages of mediational processing. The ability to tap different stages of mediation in the student must await further development of such methods as Osgood's "semantic differential."

Operation of this system would typically proceed as follows: identical stimuli from the generator will be input both to the student and to the machine itself. The output of stage 1 processing in the student will be input to stage 2 of the machine and will subsequently be processed by stage 3 in the machine. The output data that have been partially processed by the student will be compared with the data that have been processed only by the machine stages. If the student's output does not reach the standard set by the machine, the comparator will signal the generator to present coding exercises to the student. When the coding exercises have brought the student's performance to the required level, the comparator will signal the generator to present the next set of stimuli. This time the output from stage 2 in the student will serve as an input to stage 3 in the machine. Another discrepancy in the comparator would indicate trouble in the association function of the student, and association exercises will be generated for the student. When the comparator signal is null, the next set of stimuli is presented to the student. The output of stage 3 will be input directly into the comparator. A discrepancy here would indicate trouble in response formation, and the generator would exercise this function.

This system will be recognized as the troubleshooting technique of signal tracing. Extrapolations such as these will appear less speculative when viewed in the context of the following chapters, in which current work with computer-controlled teaching systems is described.

Optimal allocation of items in a simple, two-concept automated teaching model

ROBERT E. DEAR

System Development Corporation

RICHARD C. ATKINSON

Stanford University

The need for rules that dictate the best ways to branch among various types of items in automated teaching programs seems to be well recognized by researchers in this teaching field. To our knowledge, the research concerning branching procedures that has been carried out is entirely of the nature of comparative, empirical studies. In these studies several alternative branching rules and associated sets of items are developed for a particular subject-matter area, and experiments are then carried out to estimate which of the several rules considered leads to most efficient teaching.

Role of Mathematical Models of Teaching Programs

It is easily shown that as the number of items used in a program becomes even moderately large, and the branching conditions are allowed to be moderately complex, the number of possible branching patterns or item sequences rapidly becomes so large that only very partial exploration of the set of all possible sequences can be done through purely empirical research. We have chosen, therefore, to view the branching problem from the standpoint of first developing a mathematical model of a teaching program and then trying to deduce for this model the branching or item allocation rules that should be followed to achieve efficient teaching.

It seems apparent to us that very little progress toward the solution of the branching problem in teaching programs can be made unless satisfactory mathematical theories of the design of teaching programs are developed. It does not seem necessary to present any argument here in support of the use of mathematical models in social science research, as the value of this method of study is now widely accepted. However, we would like to make note of the successes that mathematical modeling has had in three related social science areas, with the hope that the researchers in these areas might be attracted to considering the branching problem in teaching programs.

The three related research areas whose problems appear to overlap considerably with the problems met in designing teaching programs are (1) mathematical learning theory, (2) the theory of item analysis and test design for aptitude or ability measurement, and (3) mathematical programming of the type that has been developed for dynamic problems such as inventory control and production scheduling. We use a certain mathematical learning theory as the principal tool for developing the teaching model that is the main topic of this report, so that we do not need to make further introductory comments about the overlap of this theory with problems in automated teaching.

There are problems, such as the control of errors of measurement and the selection of best subsets of items, that arise in the design of teaching programs, and these, of course, are central topics in mathematical theories of ability test design such as developed by Lord (1952) and Solomon et al. (1961). Numerous successful applications have been made of mathematical programming models to optimization problems which are similar to the branching problem in teaching programs. Important examples of these mathematical theories will be found in the books by Arrow, Karlin, & Scarf (1958) and Bellman (1957).

It is characteristic of mathematical studies of this kind that a number of assumptions must be made concerning basic variables of these models, such as demand functions and storage costs or item characteristic functions and distributions of ability. We recognize that the realization of these assumptions in specific applications of the mathematical theories requires careful specification of the particular variables that will be used in the models, and often a good deal of preliminary assessment must be done to insure that required properties of these variables can be assumed to hold satisfactorily. The worth of such a model in application to a particular practical problem is contingent, then, not only upon the appropriateness of the formulation of the model but also upon the appropriateness of the operational definitions of the variables used in the model.

The mathematical model of a teaching process that is developed in subsequent parts of this report is concerned with a simple situation in which only two concepts are being taught. The two concepts are embodied in two classes of statistically equivalent items. By statistically equivalent, we mean that the administration of two items from the same class at different trials can be considered as two replications of the identical statistical experiment. We shall refer to the two concepts as concept A and concept B and the items which are the components of these two classes or sets as type A items and type B items. Concept A is assumed to be easier to learn than concept B, and furthermore mastery of concept A is assumed to have positive transfer effects on the subsequent rate of learning the more difficult concept B.

Optimal Allocation of Items

We wish to examine various allocation rules or branching procedures to determine the best ways of sequencing type A items with type B items in order to achieve, in some sense, the best teaching program. Among the parameters of stochastic learning models of the kind that we are considering here two sets are directly accessible to control by the experimenter—the parameters that define reinforcement schedules and those that define conditions under which items of type A or of type B should be given at the next trial, provided that particular patterns of success or failure on the different types of items have occurred. We are concerned only with controlling the latter set of parameters. This set is referred to as the *item allocation parameters*. For our purposes, it is sufficient to assume that a fixed reinforcement schedule is followed in all situations.

A number of reasonable criteria for judging "bestness" of alternative allocation schedules could be put forth. For learning processes of the kind that we are considering in this chapter, many of the alternative criteria that seem appropriate take the form of minimizing the expected values of certain random variables. We have chosen in the present case to evaluate item allocation rules against the criterion of minimizing the expected number of trials to achieve conditioning on items of type B.

The Basic Learning Model

We have chosen to use as a model of the learning processes involved in these teaching situations a special case of a general class of models which are referred to in the literature as stimulus-sampling models. Learning models of this type were initially developed by Estes. A thorough discussion of the underlying structure of such models will be found in articles by Estes (1959a, 1959b) and in a report by Estes & Suppes (1959). We make use of a simple version of the stimulus-sampling models in this chapter. This version is frequently referred to as the single-element stimulus-sampling model. The basic axioms for single-element models are given by Bower (1961) and Atkinson & Estes (1962). This model has been found to give quite good predictions for a number of different learning situations (e.g., Suppes & Atkinson, 1960; Estes, 1961; Bower, 1961; Suppes & Ginsberg, 1961).

Single-Element Stimulus-Sampling Model

If we were considering the teaching of only a single concept, such as that represented in the type A items, then a learning model could be set up for the teaching of this concept as a two-state Markov chain. We would take as the states of this chain the elementary events that either (1) conditioning has occurred for type A items at, say, trial t (that is, concept A has been achieved at trial t) or (2) conditioning has not occurred for type A items at that trial. We designate these two states, respectively, as C_A and $\tilde{C}_A$. Within the conventional framework of the single-element stimulus-sampling theory we could then completely describe the stochastic process for passage into the state C_A or the state $\tilde{C}_A$ as a homogeneous Markov chain. Such a process is specified when probabilities of being in states C_A or $\tilde{C}_A$ at trial 0 are designated and transition probabilities for passage into one or the other of the states at trial $t + 1$, given the state of the chain at trial t, are specified.

We denote the initial state probabilities as $p_0(C_A)$ and $p_0(\tilde{C}_A)$. The transition probability matrix for this chain is specified as

$$P(A) = \begin{array}{c} \\ \text{state at trial } t \\ \\ C_A \\ \tilde{C}_A \end{array} \overset{\begin{array}{c}\text{state at trial } t + 1\\ \quad C_A \qquad \tilde{C}_A\end{array}}{\begin{bmatrix} 1 & 0 \\ \theta_A & 1 - \theta_A \end{bmatrix}}$$

The parameter θ_A in this transition probability matrix represents a conditioning or learning rate for achieving concept A at the next trial, provided that the concept has not been grasped at the present trial. The first row of this transition matrix indicates that once concept A has been assimilated it is remembered with probability 1 at the following trial.

We introduce a further set of parameters which relate probabilities of correct responses on the items to the current conditioning states. Let R_A represent the occurrence of the correct response to items of type A and, conversely, let $\tilde{R}_A$ represent an incorrect response. We define conditional probabilities of these responses, given the conditioning states at the current trial, as follows: let

$$Pr(R_A \text{ at trial } t \,|\, C_A \text{ at trial } t) = 1$$

hence

$$Pr(\tilde{R}_A \text{ at trial } t \,|\, C_A \text{ at trial } t) = 0$$

and let

$$Pr(R_A \text{ at trial } t \,|\, \tilde{C}_A \text{ at trial } t) = \rho_A \qquad 0 \leq \rho_A \leq 1$$

hence

$$Pr(R_A \text{ at trial } t \,|\, \tilde{C}_A \text{ at trial } t) = 1 - \rho_A$$

The preceding structure would specify all of the relevant parameters of our learning process if we were to concern ourselves only with the teaching of concept A.

A similar structure would obtain for the process of teaching only concept B with no preliminary or auxiliary training on type A items. We would specify—

initial state probabilities: $p_0(C_B)$ and $p_0(\tilde{C}_B)$

$$
\text{transition probabilities: } P(B) =
\begin{array}{c}
 \\
C_B \\
\tilde{C}_B
\end{array}
\begin{array}{cc}
C_B & \tilde{C}_B \\
\left[\begin{array}{cc}
1 & 0 \\
\theta_B & 1 - \theta_B
\end{array}\right]
\end{array}
$$

and

response probabilities: $Pr(R_B \text{ at trial } t \,|\, C_B \text{ at trial } t) = 1$

and

$$Pr(R_B \text{ at trial } t \,|\, \tilde{C}_B \text{ at trial } t) = \rho_B$$

To represent transfer effects in this model, we assume that the conditioning rate parameter for concept B would be different from θ_B if items of type A were interspersed with items of type B and if concept A were mastered prior to achieving concept B. When such a presentation schedule is followed, we would introduce a further conditioning rate parameter, say, θ_{BA}. For positive transfer effects it would be required that $\theta_{BA} > \theta_B$. When mastery of concept A had occurred, the following transition probabilities would obtain for the teaching of concept B:

$$P(BA) = \begin{array}{c} \\ C_B \\ \tilde{C}_B \end{array} \begin{array}{cc} C_B & \tilde{C}_B \\ \left[\begin{array}{cc} 1 & 0 \\ \theta_{BA} & 1 - \theta_{BA} \end{array} \right] \end{array}$$

The initial state of conditioning probabilities and response probabilities for type B items would not be altered by mastery of concept A.

Two-Concept Teaching Situation

The basic sets of parameters that would occur in a typical single-element stimulus-sampling model involving the acquisition of a single concept have now been specified. We must now face a fundamental problem of incorporating into our model certain parameters which will control the allocation of either a type A or a type B item for the next trial, given the information that the response on the current item was correct or incorrect. We deal with this problem by defining further conditional probabilities which we shall call *item allocation parameters*. For example, we shall specify

$$\alpha(A \,|\, R_A) = Pr \text{ (item } A \text{ at trial } t + 1 \,|\, A \text{ and } R_A \text{ at trial } t)$$

That is, $\alpha(A|R_A)$ is the probability of giving an item of type A at the next trial, provided that an item of type A had been presented at the current trial and a correct response was made. The complete set of these parameters is shown in the item allocation matrix which follows.

PROBABILITIES OF ITEM ALLOCATIONS

	Type A Item at Trial $t + 1$	Type B Item at Trial $t + 1$
Type A item at trial t and correct response made	$\alpha(A \,|\, R_A)$	$\alpha(B \,|\, R_A) = 1 - \alpha(A \,|\, R_A)$
Type A item at trial t and incorrect response made	$\alpha(A \,|\, \check{R}_A)$	$\alpha(B \,|\, \check{R}_A) = 1 - \alpha(A \,|\, \check{R}_A)$
Type B item at trial t and correct response made	$\alpha(A \,|\, R_B)$	$\alpha(B \,|\, R_B) = 1 - \alpha(A \,|\, R_B)$
Type B item at trial t and incorrect response made	$\alpha(A \,|\, \check{R}_B)$	$\alpha(B \,|\, \check{R}_B) = 1 - \alpha(A \,|\, \check{R}_B)$

Formulation of the Process as a Markov Chain

One of the most attractive mathematical features of stimulus-sampling learning models is that they lead quite naturally to expressions as finite, homogeneous Markov chains. General conditions on stimulus-sampling models that will admit formulations of the models as Markov chains have been presented by Estes & Suppes (1959). These conditions designate how the fundamental elements which describe the sample functions of the process must be treated in order to define elementary events that will be states of a Markov chain. For our model we found it necessary to specify the states as certain 3-tuples.

States of the Chain

Since it was necessary to know the conditioning state of an individual for concept A and concept B at each trial, and also the type of item that had been administered at the trial, we found that the states of our basic chain had to be defined by a triple of values. As a result, our basic Markov chain was found to consist of the following eight states:

$$(\tilde{C}_A, \tilde{C}_B, A), (C_A, \tilde{C}_B, A), (\tilde{C}_A, C_B, A), (C_A, C_B, A)$$

and

$$(\tilde{C}_A, \tilde{C}_B, B), (C_A, \tilde{C}_B, B), (\tilde{C}_A, C_B, B), (C_A, C_B, B)$$

Derivation of Transition Probabilities

The probabilities of entering the various states at trial $t + 1$, given the state of the learning process at trial t, are computed by considering, in order, (1) the response probabilities given the conditioning states, (2) the transition probabilities for the conditioning function, and finally (3) the item allocation probabilities which are dependent on the particular responses that have occurred. For example, given that the learning process is in state $(\tilde{C}_A, \tilde{C}_B, A)$ at trial t, then the probabilities of passage into the various states at trial $t + 1$ can be determined from the system of paths or tree that is shown in Fig. 1. Transition probabilities starting from state $(\tilde{C}_A, \tilde{C}_B, A)$ may be derived from this tree. One will notice that

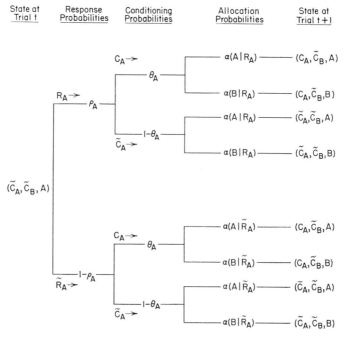

Fig. 1

the tree has two important levels of branches. The first level is determined by whether the subject makes a correct response, R_A, or an incorrect response, $\tilde{R}_A$, to the type A item that has been administered at trial t. The second level of branching indicates the probabilities that the subject will remain in the unconditioned state for concept A, $\tilde{C}_A$, or achieve mastery of concept A (i.e., move to the conditioning state, C_A).

Inspection of the tree's right-hand column reveals that only four of the eight states of the basic chain can be reached from $(\tilde{C}_A, \tilde{C}_B, A)$ in one step. Each of these four steps can be reached by two distinct paths. Adding the probabilities over the pairs of paths, we get the following four transition probabilities:

$Pr((\tilde{C}_A, \tilde{C}_B, A)$ at trial $t + 1 \,|\, (\tilde{C}_A, \tilde{C}_B, A)$ at trial $t)$

$$= (1 - \theta_A)[\rho_A \alpha(A \,|\, R_A) + (1 - \rho_A)\alpha(A \,|\, \tilde{R}_A)]$$

$Pr((\tilde{C}_A, \tilde{C}_B, B)$ at trial $t + 1 \,|\, (\tilde{C}_A, \tilde{C}_B, A)$ at trial $t)$

$$= (1 - \theta_A)[1 - (\rho_A \alpha(A \,|\, R_A) + (1 - \rho_A)\alpha(A \,|\, \tilde{R}_A))]$$

$Pr((C_A, \tilde{C}_B, A)$ at trial $t + 1 \,|\, (\tilde{C}_A, \tilde{C}_B, A)$ at trial $t)$

$$= \theta_A[\rho_A \alpha(A \,|\, R_A) + (1 - \rho_A)\alpha(A \,|\, \tilde{R}_A)]$$

and finally

$Pr((C_A, \tilde{C}_B, B)$ at trial $t + 1 \,|\, (\tilde{C}_A, \tilde{C}_B, A)$ at trial $t)$

$$= \theta_A[1 - (\rho_A \alpha(A \,|\, R_A) + (1 - \rho_A)\alpha(A \,|\, \tilde{R}_A))]$$

It is convenient to introduce notation at this point for the expected probability of allocating a type A item at the next trial, given that the conditioning state $\tilde{C}_A$ obtains at the current trial and that a type A item has been administered at the current trial. Similar notation is also introduced for the analogous expected probability of allocating type B items. We let

$$\mu_A = \rho_A \alpha(A \,|\, R_A) + (1 - \rho_A)\alpha(A \,|\, \tilde{R}_A)$$

and

$$\mu_B = \rho_B \alpha(B \,|\, R_B) + (1 - \rho_B)\alpha(B \,|\, \tilde{R}_B)$$

Using this notation for the expected allocation probabilities, the transition probabilities for the four one-step transitions which are possible from the state $(\tilde{C}_A, \tilde{C}_B, A)$ then reduce to

$Pr((\tilde{C}_A, \tilde{C}_B, A)$ at trial $t + 1 \,|\, (\tilde{C}_A, \tilde{C}_B, A)$ at trial $t) = (1 - \theta_A)\mu_A$

$Pr((\tilde{C}_A, \tilde{C}_B, B)$ at trial $t + 1 \,|\, (\tilde{C}_A, \tilde{C}_B, A)$ at trial $t) = (1 - \theta_A)(1 - \mu_A)$

$Pr((C_A, \tilde{C}_B, A)$ at trial $t + 1 \,|\, (\tilde{C}_A, \tilde{C}_B, A)$ at trial $t) = \theta_A \mu_A$

and

$Pr((C_A, \tilde{C}_B, B)$ at trial $t + 1 \,|\, (\tilde{C}_A, \tilde{C}_B, A)$ at trial $t) = \theta_A(1 - \mu_A)$

We shall not present all of the eight trees, since the example given suffices to show the general method used to construct the various trees. When the conditioning state has been achieved for one of the two types of items (i.e., that concept has been learned) and that type of item has been given at the current trial, a very simple tree consisting of only two paths results. We illustrate this point by considering the tree which emanates from the state $(C_A, \tilde{C}_B, A)$.

State at Trial t	Response Probabilities	Conditioning Probabilities	Allocation Probabilities	State at Trial $t + 1$
$(C_A, \tilde{C}_B, A)$——	$R_A \rightarrow$ ——1——	——1——	$\alpha(A \,|\, R_A)$——	$(C_A, \tilde{C}_B, A)$
			$\alpha(B \,|\, R_A)$——	$(C_A, \tilde{C}_B, B)$

TABLE 1   TRANSITION PROBABILITY MATRIX FOR THE TWO-CONCEPT TEACHING PROCESS

State at Trial t	State at Trial $t+1$							
	$(\tilde{C}_A, \tilde{C}_B, A)$	$(\tilde{C}_A, \tilde{C}_B, B)$	$(C_A, \tilde{C}_B, A)$	$(C_A, \tilde{C}_B, B)$	$(\tilde{C}_A, C_B, A)$	$(\tilde{C}_A, C_B, B)$	(C_A, C_B, A)	(C_A, C_B, B)
$(\tilde{C}_A, \tilde{C}_B, A)$	$(1-\theta_A)\mu_A$	$(1-\theta_A)(1-\mu_A)$	$\theta_A\mu_A$	$\theta_A(1-\mu_A)$	0	0	0	0
$(\tilde{C}_A, \tilde{C}_B, B)$	$(1-\theta_B)(1-\mu_B)$	$(1-\theta_B)\mu_B$	0	0	$\theta_B(1-\mu_B)$	$\theta_B\mu_B$	0	0
$(C_A, \tilde{C}_B, A)$	0	0	$\alpha(A|R_A)$	$1-\alpha(A|R_A)$	0	0	0	0
$(C_A, \tilde{C}_B, B)$	0	0	$(1-\theta_{BA})(1-\mu_B)$	$(1-\theta_{BA})\mu_B$	0	0	$\theta_{BA}(1-\mu_B)$	$\theta_{BA}\mu_B$
$(\tilde{C}_A, C_B, A)$	0	0	0	0	$(1-\theta_A)\mu_A$	$(1-\theta_A)(1-\mu_A)$	$\theta_A\mu_A$	$\theta_A(1-\mu_A)$
$(\tilde{C}_A, C_B, B)$	0	0	0	0	$1-\alpha(B|R_B)$	$\alpha(B|R_B)$	0	0
(C_A, C_B, A)	0	0	$\alpha(A|R_A)$	0	0	0	$1-\alpha(A|R_A)$	0
(C_A, C_B, B)	0	0	0	0	$1-\alpha(B|R_B)$	0	$1-\alpha(B|R_B)$	$\alpha(B|R_B)$

Thus it is evident that only two states, $(C_A, \tilde{C}_B, A)$ and $(C_A, \tilde{C}_B, B)$, can be reached in one step from $(C_A, \tilde{C}_B, A)$. The probabilities of these two transitions are

$$Pr((C_A, \tilde{C}_B, A) \text{ at trial } t + 1 \,|\, (C_A, \tilde{C}_B, A) \text{ at trial } t) = \alpha(A \,|\, R_A)$$

and

$$Pr((C_A, \tilde{C}_B, B) \text{ at trial } t + 1 \,|\, (C_A, \tilde{C}_B, A) \text{ at trial } t)$$

$$= \alpha(B \,|\, R_A) = 1 - \alpha(A \,|\, R_A)$$

The transition probability matrix for this two-concept teaching process was derived by constructing the eight trees. The results of this derivation are summarized in Table 1.

Expected Numbers of Trials to Achieve Conditioning

We are interested in determining the best set of values of the item allocation parameters for given values of the response probabilities ρ_A and ρ_B; given values of the conditioning probabilities θ_A, θ_B, and θ_{BA}; and given initial state probabilities in order to minimize the expected numbers of trials needed to teach concept B. Using this criterion, it is not necessary to consider separately the expected numbers of trials that it will take to reach the states $(\tilde{C}_A, C_B, A)$, $(\tilde{C}_A, C_B, B)$, (C_A, C_B, A), or (C_A, C_B, B). The second coordinate in the description of each of these four states, the value C_B, is the only characteristic in their description that is of critical importance to us; that is, each state of the process whose second coordinate is C_B is the state which has the property that concept B has been learned. We wish then to combine these four states, to form a single state, say $(\cdot, C_B, \cdot)$, which represents the situation that concept B has been mastered.

Combination of States

A topic of considerable importance in stochastic learning theory has been the determination of conditions that allow the reduction of Markov chains by combining or lumping various states into sets of states. It is known that one does not have complete freedom in partitioning the set of states of the original chain to form new sets of states, but, rather, certain conditions must obtain if the resulting lumped process is to be a Markov chain whose transition probabilities are independent of the initial state probabilities.

Kemeny & Snell (1960) have given a necessary and sufficient condition for a Markov chain to be lumpable with respect to a given partitioning of its set of states. The initial set of states, say $\{s_1, s_2, \cdots, s_n\}$, may be partitioned into a lumped set, say $\{A_1, A_2, \cdots, A_m\}$, where $m < n$, provided that for every pair of the new states, say A_i and A_j, $Pr(A_j$ at trial $t + 1 | s_k$ at trial $t) = $ (say) p_{ij} for every s_k in A_i. These authors show further that the satisfaction of this condition implies that there exist two matrices, say, $\underset{(m\times n)}{U}$ and $\underset{(n\times m)}{V}$ such that the transition matrix of the lumped process, call it $\underset{(m\times m)}{P_L}$, can be obtained by the following calculations:

$$\underset{(m\times m)}{P_L} = \underset{(m\times n)}{U} \quad \underset{(n\times n)}{P} \quad \underset{(n\times m)}{V}$$

The matrix U is a stochastic matrix whose ith row has equal components for states $s_k \in A_i$ and 0 for the remaining states. The matrix V has a 1 in each position in its jth column for each state $s_k \in A_j$ and 0 for the remaining states.

For our process, we wish to combine only the four states $(\tilde{C}_A, C_B, A)$, $(\tilde{C}_A, C_B, B)$, (C_A, C_B, A), and (C_A, C_B, B) into a single state $(\cdot, C_B, \cdot)$. [The remaining states $(\tilde{C}_A, \tilde{C}_B, A)$, $(\tilde{C}_A, \tilde{C}_B, B)$, $(C_A, \tilde{C}_B, A)$, and $(C_A, \tilde{C}_B, B)$ are not modified.] One sees that these four states can be combined, since the probabilities of transition from each of the four are equal for going to $(\tilde{C}_A, \tilde{C}_B, A)$, $(\tilde{C}_A, \tilde{C}_B, B)$, and $(C_A, \tilde{C}_B, A)$ and to $(C_A, \tilde{C}_B, B)$. All 16 of these transition probabilities are equal; they are all equal to zero.

The matrices $\underset{(5\times 8)}{U}$ and $\underset{(8\times 5)}{V}$ which will reduce our initial transition probability matrix $\underset{(8\times 8)}{P}$ to the matrix P_L for the lumped process $\underset{(5\times 5)}{}$ are

$$U = \begin{bmatrix} 1 & 0 & 0 & 0 & 0 & 0 & 0 & 0 \\ 0 & 1 & 0 & 0 & 0 & 0 & 0 & 0 \\ 0 & 0 & 1 & 0 & 0 & 0 & 0 & 0 \\ 0 & 0 & 0 & 1 & 0 & 0 & 0 & 0 \\ 0 & 0 & 0 & 0 & \frac{1}{4} & \frac{1}{4} & \frac{1}{4} & \frac{1}{4} \end{bmatrix} \quad \text{and} \quad V = \begin{bmatrix} 1 & 0 & 0 & 0 & 0 \\ 0 & 1 & 0 & 0 & 0 \\ 0 & 0 & 1 & 0 & 0 \\ 0 & 0 & 0 & 1 & 0 \\ 0 & 0 & 0 & 0 & 1 \\ 0 & 0 & 0 & 0 & 1 \\ 0 & 0 & 0 & 0 & 1 \\ 0 & 0 & 0 & 0 & 1 \end{bmatrix}$$

The transition probability matrix which results for the process when the four C_B states are combined into a single state $(\cdot, C_B, \cdot)$ is the following:

TRANSITION PROBABILITY MATRIX FOR THE TWO-CONCEPT TEACHING PROCESS WHEN ALL C_B STATES ARE COMBINED

State at Trial $t + 1$

State at Trial t	$(\tilde{C}_A, \tilde{C}_B, A)$	$(\tilde{C}_A, \tilde{C}_B, B)$	$(C_A, \tilde{C}_B, A)$	$(C_A, \tilde{C}_B, B)$	$(\cdot, C_B, \cdot)$
$(\tilde{C}_A, \tilde{C}_B, A)$	$(1 - \theta_A)\mu_A$	$(1 - \theta_A)(1 - \mu_A)$	$\theta_A \mu_A$	$\theta_A(1 - \mu_A)$	0
$(\tilde{C}_A, \tilde{C}_B, B)$	$(1 - \theta_B)(1 - \mu_B)$	$(1 - \theta_B)\mu_B$	0	0	θ_B
$(C_A, \tilde{C}_B, A)$	0	0	$\alpha(A \mid R_A)$	$1 - \alpha(A \mid R_A)$	0
$(C_A, \tilde{C}_B, B)$	0	0	$(1 - \theta_{BA})(1 - \mu_B)$	$(1 - \theta_{BA})\mu_B$	θ_{BA}
$(\cdot, C_B, \cdot)$	0	0	0	0	1

Derivation of Expected Numbers of Trials to Learn Concept B

Inspection of the transition probability matrix which results when four of the states are combined to form the single state $(\cdot, C_B, \cdot)$ reveals that ultimately this state can be reached from each of the remaining states, $(\tilde{C}_A, \tilde{C}_B, A)$, $(\tilde{C}_A, \tilde{C}_B, B)$, $(C_A, \tilde{C}_B, A)$, and $(C_A, \tilde{C}_B, B)$. The chain is also seen to be an absorbing chain with the single absorbing state $(\cdot, C_B, \cdot)$, because once this state is reached it is always returned to with probability 1. The remaining four states of the combined learning process are therefore all transient.

The expected numbers of steps to reach the absorbing state, starting from each of the transient states, can be calculated as the row sums of a certain inverse matrix. The underlying theory for this procedure is developed in Kemeny & Snell (1960); we summarize the development here.

First, it is necessary to introduce notation for the absolute state probabilities of being in the various transient states at each trial t ($t = 0, 1, 2, \cdots$), given that the process was started in one of the transient states. Let $s_1 = (\tilde{C}_A, \tilde{C}_B, A)$, $s_2 = (\tilde{C}_A, \tilde{C}_B, B)$, $s_3 = (C_A, \tilde{C}_B, A)$, and $s_4 = (C_A, \tilde{C}_B, B)$ and then define for $i, j = 1, 2, 3,$ or 4 the random variable

$W(t, s_i, s_j) = 1$ if the process is in the transient state s_j at trial t and was in the transient state s_i at trial 0

$W(t, s_i, s_j) = 0$ otherwise

We denote the absolute state probabilities of being in the transient state s_j at trial t, given that the process was in the transient state s_i at trial 0, as $q_{i,j}^{(t)}$ and let $q_{i,i}^{(0)} = 1$ for all transient states s_i. The expected number of trials that the process will be in the transient state s_j, when it was started in the transient state s_i, is

$$E[W(t, s_i, s_j)] = \sum_{t=0}^{\infty} (1q_{i,j}^{(t)} + 0(1 - q_{i,j}^{(t)}))$$

$$= \sum_{t=0}^{\infty} q_{ij}^{(t)}$$

The set of all of these expected values of the random variables $W(t, s_i, s_j)$, defined for each of the transient states, may be represented by the following infinite series of matrices

$$\{\sum_{t=0}^{\infty} q_{ij}^{(t)}\} = \sum_{t=0}^{\infty} Q^{(t)} \qquad (i, j = 1, 2, 3, \text{ or } 4)$$

Kemeny and Snell have shown that this set of expected numbers of times that the process is in each of the transient states is equal to the inverse of the matrix $N = I - Q$; that is, this set of expected values is given by

$$N^{-1} = \sum_{t=0}^{\infty} Q^{(t)}$$

For our model of a two-concept teaching process, the N matrix is

$$\underset{(4\times4)}{N} = \begin{bmatrix} 1-(1-\theta_A)\mu_A & -(1-\theta_A)(1-\mu_A) & -\theta_A\,\mu_A & -\theta_A(1-\mu_A) \\ -(1-\theta_B)(1-\mu_B) & 1-(1-\theta_B)\mu_B & 0 & 0 \\ 0 & 0 & 1-\alpha(A\,|\,R_A) & \alpha(A\,|\,R_A)-1 \\ 0 & 0 & -(1-\theta_{BA})(1-\mu_B) & 1-(1-\theta_{BA})\mu_B \end{bmatrix}$$

We expressed the inverse of the N matrix in terms of the elements of N which are not necessarily zero. These elements, it can be seen, are functions of the various parameters of the teaching process. We computed the determinant of N and the adjoint matrix of N to obtain the inverse of N by the well-known relation $N^{-1} = \text{adj } N/|N|$.

The determinant of N turns out to be

$$|N| = (n_{11}n_{22} - n_{12}n_{21})(n_{33}n_{44} - n_{34}n_{43})$$

whereas the adjoint of N is the matrix

$$\text{adj } N = \begin{bmatrix} n_{22}d_2 & -n_{12}d_2 & -n_{22}d_4 & n_{22}d_3 \\ -n_{21}d_2 & n_{11}d_2 & n_{21}d_4 & -n_{21}d_3 \\ 0 & 0 & n_{44}d_1 & -n_{34}d_1 \\ 0 & 0 & -n_{43}d_1 & n_{33}d_1 \end{bmatrix}$$

where
$$d_1 = n_{11}n_{22} - n_{12}n_{21}$$
$$d_2 = n_{33}n_{44} - n_{34}n_{43}$$
$$d_3 = n_{13}n_{34} - n_{14}n_{33}$$
and
$$d_4 = n_{13}n_{44} - n_{14}n_{43}$$

The elements of this N^{-1} matrix represent the expected numbers of trials that the process will be in each of the transient states (states such that concept B has not been learned). The elements in the first row of N^{-1} represent the expected numbers of trials that the process will be in each of the four transient states when the process was in the state $(\tilde{C}_A, \tilde{C}_B, A)$ at trial 0. The elements in the second row give these expected values when the process was started in the state $(\tilde{C}_A, \tilde{C}_B, B)$; similarly, the third and fourth rows of N^{-1} give these expected numbers of trials that the process will be in each of the various transient states when it was started, respectively, in the state $(C_A, \tilde{C}_B, A)$ and the state $(C_A, \tilde{C}_B, B)$.

We now define random variables that will represent reaching the state $(\cdot, C_B, \cdot)$ for the first time when the process is started in each of the four transient states. Let

$Z(t, s_i) = 1$ if the process reached the state $(\cdot, C_B, \cdot)$ for the first time at trial t and was in the transient state s_i at trial 0

$Z(t, s_i) = 0$ otherwise

The expected values of these random variables are the expected numbers of trials that are required to learn concept B when the teaching process is started in the various transient states. Our principal objective is to minimize each of these four expected values by appropriate choice of the item allocation probabilities.

It is readily seen that the expected numbers of trials required to learn concept B, starting from the transient state s_i, is equal to the sum over all of the transient states of the expected numbers of trials that the process will be in each of the transient states when it was started in the state s_i; that is,

$$E[Z(t, s_i)] = \sum_{j=1}^{4} E[W(t, s_i, s_j)]$$

and consequently

$$E[Z(t, s_i)] = \sum_{j=1}^{4} n^{ij}$$

The four expected numbers of trials to learn concept B, which are obtained as the row sums of N^{-1}, were found to simplify to the following equations:

$$E[Z(t, (\tilde{C}_A, \tilde{C}_B, A))]$$

$$= \frac{\left\{ \begin{array}{l} (1-\alpha(A\,|\,R_A))\{\theta_{BA}[1-(1-\theta_B)\mu_B+(1-\theta_A)(1-\mu_A)]\} \\ \qquad +\theta_A[1-(1-\theta_B)\mu_B]\} \end{array} \right\}}{(1-\alpha(A\,|\,R_A))\theta_{BA}[\theta_A+\theta_B-\theta_A\theta_B-\theta_B(1-\theta_A)\mu_B-\theta_A(1-\theta_B)\mu_A]}$$

$$+ \frac{\theta_A[1-(1-\theta_B)\mu_B][\theta_{BA}(\mu_A+\mu_B-1)+(1-\mu_B)]}{(1-\alpha(A\,|\,R_A))\theta_{BA}[\theta_A+\theta_B-\theta_A\theta_B-\theta_B(1-\theta_A)\mu_B-\theta_A(1-\theta_B)\mu_A]}$$

$$E[Z(t, (\tilde{C}_A, \tilde{C}_B, B))]$$

$$= \frac{\left\{ \begin{array}{l} (1-\alpha(A\,|\,R_A))\{\theta_{BA}[(1-\theta_B)(1-\mu_B)+1-(1-\theta_A)\mu_A]\} \\ \qquad +\theta_A(1-\theta_B)(1-\mu_B)\} \end{array} \right\}}{(1-\alpha(A\,|\,R_A))\theta_{BA}[\theta_A+\theta_B-\theta_A\theta_B-\theta_B(1-\theta_A)\mu_B-\theta_A(1-\theta_B)\mu_A]}$$

$$+ \frac{\theta_A[(1-\theta_B)(1-\mu_B)][\theta_{BA}(\mu_A+\mu_B-1)+(1-\mu_B)]}{(1-\alpha(A\,|\,R_A))\theta_{BA}[\theta_A+\theta_B-\theta_A\theta_B-\theta_B(1-\theta_A)\mu_B-\theta_A(1-\theta_B)\mu_A]}$$

$$E[Z(t, (C_A, \tilde{C}_B, A))] = \frac{2 - \alpha(A\,|\,R_A) - (1 - \theta_{BA})\mu_B}{(1 - \alpha(A\,|\,R_A))\theta_{BA}}$$

$$E[Z(t, (C_A, \tilde{C}_B, B))] = \frac{2 - \alpha(A\,|\,R_A) - \theta_{BA} - (1 - \theta_{BA})\mu_B}{(1 - \alpha(A\,|\,R_A))\theta_{BA}}$$

Best Item Allocation Policies

Having obtained the four expressions for the expected numbers of trials to learn concept B, starting from each of the transient states, we wish now to determine if there are best settings of the item allocation probabilities which will minimize each of these four expected values. It turns out that the basic quantities which must be considered for these minimizations are μ_A, μ_B, $\alpha(A\,|\,R_A)$, and, in addition to the item allocation probabilities, the probability of guessing correctly on A items, ρ_A.

Minimization of $E[Z(t, (C_A, \tilde{C}_B, B))]$

We present these minimizations, starting with the simplest case first. It will be seen that in all four instances the quantity μ_B should be set equal to 1. In this particular expected value it can be seen that putting $\mu_B = 1$ reduces the numerator and does not affect the denominator, to give the result

$$\min E[Z(t, (C_A, \tilde{C}_B, B))] = \frac{1 - \alpha(A \mid R_A)}{(1 - \alpha(A \mid R_A))\theta_{BA}} = \frac{1}{\theta_{BA}}$$

Thus, setting $\mu_B = 1$ will minimize $E[Z(t, (C_A, \tilde{C}_B, B))]$ independent of the value of $\alpha(A \mid R_A)$, the other allocation parameter which appears in this expression. Since by definition $\mu_B = \alpha(B \mid R_B)\rho_B + \alpha(B \mid \tilde{R}_B)(1 - \rho_B)$, it is evident that the setting $\mu_B = 1$ can always be achieved by setting $\alpha(B \mid R_B) = \alpha(B \mid \tilde{R}_B) = 1$. This means that a B item will always be repeated after a B item, whether success or failure occurs.

The policy of setting $\alpha(B \mid R_B) = \alpha(B \mid \tilde{R}_B) = 1$ does not, of course, represent any surprising result. This policy simply dictates that if concept A has already been mastered at the outset and a B item was the first item administered, one should never waste trials with any more A items, since the learning rate θ_{BA} is already in effect.

Minimization of $E[Z(t, (C_A, \tilde{C}_B, A))]$

For the minimization of the remaining three expected numbers of trials to learn concept B, an argument concerning general conditions for the minimization of the ratio of two linear functions of a single variable will be needed. For example, if $a + bx$ and $c + dx$ are two linear functions of a continuous variable x, with x restricted to a finite interval (in the present case the closed unit interval $[0, 1]$ is the interval of interest), and if we let $g(x; a, b, c, d)$ be the function

$$g(x; a, b, c, d) = \frac{a + bx}{c + dx} \qquad 0 \le x \le 1$$

then it is easily shown that the minimum of g occurs at the following points:

(i) the minimum of g occurs at $x = 0$ if $bc - ad > 0$,

(ii) the minimum of g occurs at $x = 1$ if $bc - ad < 0$,

(iii) g does not have a minimum if $bc = ad$.

It is clear that μ_B should be set equal to 1 to minimize $E[Z(t, (C_A, \tilde{C}_B, A))]$. When this is done, this expression reduces to

$$E[Z(t, (C_A, \tilde{C}_B, A))] = \frac{(\theta_{BA} + 1) - \alpha(A \mid R_A)}{\theta_{BA} - \theta_{BA}\alpha(A \mid R_A)}$$

Thus $E[Z(t, (C_A, \tilde{C}_B, A))]$ may be regarded as the ratio of two linear expressions in the variable $\alpha(A\,|\,R_A)$. In this instance, then, $bc - ad = (-\theta_{BA}) + (\theta_{BA} + 1)\theta_{BA} = \theta_{BA}^2 > 0$; hence this expected value is minimized by setting $\alpha(A\,|\,R_A) = 0$. The resulting minimum value of the expectation is

$$\min E[Z(t, (C_A, \tilde{C}_B, A))] = \frac{\theta_{BA} + 1}{\theta_{BA}} = 1 + \frac{1}{\theta_{BA}}$$

One sees that if the first item administered is an A item, but concept A has already been mastered, then the subject should immediately be switched to B items (by setting $\alpha(A\,|\,R_A) = 0$) and only B items should be administered from then on (by setting $\mu_B = 1$, which is in turn accomplished by setting $\alpha(B\,|\,R_B) = \alpha(B\,|\,\tilde{R}_B) = 1$). The resulting minimum expected number of trials to learn concept B turns out to be one greater than the corresponding minimum starting from state $(C_A, \tilde{C}_B, B)$. The one extra trial has, so to speak, been wasted by starting with an A item when concept A had been mastered.

Minimization of $E[Z(t, (\tilde{C}_A, \tilde{C}_B, A))]$ and $E[Z(t, (\tilde{C}_A, \tilde{C}_B, B))]$

The derivations of the minimum expected numbers of trials for the two states in which neither concept A nor concept B had been mastered at the beginning of the teaching program are considerably more lengthy to show in detail, although the same argument about minimizing the ratio of two linear functions of a single variable suffices to locate these minima. For these two expected values we seek in turn the best settings of $\alpha(A\,|\,R_A)$, μ_A and μ_B for each of the two expectations. We have conjectured that the iterative search for the minimum of these expected numbers by fixing, for example, μ_A and μ_B and solving for the minimizing value of $\alpha(A\,|\,R_A)$ and then perhaps fixing μ_B and $\alpha(A\,|\,R_A)$ and solving for the minimizing values of μ_A, etc., will give a resulting setting of these three parameters which is equal to the setting that would be obtained by simultaneous minimization of all three parameter settings. We have not been able to give a proof of the equivalence of these two minimization procedures for this problem; however, computations of the values of these expected numbers of trials were done for wide ranges of values of all the parameters in the expressions. These computations showed no contradictions of the settings that are obtained by using the iterative minimization procedure.

The parameter μ_B is not a function of any of the arguments of μ_A, nor is it a function of $\alpha(A\,|\,R_A)$. However, μ_A is restricted by the value of

$\alpha(A \mid R_A)$ unless we also allow the guessing probability ρ_A to vary. With this additional freedom for variation of μ_A, we may then use the argument that has been presented for the minimization of the ratio of two linear functions of a single variable successively for $\alpha(A \mid R_A)$, μ_A, and μ_B. We know from the conditions (i), (ii), (iii) that either the minimizing values will occur at 0 or 1 or there is no minimizing setting.

It appears that for the minimization of $E[Z(t, (\tilde{C}_A, \tilde{C}_B, A))]$ the allocation probability $\alpha(A \mid R_A)$ must be set equal to zero. The appropriate values of μ_A and μ_B under certain restrictions on the relative values of θ_A, θ_B, and θ_{BA} are then both found to be the value 1. The resulting minimum for $\alpha(A \mid R_A) = 0$ and $\mu_A = \mu_B = 1$ is

$$\min E[Z(t, (\tilde{C}_A, \tilde{C}_B, A))] = 1 + \frac{1}{\theta_A} + \frac{1}{\theta_{BA}}$$

The value of this minimum is one trial larger than could be obtained if, under the condition that $\rho_A = 0$, the policy were followed to start with an A item and continue with A items until the first successful response occurs and then immediately switch to B items for the rest of the program. The source of this extra trial can be seen by inspection of the transition probability matrix, where it is made evident that the particular settings of $\alpha(A \mid R_A)$, μ_A, and μ_B have the result that no transitions from the state $(\tilde{C}_A, \tilde{C}_B, A)$ to $(\tilde{C}_A, \tilde{C}_B, B)$ are possible. The absorbing state $(\cdot, C_B, \cdot)$ can be reached, of course, only through the state $(\tilde{C}_A, \tilde{C}_B, B)$ or through the state $(C_A, \tilde{C}_B, B)$. The settings $\alpha(A \mid R_A) = 0$ and $\mu_A = \mu_B = 1$ result in reaching $(\cdot, C_B, \cdot)$ from $(\tilde{C}_A, \tilde{C}_B, A)$ only along the path $(\tilde{C}_A, \tilde{C}_B, A) \rightarrow (C_A, \tilde{C}_B, A) \rightarrow (C_A, \tilde{C}_B, B) \rightarrow (\cdot, C_B, \cdot)$. One trial is wasted, on the average, because of the necessary detour through $(C_A, \tilde{C}_B, A)$.

For the minimization of $E[Z(t, (\tilde{C}_A, \tilde{C}_B, B))]$ we found it again necessary to set $\mu_A = \mu_B = 1$; however, there is no minimizing setting of $\alpha(A \mid R_A)$—any value in the interval $0 \leq \alpha(A \mid R_A) < 1$ will do. The resulting minimum of this expectation is

$$\min E[Z(t, (\tilde{C}_A, \tilde{C}_B, B))] = \frac{1}{\theta_B}$$

This expected number of trials is the value that one would anticipate if the teaching program started with a B item and A items were never administered (the situation which results when $\mu_B = 1$ and a B item is administered at the outset).

A Uniform Item Allocation Policy

The results of the minimizations of each of the four expected numbers of trials to learn concept B indicate that a uniform item allocation policy can be stated that will serve to minimize all four of the expected numbers. The policy consists of setting $\alpha(A|R_A) = 0$, $\mu_A = 1$, and $\mu_B = 1$. We have seen that because of the functional dependence between $\alpha(A|R_A)$ and μ_A it is necessary to insist that $\rho_A = 0$. This last requirement, we recognize, is an idealization that would be very difficult to realize in practice, but it does further support the well-accepted test-construction principle that items should be designed to minimize the probability of guessing correct answers when the subject does not know the correct answer.

We have also investigated item allocations under the conditions that the guessing probabilities ρ_A and ρ_B are given fixed values. With these restrictions μ_A and μ_B cannot always be set to any value in the unit interval $[0, 1]$ by controlling the item allocation parameters alone. We have found that the minimum expected numbers of trials to teach concept B when the guessing probabilities are considered fixed are in general larger than the minima obtained by allowing the guessing probabilities to vary. Furthermore, when the guessing probabilities are considered fixed, the best settings of the item allocation probabilities are not unique. The minimization of the various expected numbers of trials to teach concept B when the guessing probabilities are fixed is a much more difficult mathematical problem than the minimizations that have been discussed in this section. We plan to publish further results concerning minimizations for given guessing probabilities in a subsequent report.

Except for the minimization of $E[Z(t, (\tilde{C}_A, \tilde{C}_B, A))]$, there are no particularly subtle branching patterns that result from the use of our item allocation policy. We feel that the important point that this study has made, however, is that purely analytical techniques can be used to determine best item allocation policies in teaching programs. The particular learning model that was formulated in this research is admittedly a very simple example of a model of a teaching program. It is our intention to consider next some more sophisticated models of teaching programs and perhaps other criteria for measuring efficient teaching. It is our hope that the rudimentary beginning toward analytic study of branching problems in the design of teaching programs that we have presented here will stimulate others who are of a similar disposition to entertain these problems.

REFERENCES

Arrow, K. J., Karlin, S., & Scarf, H. *Studies in the mathematical theory of inventory and production.* Stanford, California: Stanford University Press, 1958.

Atkinson, R. C., & Estes, W. K. Stimulus sampling theory. In R. R. Bush, E. Galanter, & R. D. Luce (Eds.), *Handbook of mathematical psychology.* New York: Wiley, in preparation.

Bellman, R. *Dynamic programming.* Princeton, New Jersey: Princeton University Press, 1957.

Bower, G. H. Application of a model to paired-associate learning. *Psychometrika,* 1961, **26,** 225–280.

Estes, W. K. Component and pattern models with Markovian interpretations. In R. R. Bush & W. K. Estes (Eds.), *Studies in mathematical learning theory.* Stanford, California: Stanford University Press, 1959a.

Estes, W. K. The statistical approach to learning theory. In S. Koch (Ed.), *Psychology: a study of a science.* New York: McGraw-Hill, 1959b. II, pp. 383–491.

Estes, W. K. New developments in statistical behavior theory: differential tests of axioms for associative learning. *Psychometrika,* 1961, **26,** 73–84.

Estes, W. K., & Suppes, P. *Foundations of statistical learning theory. II. The stimulus sampling model for simple learning.* Stanford University: Institute for Mathematical Studies in the Social Sciences, Applied Mathematics and Statistics Laboratories, 1959. [Technical Report No. 26, Contract Nonr 225(17).]

Kemeny, J. G., & Snell, J. L. *Finite Markov chains.* Princeton, New Jersey: D. Van Nostrand, 1960.

Lord, F. L. *A theory of test scores.* Psychometric Monog. No. 7, Philadelphia: G. S. Ferguson, 1952.

Solomon, H. (Ed.), *Studies in item analysis and prediction.* Stanford, California: Stanford University Press, 1961.

Suppes, P., & Atkinson, R. C. *Markov learning models for multiperson interactions.* Stanford, California: Stanford University Press, 1960.

Suppes, P., & Ginsberg, R. *A fundamental property of all-or-none models.* Stanford University: Institute for Mathematical Studies in the Social Sciences, Applied Mathematics and Statistics Laboratories, 1961. (Technical Report No. 39.)

New directions in teaching-machine research

JAMES G. HOLLAND

Harvard University

Since the publication of Skinner's article "The Science of Learning and the Art of Teaching" in 1954, programmed instruction has advanced at an accelerated pace which promises great improvement in education. These programs have usually followed the format dictated by a single type of machine. Such a machine presents printed material and provides for a student's response to small units of material. Nearly every academic subject matter has some program development underway in this manner. Such work commonly uses a standard, favorite text as the accepted definition of what should be taught. This type of expedient program is indeed an important contribution to immediate educational needs; but, although the author intends no depreciation of this important effort, it misses a possibly greater potential contribution of the new behavioral technology which is now ready to begin the analysis of fundamental skills and the development of techniques for establishing them.

It is true that workable principles have been developed for expedient programming and that these have, in turn, bred their own particular type of research effort, namely, hypothesis testing. With research talent already drained by expedient programming, it is a shame to see it further drained by the type of research being carried out. Such pedestrian problems as response mode and comparisons of "programmed

The preparation of this manuscript, and much of the research reported, was supported by grants from the U. S. Office of Education and from the Carnegie Corporation.

instruction" and "conventional methods" are investigated. Aside from the overgeneralization inevitable from such ill-defined variables, even these relatively uninteresting problems are inadequately treated. Despite the overwhelming recognition of the importance of quality in the program, we are seldom given information for evaluating the program. Indeed, the importance of this point has been illustrated by a demonstration (Holland, 1960) that the difference between using a program and simply reading the same completed statements can be abolished by such a minor change in the program as leaving less appropriate parts of the statement blank for the student to complete. Moreover, hypothesis-testing studies in teaching-machine research often use only 100 or 200 items which, for the variables studied, should and do yield negative results. In the face of these obvious difficulties, it is all the more surprising when the researchers eagerly accept the null hypothesis.

As important as expedient programming is, a real revolution in education can be brought about by an experimental analysis of techniques to establish fundamental skills. Techniques must be developed to teach people to speak and write correctly rather than simply to teach *about* English. Techniques must be developed to teach persons to behave in a foreign language without necessarily teaching them about the language and without teaching them English equivalences which interfere with eventual "thinking" in the language. Techniques must be developed to teach logical speech and action rather than merely to teach about a formal discipline that logicians have developed. Techniques must be developed to establish such fundamental skills as attentive reading, observation of displays for later recall, inductive reasoning, and a host of discriminative capacities. This effort will require the experience accumulated over the years in the behavioral laboratories. It is known that gradual progression, control of the student's observing or mediating behavior, and variation of material are all important general principles that should apply. But the specific form that the application will take will be an experimental matter to be worked out by careful experimental analysis. Such research attempts to discover conditions under which a skill can be created; it attempts to discover new methods and techniques. Work of this type is carried out with extreme care and with careful observation and sensitivity to all possible influences. The experimenter cannot be bound by an existing format, type of material, or existing machine in his endeavors to meet these goals.

the (s) sound occurs in all positions within the words used and, further-more, the tasks vary—there is identification of isolated sounds; dis-crimination of words containing (s) sounds, discrimination of position of (s) sounds within words, and discrimination of correct from mis-articulated (s) sounds within words.

When children with defective (s) discrimination and articulation worked through this program, their ability to discriminate (s) sounds improved drastically. In addition, even though there had been no work on their actual articulation, a week after completing the program there was a significant improvement in their (s) articulation.

Inductive Reasoning

Some work currently underway by Eugene Long and the present writer illustrates an effort to develop procedures which may enable training of "mental abilities." The instrument used is shown in Fig. 1.

Fig. 1. The subject's panel. The upper window displays the problem and the lower five windows the response alternatives. The globe at the top lights when a response is correct.

There is a top window and five smaller choice windows which serve both as stimulus displays and response keys. A slide projector trans-illuminates these keys. When the top window is pressed, a shutter opens to expose the projected images on five small choice windows. Photocells in the projector, operated by a hole punch coding system, determine which of the five bottom windows will be scored as correct. When the student presses the bottom window that is correct for the problem presented in the top window, the shutters close, the slide changes presenting the next frame, and simultaneously a red light at the top of the instrument lights and a gong sounds. If, instead, the subject presses an incorrect window, only the bottom shutter closes. He must then press the top window, again opening the bottom shutter, and respond to the same problem once more. If he is now correct, the slide changes, the light goes on, and the gong sounds; but instead of presenting the next frame in the sequence, the projector presents the previous frame. If he is now correct on this frame, the material advances to the frame that he previously missed, and if he is then right on his very first choice the material advances to the next item in the sequence.

The details of this procedure were *not* arbitrarily decided upon. Considerable exploratory work carried out at the Walter E. Fernald State School for the Mentally Retarded enabled the evolution of this procedure. The red light and gong were added to provide clear-cut stimuli following correct responses. Candies (M & M's) were tried as reinforcers and discarded. Requiring a first correct response before moving ahead prevents the subject from getting through long, difficult sequences of the program by essentially chance or random choices. Thus the procedure decreases the danger of fortuitously reinforcing sequential patterns on the keys and other nonstimulus related responses. Moreover, when this procedure was not used, the student who had advanced by such fortuitous responding had difficulty later in the sequence even if he attempted to use the stimuli. This was because he was then faced with more advanced problems than he had seen when he initially began his random responding.

Samples of the material used to establish inductive reasoning are shown in Fig. 2. The child is presented with a sequence of forms in the problem window. The child's task is to press the bottom window which displays a form that could be added to extend the series correctly one element to the right. This material, incidentally, is somewhat similar to test material on inductive reasoning in which the

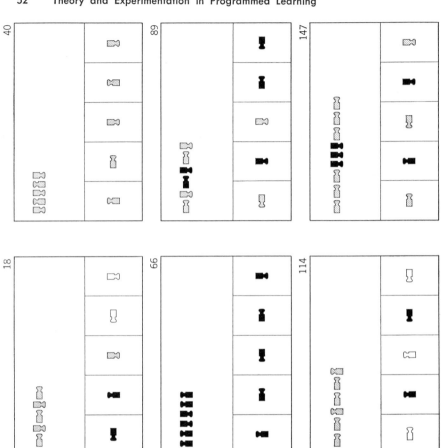

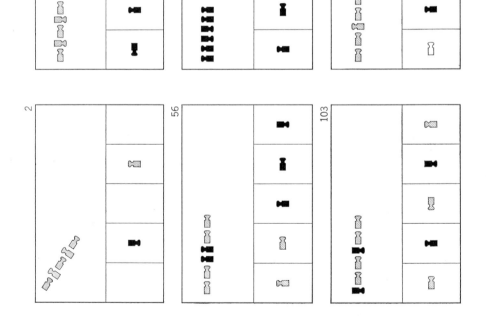

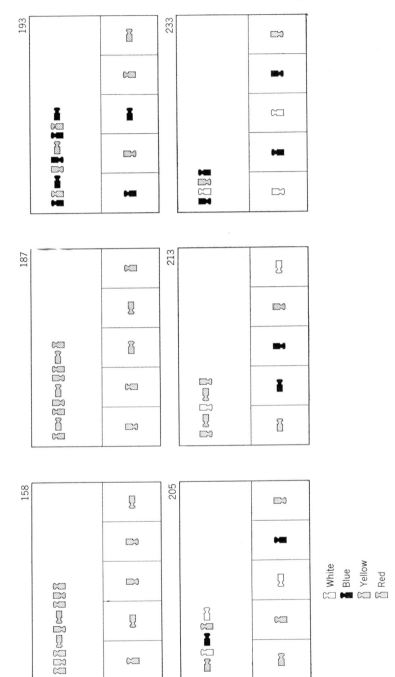

Fig. 2. Sample items from the inductive reasoning experiment. The number above each item indicates its position in the 234-item sequence. The correct alternatives (in order) of these items are 4, 3, 3, 5, 4, 4, 1, 4, 2, 1, 2, 4, 5, and 1.

child's task is to determine what would follow next in a sequence. There are also a small number of very simple problems of this type and an ingenious set of booklets developed by Thelma Thurstone (1948) to teach primary mental abilities. The other frames shown in Fig. 2 are taken from various points throughout the program and the number above them indicates their position in the program. At present 234 items in this program carry the student to the level indicated by number 233 in Fig. 2. The last 31 frames of the program are of the general type illustrated by number 233 in Fig. 2, in which the correct alternative (window number 1) shows a sample not actually shown in the problem window because the problem sequence was not extended far enough to include it. The progression from simple to difficult problems is obvious in the figure. Within each type of problem a progression of difficulty is provided by making the incorrect alternatives progressively more difficult (contrast number 18 with number 40), and by occasionally decreasing from two to one the number of relative dimensions (direction and color) enabling solution.

The program as it now stands is in transition. Additional revisions will be made, with considerable extension into more difficult problems and different types of material. The data shown in Fig. 3 were obtained with an earlier version of the program consisting of 187

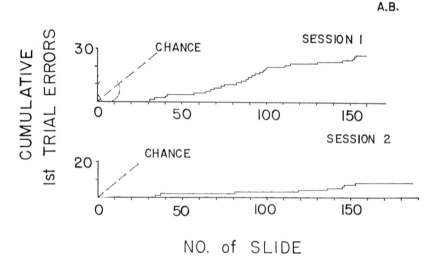

Fig. 3. *Cumulative first trial errors for a single subject. Session 1 is the subject's performance on the 187-item sequence. Session 2 is the same subject on a revised 234-item sequence.*

frames. The practice has been to try initial material and to modify it immediately from experience with a few subjects, try the revision and again modify it, and so forth until material has been developed to establish the behavior desired. In Fig. 3 there are two sessions shown for a single subject. The first session uses the 187-item version. The data shown are a plot of cumulative first-trial errors. On the horizontal axis the unit is the individual slide in its proper place in the sequence. When on an individual trial the slide is presented and an incorrect response is made, there is a step up of one unit. When another error is made on the presentation of another new slide, there is another upward step, resulting in a cumulative plot of first trial errors during the session. This means of presenting the data shows each area in which errors are clustered. The slope in any portion of the graph indicates error rate in that region. The line labeled "chance" is the slope that the record would take if the child's responses were under no stimulus control at all. In this subject's first session he made no errors until slide #31. An appreciable cluster of errors occurred in the region of slide #70 when the problem was double alternation in one dimension and single alternation in the other. It should be noted, nevertheless, that even in this area his performance was considerably better than chance. Again, another area of difficulty appeared around slide #90 when the problem was of the one-two-one nature; the errors between #90 and #100 resulted from inadequate bridging material from double to triple alternation, and the cluster of three errors near the end of the sequence occurred for the items in which the correct response was not directly seen in the sample (that is, the difficult problems like that shown as number 233 in Fig. 2).

On the basis of this performance, the sequence was improved. In no case were difficult slides removed. Improving the material consisted entirely of rearrangements in order and additions of other slides to provide smooth progression. Incidentally, in the final portion of the program, more difficult items were also added. Even if the material had not been changed, some improvement would have been expected. But experience has demonstrated that errors made in this kind of material are likely to be repeated in another session. Simple drill procedures with similar materials show only a very gradual reduction in errors and slow approach to criterion. At any rate, if no reduction had been shown, the experimenters would have learned that they had effected no improvement. In the second session only nine errors were made in the longer version and the places in which clusters of errors occurred previously had few errors.   In what would have been the first cluster of six errors above only one error was made; in the third cluster, one error; and in the final cluster, one error.

The sequence of 234 frames developed was used with naïve, normal subjects ranging from 6 to 9 years of age.   The results for a single session are shown in Fig. 4.   One subject, D. W., age 9, made only two errors in the entire program, and those were in the most difficult material at the end.   Subject B. M., age 6, made only nine errors in the entire sequence and only five of these were on the 31 difficult problems near the end of the program.   J. D., age 7, made 11 errors. Interestingly only one of these was on the last 20 frames.   This is possibly related to the two short rest periods allowed him because of signs of restlessness.   Subject R. M., age 8, made 13 errors and remained considerably better than chance even near the end of the program where more than half of his errors occurred.   D. W. and C. D., both 7, also did well during most of the program but revealed deficiencies near the end where they performed at near chance for the

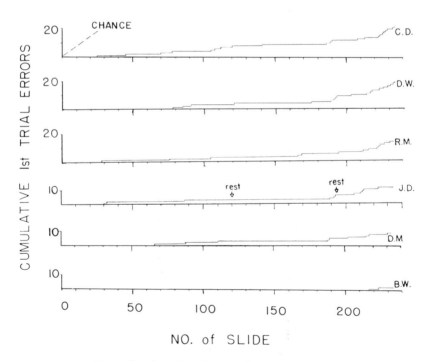

Fig. 4. *Cumulative first-trial errors for six naïve subjects.*

last 10 frames. Several of the subjects also revealed a deficiency in the material in the region of frames 185 to 195.

This research has successfully developed a procedure that will establish an ability to solve an inductive sequence of medium difficulty. The work, however, is not complete. Aside from the small revisions which must be made in view of the foregoing data, other types of problems need to be included and considerably more difficult material must be added. Beyond this phase it would be of interest to posttest with standardized abilities tests and to investigate further the limits of transfer.

This approach to learning research is novel in that it is directed toward development of techniques that will establish a given behavior. It can be contrasted with research directed toward discovering some supposed "learning function" or to discover whether one arbitrary condition is better than another arbitrary condition. Through careful analytical research of procedures, one can often attain behavioral control. The real product of such work is a technique and procedure for establishing such control rather than the usual confirmation of an hypothesis. One understands language behavior when he knows in detail how to produce it. One understands inductive reasoning when he knows how to create the ability. Although the interests of the investigators are primarily those of pure science, it is, of course, conceivable that the day may come when preschool children will play with learning material that will establish a wide range of important skills.

REFERENCES

Evans, J. Teaching machines. Paper read at Amer. Psychol. Assoc., New York, September, 1961.

Holland, Audrey, & Matthews, J. The use of a teaching machine in training speech sound discrimination for articulation therapy. In preparation.

Holland, J. G. Design and use of a teaching machine program. Paper read at Amer. Psychol. Assoc., Chicago, September, 1960.

Holland, J. G., & Skinner, B. F. *The analysis of behavior*. New York: McGraw-Hill, 1961.

Thurstone, Thelma. *Learning to think series*. Chicago: Science Research Associates, Inc., 1948.

Intrinsic and extrinsic programming

NORMAN A. CROWDER

Educational Science Division

U. S. Industries, Inc.

The major theme of this book, the application of modern computing techniques to teaching machines, brings us at once to some very fundamental issues in the field of automated instruction. As a beginning, we should distinguish clearly the structural differences between linear, or what I shall call "nonresponsive" programming techniques, and branching, or "responsive," programming techniques. We must also examine the theoretical basis for these differences in structure.

It is characteristic of all teaching-machine methods that they require, or at least provide an opportunity for, an active response on the part of the student at frequent intervals throughout the program of instruction. There have long been two schools of thought regarding the primary reason for eliciting the student's response. Indeed, the two schools represent historically independent developments and spring from differing theoretical backgrounds.

One school of thought, having its roots in classical experimental psychology, views the student's response as an integral part of the learning process and therefore as a legitimate end in itself. The adherents of this school are satisfied, in general, to make no further use of the student's response other than for its assumed effect on the student. Since the student's response is not used to control the program, the resulting programs are the linear, or nonresponsive, type.

The other school, having its roots in differential psychology, is primarily interested in using the student's responses to control the course of the programmed material presented to that particular student. Adherents of this second school have generally preferred to beg the question of exactly how the learning was to take place in order to focus attention on being able to determine, from step to step in the program, whether learning has taken place. When this information is available in usable form, it is then possible for the program to be automatically modified until the desired result is attained for that student at that time. This second school is interested in the student's response as the primary datum required to operate a branching, or responsive, program.

We should not ignore the effect of the student's response on the student, any more than we should ignore its possible use in automatically controlling and modifying the instructional program. Nonetheless, when we consider the use of computing apparatus to modify the instructional program for an individual student, we are primarily interested in the use of the student's response to control branching. In order to make full use of whatever computing capability we employ, we need to realize that a branching program has definitely different structural characteristics than a linear program and also has different capabilities.

I have deliberately emphasized the fact that computer control implies branching programs; my reason for this emphasis is that a widespread interest in branching or responsive programs is a relatively recent development. Not very many months ago I heard someone refer to those of us who were interested in branching programs as a "vociferous minority" and suggest that our members should not be judged directly by the amount of noise we made. I take it, by the attendance at this conference, that the ranks are swelled somewhat, although perhaps with quieter members.

There are two important aspects of branching, or responsive, programming that I wish to consider before discussing my major topic, which is the choice of techniques within the general area of responsive programming. The first point is that branching programs will, I predict, use multiple-choice rather than completion questions for a purely practical reason. It is simple and convenient to let the teaching machine, whatever form it takes, know which of several alternatives a student has chosen and to cause it to take appropriate action on the basis of this choice. It is virtually impossible, in the present state of the art, to let a teaching machine "know" what answer a student has given when the student has written out or "constructed" his answer. This purely practical consideration was, of course, my reason for originally preferring the multiple-choice response mode; moreover, if I understand the research of the last year correctly, the theoretical reasons for preferring the constructed response mode have been swept away by the experimental evidence. To use, I believe, James Evans' phrase, multiple-choice responses are now allowed to sit at the same lunch counters as constructed responses. At least this seems to be true any place south of Boston and environs.

In some curious cases there is no difference between the multiple-choice and the constructed response format. These are those cases in which the universe of sensible responses is strictly limited to a finite number. There are only 26 possible alternatives for the next letter in a spelling problem, 10 alternatives for the next digit in a problem in decimal arithmetic, and only two in problems in binary arithmetic. In these cases the distinction between the multiple-choice and constructed response format disappears.

My second major point about branching programs is that when we focus attention on the student's response as the primary datum need to operate our branching program, rather than as a part of the learning process *as such,* we become aware that the questions in our program may serve a variety of different functions and that these different functions require different types of questions. A routine question on a routine step in the program should serve

1. to determine whether the student has learned the material just presented;

2. to select appropriate corrective material if the student has not learned;

3. to provide desirable practice with the concept involved;

4. to keep the student actively working at the material; and,

5. to fill a desirable motivational purpose if the student answers the question correctly.

It is quite possible, however, that we will, in preparing branching programs, write questions that serve none of these purposes. We may want a very difficult question, or a short series of difficult questions, to determine whether a student should skip a whole block of material. Such a question may not accomplish any of the purposes served by the question used in a routine program step. Although this point may seem obvious, I wish to indicate that it is not necessary to view each program step, and the associated question, as having the same function and therefore the same structural and statistical properties. For example, I think it desirable that on a routine program step (if there is such a thing) no more than 15% of the students should select a wrong answer. However, a major program branch might have a question that would be failed by 90% of the students.

It may be somewhat less obvious that the alternatives provided in a single multiple-choice question may also serve different purposes and have different consequences. One alternative may be provided to catch a particular procedural error and lead to a single corrective presentation; a second may lead to a correctional subsequence; whereas a third alternative may detect an error of interpretation on a point made previously and lead the student back to that point in the program to work his way up again. It is fairly simple to provide for all such contingencies.

After this unconscionably long preamble about the rationale of responsive programs, I should like to consider now the several means of accomplishing branching programming. We may distinguish two basic types of branching programs. In one type there is a one-to-one correspondence between the student's answer choice and the next material he sees. Thus the student's answer choice leads him to turn to a particular page in a scrambled book, or to press a particular button on a machine, at which point a particular, predetermined presentation appears to the student. This type of responsive programming requires no intermediate computation between the student's answer choice and the decision as to what material he will see next. I call this type of responsive programming "intrinsic programming." When, in addition to the student's response alone, we use other data, such as the student's response history, and perform further computation to select the next material the student should see, we have what I call "extrinsic programming."

I would like to inject a historical note at this point. When I first began to work in this field in 1955, I assumed that any type of auto-instructional program could usefully be classified according to the technique used to provide the branching and therefore coined the terms "intrinsic" and "extrinsic" programming to distinguish the two types of program control I have just discussed. It did not occur to me that anyone would seriously propose an autoinstructional program that did not provide any means to vary the program automatically to accommodate the needs of different students.

The intrinsic programming technique has the obvious advantage that no complex computing equipment is required for its implementation. With relatively simple devices (compared to the complex computers now being proposed), quite complex kinds of branching programs can be achieved. The simplest device using intrinsically programmed materials is the "scrambled book" or TutorText.*

* Trademark.

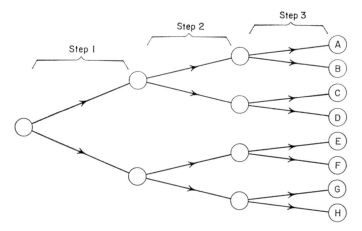

Fig. 1. Branching program for scarmbled book: three steps with two choices at each step.

In principle, the scrambled book can accommodate any branching program that depends only on the history of the student's choices; this should be obvious from Fig. 1.

Figure 1 shows a three-step program with two choices at each step. Each of the students arriving at a different point on the third step has a different history, yet in no step have we considered any data beyond the student's present location and his immediate choice.

It would appear from Fig. 1 that the number of pages or locations to be provided becomes very large if the program is more than a few steps long. In practice, however, this is not the case; most of the student's history is probably irrelevant for the selection of the student's path at any given point in the program. If we carry this idea to its extreme, we get the kind of pattern shown in Fig. 2, which is the simplest kind of branching pattern.

In this pattern branches representing errors are "cut off," and the student, after correction, is returned to the point at which he branched,

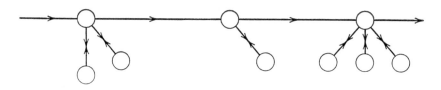

Fig. 2. Simplified branching program for scrambled book.

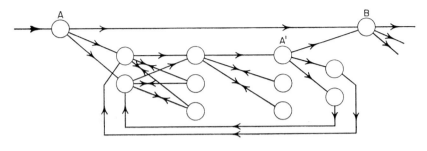

Fig. 3. Branching program with remedial subsequence.

as implied by the double arrows on the branches. With this type of sequence, the number of pages becomes manageable.

A more complex but still practically useful sequence is shown in Fig. 3.

The chief characteristic of the sequence shown in Fig. 3 is that a student making any error on step A is placed in a subsequence which will lead him eventually to the next step (step B), but only if he passes the criterion question at A^1, which covers essentially the same material as question A. Again, notice that in this sequence the only data required to determine where the student should go next are his present location and his immediate choice. The branching program can therefore be accommodated in such a simple device as a scrambled book.

A somewhat more complex device, the AutoTutor * Mark II, shown in Fig. 4, handles similar material but adds some new dimensions of control. The actual material is handled on a roll of 35-mm microfilm. The student sees this material projected on a view screen and has 10 response buttons which he uses to answer the questions. The actual effect of each of the 10 buttons is as follows:

Button I—rewinds film 19 steps
Button H—advances film 15 steps
Button G—advances film 13 steps
Button F—advances film 11 steps
Button E—advances film 9 steps
Button D—advances film 7 steps
Button C—advances film 5 steps
Button B—advances film 3 steps
Button A—advances film 1 step
Button R—cancels previous excursion

* Trademark.

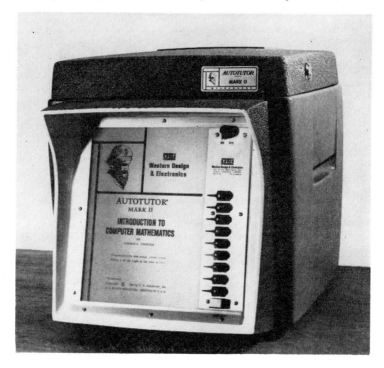

Fig. 4. AutoTutor Mark II.

Buttons A through H are the ones normally used by the student to answer multiple-choice questions. Each button advances the film the number of steps shown. If the student has chosen the correct answer to a question, the film frame on which he lands will contain new information and a new question. When the student again presses one of the A through H buttons to answer the new question, the film will advance from the new location. If the student has chosen an incorrect answer, the material he sees will, in the simplest case, present correctional material; it will then direct him to press the R or RETURN button, which will reverse the excursion the machine has taken immediately before and put the student back on the original question frame for another try at the question. This is the sequence of events, somewhat more conveniently arranged, that would occur if the student were using a scrambled book. However, having the material inside a machine, under mechanical control, we are able to add some very interesting new control features to the material. These controls are brought about by a code on each film frame that determines the buttons on the machine that will be allowed to operate when the student is viewing the frame. Four codes are available on the Mark II AutoTutor, with the following functions:

Code X. All buttons operate. This is the code used routinely on a right-answer frame. The student has just chosen the correct answer to the preceding question; we are satisfied with his performance and have no reason to restrict the student's activity, nor has the student any reason to do anything but what we want him to do, which is to choose an answer to the new question. If the student should want to review the preceding right-answer frame, he may do so by pressing the RETURN button, which we allow to operate.

Code Z. Only the RETURN button works. All other buttons are dead. This is the code normally used on a simple wrong-answer frame. The student on such a frame has made an error, and we want him to read the correctional material and then return to the question page. We set conditions so that only the RETURN is allowed.

Code Y. Only buttons A through H work. This code is used on a wrong-answer frame that introduces a correctional subsequence. The student has made an error; we want him to work forward through a correctional subsequence. In particular, we do *not* want him to return to the question to try another answer. Therefore, we do not allow the RETURN button to work from this frame.

Code W. Only the I button works. The I button on the Mark II is the only button that runs the film backwards. It, with the W code, is used to run the student back in the program, to review material previously studied. It may be used for very simple review of material previously covered or, in a sequence of backward excursions, to bring the student back to the beginning of a complete section of the program.

With the use of these film codes, which appear on each frame of instructional material and are read by two photocells in the machine, it is possible to achieve great flexibility and at the same time exercise complete control over the options available to the student. Figure 5 shows this coding applied to the sequence of steps shown in Fig. 3. It is literally impossible for the student to advance from frame 1 to, say, frame 400 of a program until he achieves the criterion performances we have required on the way.

It may be a nice point whether the Mark II AutoTutor, with the

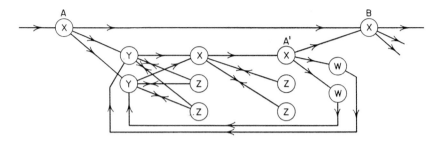

Fig. 5. Application of AutoTutor film codes to branching program.

film codes described, uses intrinsic or extrinsic programming. Whatever conclusion we might come to on this question of definition, it is nonetheless true that we use only data derived from the student's present position, the film frame he is presently viewing, and his immediate choice to determine what will happen to him next. I present this information about the scrambled book and AutoTutor in this much detail to give some idea of the complexity of programming that can be accommodated without involving the more complex types of computing apparatus. Actually, what I have illustrated in this paper are not entire program sequences but small sections of actual sequences.

I would like to make one final point bearing on this matter of complex control of teaching machines. To my mind it is the logic of the subject matter itself that must always be allowed first consideration in designing a program. No amount of computing capability can substitute for clear, well-written programmed material. This is unfortunate because it is easier to draw logic diagrams for computer programs than it is to write effective program material. Nonetheless, it is the material that will ultimately determine the success of the program. I believe that the field of programmed instruction is now beginning to free itself from the restrictions resulting from adherence to a grossly oversimplified learning paradigm; I would hate to see it immediately succumb to a second type of restriction imposed by the possibility of using very complex formal control at the expense of paying close attention to the material to be taught.

Some research problems in automated instruction: instructional programming and subject-matter structure

ROBERT GLASER

University of Pittsburgh and American Institute for Research

It seems highly probable that work on instructional programming will interact with the structuring and analysis of knowledge. In the context of this presumed interaction I shall consider three general problems: (1) the analysis of subject matter or knowledge for converting it into programmed learning sequences, (2) the restructuring of subject materials in order to facilitate the attainment of the objectives of instruction, and (3) the use of learner responses as an indicator of attainment of knowledge. These problems are discussed in relation to work performed in research projects at the University of Pittsburgh. One project was conducted under the sponsorship of the Cooperative Research Branch of the Office of Education, for which Dr. Julian Taber was associate project director and Dr. Lloyd Homme and Dr. James Evans were co-workers previously; the other project was carried out under contract with the Training Research Branch, Aeronautical Systems Division of the Air Force Systems Command, for which Dr. Halmuth Schaefer was associate project director.

The Analysis of Knowledge for Instructional Programming

A problem that arises when one starts to build a programmed learning sequence is the analysis of the knowledge domain to be covered.

This report was written under the sponsorship of the Cooperative Research Branch, U. S. Office of Education, and the Training Research Branch, Aeronautical Systems Division, U. S. Air Force.

Knowledge must be analyzed into units that can provide the building blocks by which the learner goes through an instructional program. The problem of sequencing and flow of these units is discussed later. My first concern is with the nature of the blocks themselves.

The Ruleg System

Some two years ago, Evans, Homme, and I (1960) attempted to approach the analysis of knowledge by beginning with the humble premise that all verbal subject matter that appears in a program can be classified into two groups of statements, rules and examples. We called rules *ru*'s and examples *eg*'s and talked about the "Ruleg System." The definitions of *ru*'s and *eg*'s are relative ones, and sometimes a rule can be an example and an example a rule. In general, a *rule* can be a definition, a mathematical formula, an empirical law, a principle, axiom, postulate, or hypothesis from any area of knowledge. The invariant feature of a rule is that it is a statement of some generality for which substitution instances or examples can be obtained. An *example* can be a description of a physical event, a theorem or deduction, or a statement of a relationship between physical or conceptual objects. The invariant feature of all *eg*'s is that they are statements of some specificity derived from more generalized rules. The clearest example of rules and their corresponding *eg*'s are, of course, in mathematics. The algebraic statement that $a + b = b + a$ is a rule that summarizes an infinite number of substitution instances, so that an example is $7 + 2 = 2 + 7$. The latter statement is in turn a rule for an example of such a statement as 7 stones + 2 stones = 2 stones + 7 stones. It is also possible that the initial algebraic statement $a + b = b + a$ is an example of a rule in group theory such as $a \text{ o } b = b \text{ o } a$ in which neither the objects nor the operator are specified and $a + b = b + a$ becomes an example. Similar examples can be easily generated in different subject-matter domains.

The Ruleg System suggests that in the preparation of a program we write down the rules we wish to teach and arrange them in some order. The nature of the ordering and the necessity for ordering the rules in a particular way is a function of the extent to which the subject matter is structured. In certain subject matters it appears that certain things "logically" come before others. Rules may be ordered on some continuum of simplicity to complexity, as in a physics program. In a geography program the ordering may be along some spatial continuum. Some subject matters appear to require a definite ordering and others may not. Perhaps some thought should be given to the invention of an index of ordering or sequentialness for various subject matters, which would bear some relationship to the sequential dependencies required in a program.

According to the Ruleg System, the rules should, after a preliminary ordering, be arranged in a matrix somewhat as shown in Fig. 1. This matrix is based on the conception that an expert in a particular domain of knowledge manifests his expertness by an ability to integrate the concepts in his field. The *ru* matrix permits the examination of similarities, differences, and possible confusions between the rules and other interverbal connections which must be learned by the student. Upon this matrix we can impose different operators for interrelating the *ru*'s. A very general operator is *relation*. We might ask how rule 1 is related to rule 2 and how rule 2 is related to rule 1. Some cells will be of no consequence and some cells will be redundant, but we might attain some systematic structuring of the knowledge domain. The diagonal cells, which relate each rule to itself, can be called *definition* cells in which a particular rule is explained in terms of previous behavior that exists in the student, so that the definition can be made meaningful in terms of his existing repertoire. Another operator might

	RU 1	RU 2	RU 3	• • •
RU 1				
RU 2				
RU 3				
• • •				

Fig. 1. A rule matrix.

be *discrimination,* in which we can ask, for any particular cell, how one rule is different from another; this may facilitate discrimination training.

An important part of the Ruleg System is that each cell in the matrix would contain an example of the statements in that cell, and within each cell a series of examples could be generated which would be used to teach understanding and manipulation of the rule involved. The cells and the rules could then be organized in some desired sequence in an instructional program. The nature of this sequence is some function of the structure of the knowledge domain and of the behavioral characteristics of sequences which best facilitate retention, creativity, and so forth. The Ruleg System may be considered in relation to such programming principles as fading, discrimination training, prompting, and so forth; in this chapter I wish to indicate only that the Ruleg System has been one rough attempt to analyze a knowledge domain, prior to the development of an instructional program, to facilitate the preparation of such a program. It also might provide some orderly framework which could be specified for computer analysis.

Mechner's System

Another procedure for outlining a knowledge domain in a relatively systematic fashion has been described in a preliminary mimeographed paper by Dr. Francis Mechner (1961) of Basic Systems, Inc., who suggests the following procedure: begin by outlining a subject in terms of 5 to 20 major headings which might correspond loosely to chapter headings of a textbook; write them on red index cards and order them in some rational sequence. Next, break down each of these headings into several subheadings, write them on yellow index cards, and again order them. Do this again with green and then once again with blue index cards. The criterion for the words, phrases, and concepts written on the blue index cards is that they "should be the atoms of the subject, so to speak." They should be elementary enough so that they can be introduced every 5 to 10 frames in a program. This is, of course, an average rate, since several blue concepts might be involved on one frame, and some concepts might require more frames than others. As an example, using set theory, Mechner gives the picture shown in Fig. 2. This provides an illustration of the contents of the various subcategories.

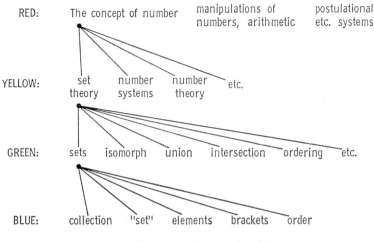

Fig. 2. An illustrative subcategory breakdown.

Mechner then introduces the notion of a flow chart to facilitate the initial introduction and manipulation of a particular unit of knowledge or subject-matter stimulus. The basic concept of the flow chart centers around the systematic "thinning out" of material to be learned and reviewed. The nature of this thinning-out process in the course of an instructional program is specified by an exponential decay function, and the rate of change in this function varies according to the complexity of the concept involved. The flow of a concept in the course of a program is diagrammed in Fig. 3. Every dot represents a response by the student. Several dots vertically above the other lying below a particular frame would indicate that several concepts should be integrated in the frame.

In both of the two crude systems described for ordering subject matter for programming I have emphasized the structure of the subject matter, or what can be called the "logical or epistemological arrangement," and I have suggested that for the analysis of this kind of formal subject-matter structure it might be possible to obtain the assistance of computer programming. However, there is another kind of program ordering based upon a "learning structure." This is the ordering of subject-matter stimuli and responses which have been empirically discovered to produce certain kinds of desirable subject-matter behaviors, such as retention, the manipulation of concepts for problem solving and model building, and creativity and invention with the subject matter. It is up to the experimental psychologist to

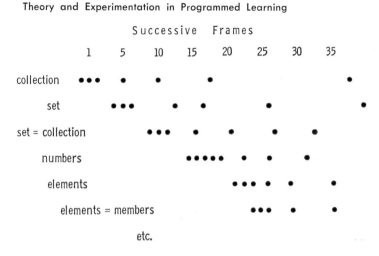

Fig. 3. A program flow chart.

use what he knows about learning and to discover more about learning, so that these appropriate learning sequences can be incorporated with the epistemological structure of the knowledge domain in order to produce an ideal acquisition of knowledge. It is difficult to predict the form of these sequences for particular subject matters. I believe, however, that revised knowledge structures and revised subject material presentation sequences will result from the interaction between subject-matter structure and the structure we learn to use from experience in shaping behavior.

Restructuring Subject Materials

The emphasis just placed on the structuring of subject-matter presentation, where this structure is based on knowledge of what is required to shape the behavior of the learner, leads into the second problem: that is, restructuring subject materials for the attainment of desired terminal behavior. The methods of presenting subject-matter stimuli to the learner, and the ways in which he responds to them, may be different from those in conventional subject-matter presentation. These methods also suggest innovations in the format and style of our present conceptions of a program frame. Let me give three examples here: one is redundancy programming, the second is the use of literal and transliteral prompts, and the third is a spiral program.

Redundancy Programming

A good example of an unconventional presentation of subject material is a foreign language vocabulary program, using language redundancy, constructed by Schaefer (1961). This programming procedure has been developed to teach a reading vocabulary in German to American college students. The procedure is based on the fact that a verbal utterance contains redundant parts which may be eliminated without loss of information. Redundant parts of a sentence may be replaced by nonsense words without loss in the reader's understanding of the content. If the "nonsense" words are words of a language presently unknown to the reader, then consistent use should equate them to their equivalents in the reader's language. Similarly, the grammatical structure of a new language may be acquired to some degree by phrasing the words of the known language according to the grammatical rules of the new language insofar as possible. In trying out this form of programming, Schaefer used stories by Edgar Allen Poe; new German words were introduced gradually in place of English words, and German word order was similarly introduced. The form of the program is shown in Figs. 4, 5, and 6. Figure 4 is an early phase which introduces certain key words. Figure 5 is the second phase in which it is assumed that many of the key words are known to the reader, and in this stage the programmer begins to use the grammatical form of the new language. Few new words are intro-

True! - nervous, very, very dreadfully nervous, ich, had been, and am; but why will you say that ich am mad? The disease had sharpened meine senses - not destroyed, not dulled them. Above all was der sense of hearing acute. Ich heard all the things in dem heaven and der earth. I heard many things in hell. How, then, am ich mad? Hearken! Und observe how healthily--how calmly ich can tell die whole story.

Fig. 4. Redundancy programming: first phase.

Der second und third day went by und yet showed himself mein tormentor

nicht. Again could ich as free man breathe.   Das monster was apparently

in great terror run away!   Never again would ich es see!   Meine happiness

was complete!   Die guilt der black deed disturbed mich but little.   Some

questions were asked und readily answered.   Eine search was even under-

taken, but, of course, could nichts be found.   Ich looked einer safe future

toward.

Fig. 5. Redundancy programming: second phase.

duced in this phase; instead, the emphasis is on the appearance of an unfamiliar grammatical order. Figure 6 is a third phase, in which new words are introduced and sentences must be rewritten and simplified in order to utilize the existing response repertoire. Gradually, as the vocabulary increases, the grammatical form of the native language turns more and more into the grammatical form of the new language. The details of this method are described in a recent report (Schaefer, 1961).

Discriminative Transfer Programming

A second example of an unconventional form of subject-matter presentation, but more in the usual context of a program frame, is a procedure worked out by Taber (1961); this procedure results from the application of the discrimination-training paradigm to human

Die slope seiner Wände wurde von Moment zu Moment smaller, und der bottom

der Vortex seemed sich gradually zu lift.   Der sky war klar, die Winde hatten

sich died, und der moon went brightly im Westen down, als ich mich auf dem

surface des Ozeans facing die coast von Lofoden found, exactly über der place,

wo der Trichter des Moskoestromes gewesen war.

Fig. 6. Redundancy programming: third phase.

learning. In bringing about discriminative control, the method requires that a response be elicited in the presence of the stimulus which is to acquire discriminative properties and that reinforcement must be contingent upon such an appropriate occurrence. At the beginning of discrimination training, the response, over which control is sought, is assumed to exist at some strength in the repertoire of the organism. If the response is weak or improbable, it can be elicited in the presence of the discriminative stimulus by presenting in addition some stimulus which previously was brought to control the response. Such auxiliary stimuli, which are initially used to prompt the response, may, as training proceeds, be gradually dropped and the control of the response transferred to the new stimulus. This is the basic paradigm for the programming procedure which can be called discriminative transfer programming.

Using this procedure with verbal behavior, it is possible to substitute one stimulus for another in cases in which both stimuli evoke the same form of behavior. For example, a picture of a house and the word "house" can be used to evoke the same verbal response. If one wishes to bring the verbal response under the control of a written word, the discrimination-training paradigm suggests that the picture be presented together with the word and that the picture be gradually faded or dropped from the situation. This is, of course, not new to programmers; however, a literal application of this procedure has resulted in an interesting program for the teaching of color words to first-grade students.

Figure 7 outlines the program which was designed to teach eight color names. The figure shows the characteristics of various program cycles for a particular color; such cycles were interspersed with similar cycles for other colors. The figure shows how the color prompt for the word "blue" was vanished throughout the program sequence. Squares in the figure illustrate the form in which each of the eight words appeared in cycles 1, 3, 5, 7, 8, and 10. In going through the program, a child read each of the eight words a total of 11 times, the order in which the words appeared was varied from cycle to cycle, and the entire experimental program consisted of a total of 74 frames. This programming procedure appears to be quite an efficient method and may be generally applicable to other subject matters. For example, an early frame in a number-reading program may appear as shown in Fig. 8. Perhaps elementary-reading training could be carried on when words such as "dog," "cat," and "dance" are associated with

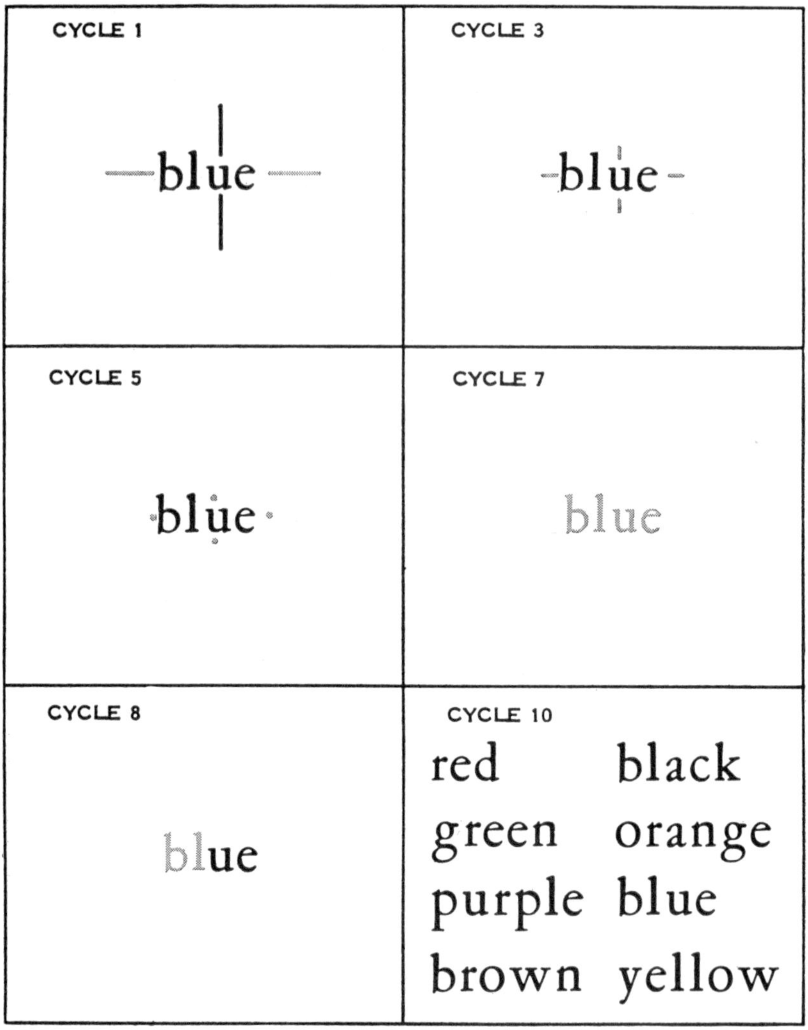

Fig. 7. Discriminative transfer programming: learning color words. Blue coloring (represented here by shaded portions of the figure) was used as vanishing "prompt."

pictorial representations of the real object or figures illustrating the action referred to by a verb.

A more complex example of the discriminative transfer technique is illustrated in a program developed by Attila Csanyi (1961). Mr. Csanyi has programmed oral responses, specifically the pronunciation of

7

7 SEVEN 7

7

Fig. 8. Discriminative transfer programming: an illustrative number-reading frame.

<u>Read out loud</u>:

1.	f (a) <u>a</u> t h e r	a	a	a
2.	b r (ea) <u>e</u> k	e	e	e
3.	c h (ie) <u>i</u> f	ī	ī	ī
4.	(o) <u>o</u> l d	o	o	o
5.	b l (ue) <u>u</u>	u	u	u
	a,	e,	i,	o	u

Fig. 9. Transliteral prompting: early phase.

sounds in the Spanish language, along with the appropriate accent and stress. The program was designed to teach pronunciation of Spanish letters, syllables, and words. In teaching pronunciation, a teacher often uses the previously established English pronunciation to cue or prompt the to-be-learned foreign language pronunciation. Figure 9 is an example of what we have come to call "transliteral prompting." Here a previously learned English word is used to prompt the pro-

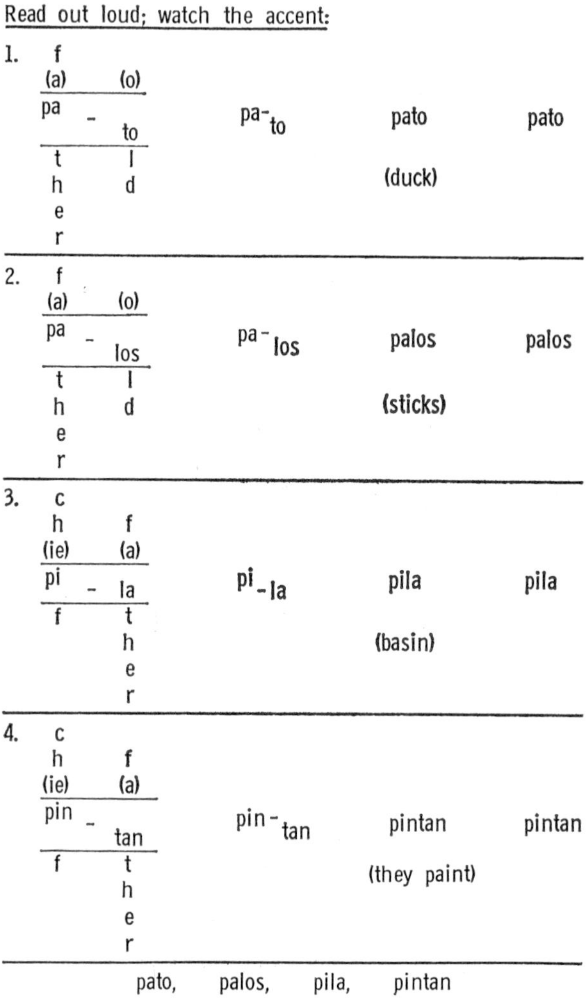

Read out loud; watch the accent:

1. f
   (a)   (o)
   pa   -   pa-_{to}   pato   pato
             to
   t   l
   h   d   (duck)
   e
   r

2. f
   (a)   (o)
   pa   -   pa-_{los}   palos   palos
             los
   t   l
   h   d   (sticks)
   e
   r

3. c
   h   f
   (ie)   (a)
   pi   -   pi-_{la}   pila   pila
             la
   f   t
            h   (basin)
            e
            r

4. c
   h   f
   (ie)   (a)
   pin   -   pin-_{tan}   pintan   pintan
             tan
   f   t
            h   (they paint)
            e
            r

pato,   palos,   pila,   pintan

Fig. 10. *Transliteral prompting: later phase.*

nunciation of a particular foreign language letter or character. Using material like that shown in Fig. 9, the student is required to look at the English words which are written vertically and to transfer the sound of the vowels written in parentheses to the letter between the horizontal lines. Thus the student reads "father," "break," "chief," "old," and "blue" and pronounces the vowels as in Spanish, /ah/, /eh/, /ee/, /oh/, and /oo/. The program progresses from sounds to syllables to Spanish words by themselves. Words are shown in Fig. 10.

Obviously there are some problems in this kind of programming, since what is learned is only an approximation of native pronunciation and transliteration may never be exactly precise; there is also the case of sounds which have no English equivalent. However, we have found that instruction in mouth and tongue placement may be helpful here. For the early stages of approximating pronunciation, however, Csanyi's procedure appears to be useful.

"Spiral" Programming

A further example of subject-matter restructuring is a recently completed program in junior high school general science (Glaser & Schaefer, 1961). Two forms of the program were constructed. In one program, called a "block program," 10 topics were covered in the order presented in Fig. 11. A second version of the program, called a "spiral program," was also constructed. The notion of a spiral program concerns itself with two aspects; one is the spacing of practice and review and the other is the interrelationships between the various topics of the general science course. In the usual textbook presentation, in which each topic has a chapter devoted to it, a student studies one topic for a time and then moves on to the next topic. In the general science course it seemed possible to slice off the basic parts of all topics covered, then take a second slice of the next advanced parts of these topics, then a third slice, and so on. In a sense, the student is still working on the first chapter of a course while beginning the last chapter.

Spiraling can involve two possible advantages. One is the spacing of practice throughout the entire course and the gradual fading of the prompts involved in this practice over a longer period than in a more condensed presentation. The second possible advantage is that the conventionally practiced division of what is called "general science" into the topics shown in Fig. 11 is only one possible mode of presentation and may not be the one that leads to the greatest degree of generalization for the student. The boundaries of the various topics are not well defined lines; it may not be desirable to impose strict boundaries. We felt, however, that a prime goal of instruction in general science was that the student gain understanding and facility with such concepts as gravity, entropy, inertia, cycles, and waves. He should also understand how these topics play a role in the conventional topical divisions. Gravity, for example, plays a role in biology in determining the structure of stems and the position of flowers; in chemistry, in separating mixtures and in weighing compounds; in astronomy, in keeping planets in orbit; in meteorology, in keeping the atmosphere from leaving the planet; and so forth. In working with the spiral program, it was tempting to reorganize the subject matter along these lines. However, we set this formidable task aside for another day and built the spiral program in a fairly mechanical way by breaking each topic, such as biology or chemistry, into component topics and ordering these topics in terms of difficulty. We thus achieved a program which to a large extent first presents the simplest concepts in the 10 topics and then presents the next difficult concepts in these same topics, and so on, until the material is covered. Between, and in the course of, each spiral of the 10 topics, review and fading are introduced. We thus had a program which was comparable

1. Measurement	235	frames
2. Chemistry	825	frames
3. Sound	230	frames
4. Electricity	763	frames
5. Meteorology	784	frames
6. Astronomy	843	frames
7. Communication	250	frames
8. Light	349	frames
9. Work and Machines	1227	frames
10. Biology	1271	frames

Fig. 11. The order of topics covered in the general science block program.

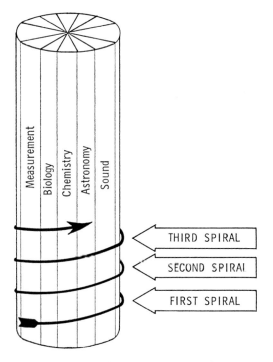

Fig. 12. A model of the general science spiral program.

to the more conventional block program but in which we could study the advantage of the more spaced practice and review.

The spiral program is shown in Fig. 12. The student starts on one section and goes to the next on the low level at first and covers all the topics in their simplest context. He then begins the next round of topics on a new difficulty level. In doing so he looks once more through the review sections of what he saw during the first round. At the present time, students are working on both forms of the program, the block and the spiral, but experimental results are not yet available.

Response Mode as an Indicator of the Attainment of Knowledge

The third problem on which I should like to comment briefly concerns the use of different forms of response to indicate the attainment of knowledge. Almost two years ago (Evans, Glaser, & Homme, 1960), a comparison was made of two different response modes in a program in symbolic logic. One group wrote out, that is, constructed, their responses, and another group employed multiple-choice responses. Criterion performance indicated no significant differences between the modes of responding. Similar findings were obtained in a study by Coulson & Silberman (1959), and these findings have been repeated since in studies by others (see the chapter by Briggs, Goldbeck, Campbell, & Nichols in this book). On the basis of these studies, one might hypothesize that organisms display "topological generalization," that is, response generalization from the performance of a response with one set of muscles to performance with another set of muscles.

A striking example of this was given by Evans in a recent talk at the American Psychological Association (Evans, 1961). He displayed data (Fig. 13) showing the results of a program (called a multiple-

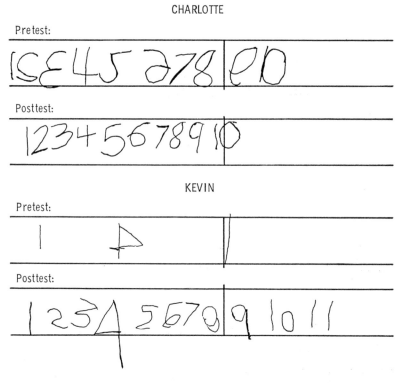

Fig. 13. Pre- and posttests for multiple-choice discrimination programming.

choice discrimination program) which, among other things, involved learning to write numbers. The pretest top lines show the performance of two students before the program; the posttest lines show their performance at the end of the program. Throughout the course of the program no numbers were *actually* constructed by writing; the child responded in multiple-choice discriminations either by circling a correct matching response on a constructed-response teaching machine or by pushing an appropriate button on a multiple-choice machine. The children learned to construct numbers fairly well, possibly because their learning of appropriate discriminations made it possible for them to monitor their own constructed responses.

If a program leads, as a good program does, to high probability responses, then the problem of channeling these responses into a number of response modes may be almost trivial. This is especially true of an adult; if the adult can make a response such as "Office of Naval Research," then the correlation of responses will be high when he is required to write it, type it, or recognize it from a list. For low probability responses of the kind that occur in nonprogrammed learning situations, this topological generalization is probably less likely; it is more desirable in such situations that response modes in the course of instruction be similar to the criterion behavior.

Some Further Problems

In concluding, there are two further research problems I should like to mention. One concerns the notion of "intrinsic" reinforcement. It is possible that the emphasis on providing confirmation and feedback to the student as he goes through a program has led us to overlook the notion that much of human learning is intrinsically reinforcing; that is, the response has reinforcing properties and the student needs only to make a response which provides reinforcing stimuli. In the programs mentioned above, the redundancy program and the discriminative transfer programs, a stimulus was presented to which the student re-responded, but there was no special frame supplying printed response feedback. A study by Scharf (1961) and another by Evans, Glaser, & Homme (1960), in which the amount and delay of reinforcement were varied, have shown no significant differences in criterion performance. It seems that in the high probability response context of a program use can be made of reinforcers that are inherent in responding to the subject matter. In many well-constructed frames there is little doubt that the student, after having made a response, can check or monitor himself regarding the correctness of his response without the necessity for frequent response confirmation frames. In the redundancy program, for example, the response may be considered "self-reinforcing," perhaps in the same sense that a student is reinforced when he is led to discover something or make what he considers to be an ingenious response to a situation.

The notion I am trying to convey here is similar to O. K. Moore's term "autotelic," which he coined to describe the quality of an instructional sequence which becomes an end in itself so that performing the sequence is "intrinsically" reinforcing. If a frame offers a stimulus which has a high probability of eliciting the desired response, the foundation for an autotelic frame has been laid. Finishing such a frame (i.e., giving the correct response) is an end in itself. In this sense a frame that is "peaked" in difficulty (neither too easy nor too difficult) can provide a stimulus for an "intrinsically reinforcing frame"—particularly if the program is tried and tested and especially constructed for one subject. When the program is to be used with a number of subjects, the frame is not quite peaked for the individual subject, hence may require confirming stimuli. Perhaps frames can be made more autotelic if they are written with various degrees of prompting so that a subject can, before making a response, select that frame which most probably assures him of making the correct response. Such a procedure is akin to the notion of branching. We are working with a program in which, for every frame, several frames have been written; with this arrangement, the student can skip frames until he comes to the one which makes the response "almost" obvious (Glaser & Schaefer, 1961).

The final research problem I wish to discuss is very general. Programs can become research apparatus in the same sense that "paired associate" and "serial" word lists have been. If this is to be the case, we need two things: (1) a set of terms or a taxonomy for describing the properties of a particular program and the differences between programs and (2) some standard programs for general research use. At the present time it is difficult to interpret the results of a study when an investigator reports that he has used a "Skinner-type" program. In our work at the Programmed Learning Laboratory some attempt has been made to construct a "standard" program (Evans, Glaser, & Homme, 1960).

The importance of the need for a descriptive terminology for programs is highlighted when we consider that one of the goals of programmed learning is the development of a "theory" of the instructional process that helps produce a specifiable teaching technology. One approach to such a theory is the development of programmed learning sequences for certain subject matters in which the frames can be identified by their psychological and pedagogical characteristics. Once we can specifically identify such characteristics of an instructional sequence, we will have gone a long way toward increasing our knowledge of learning and teaching.

REFERENCES

Coulson, J. E., & Silberman, H. F. *Results of an initial experiment in automated teaching.* Santa Monica, California: System Development Corporation, 1959. Also in A. A. Lumsdaine & R. Glaser (Eds.), *Teaching machines and programmed learning: A source book.* Washington, D. C.: National Education Association, 1960. Pp. 452–468.

Csanyi, A. P. An investigation of visual versus auditory programming in teaching foreign language pronunciation. In R. Glaser & J. I. Taber (Eds.), *Investigations of the characteristics of programmed learning sequences.* Pittsburgh: University of Pittsburgh, 1961. Report issued under Cooperative Research Project 691(9417).

Evans, J. L. Multiple choice discrimination programming. Paper read at Amer. Psychol. Assoc., New York, September 1961.

Evans, J. L., Glaser, R., & Homme, L. E. *An investigation of teaching machine variables using a program in symbolic logic.* Pittsburgh: University of Pittsburgh, 1960. A report issued under Cooperative Research Project 691(9417).

Glaser, R., & Schaefer, H. H. *Final report: Principles of programming printed materials.* Pittsburgh: University of Pittsburgh, 1961. A report issued under AF 33(616)-7175.

Mechner, F. *Programming for automated instruction.* New York: Basic Systems, Inc., 1961. (Mimeo.)

Schaefer, H. H. *A vocabulary program using "language redundancy."* Pittsburgh: University of Pittsburgh, 1961. A report issued under Cooperative Research Project 691(9417).

Scharf, Eugenia S. A study of the effects of partial reinforcement on behavior in a programmed learning situation. In R. Glaser & J. I. Taber (Eds.), *Investigations of the characteristics of programmed learning sequences.* Pittsburgh: University of Pittsburgh, 1961. Report issued under Cooperative Research Project 691(9417).

Taber, J. I., & Glaser, R. *An exploratory evaluation of a discriminative transfer learning program using literal prompts.* Pittsburgh: University of Pittsburgh, 1961. A report issued under Cooperative Research Project 691(9417).

Experimental results regarding form of response, size of step, and individual differences in automated programs

LESLIE J. BRIGGS, ROBERT A. GOLDBECK, VINCENT N. CAMPBELL, and DARYL G. NICHOLS
American Institute for Research

The very different conceptions of learning held by Skinner (1958) and Crowder (1959) are reflected in the programming techniques used by these two investigators. Experimental analysis of these techniques requires that they be broken down into their component operational characteristics. Although this analysis may do some violence to the total systems of programming advocated by Skinner and Crowder, we feel that study of single programming characteristics and of interactions among these characteristics is necessary to develop explanatory principles of the learning produced by automated instruction. Such research also should result in improvements in either the time efficiency or the learning level attainable, by developing optimum combinations of characteristics.

Form of Response

Our research initially concerned the different roles assigned to the reading material by various programmers. Skinner uses the stem of

Research in form of response sponsored by the Office of Naval Research, Contract Nonr-3077(00).
Research in size of step sponsored by the U. S. Office of Education, Grant 736134.01.
Research in individual differences in automated programs sponsored by the U. S. Office of Education, Grant 736103.00.

the frame to evoke the overt response required. Crowder, regarding programming as a problem in effective communication, stresses the reading material as something to be read and understood by the subject; overt responses are required mainly to see if the communication has been effective and to determine which frame the student should read next. As a result, the amount of reading per overt response differs between the two kinds of programs.

While recognizing that the assumed role of reading is different in the two kinds of programs, we doubted that frequent overt responding and short, easy frames constituted an ideal pair of conditions for effective learning, as proposed by Skinner. First, we thought that writing responses to easy frames requires undue time; second, we thought the degree of redundancy and the direct prompting employed to make the frames easy tend to eliminate the need for response construction.

In an early experiment (Goldbeck, 1960) we used independent frames of factual material in which the number of words in the stem per response term was quite small, as is typical in Skinner-type programs. The hypothesis was that success on a criterion test following the learning would be a function of both difficulty of the material and form of response. We used a 3 x 3 design with three levels of item difficulty (established by varying degrees of cueing) and three modes of responding: constructed (overt) responding, covert responding, and simply reading. Each frame for the overt and covert groups was identical, the instruction to write or not write the responses in the blanks being the only difference in the two sets of experimental materials. On the page following the "frame," the correct answer was supplied as feedback. For the reading group, all the information was given in the frame; the "response" term was supplied and underlined, corresponding to "blanks" in frames for overt and covert groups. There was no "feedback" page for the reading group. In all nine experimental conditions each subject worked once through the program at his own pace and received a test immediately upon completion of the learning trial. Time taken for the learning trial was recorded separately for each subject.

Covariance analysis of posttest scores, using scores on the California Reading Maturity Test as the covariable, indicated a significant interaction ($P < .01$) between response mode and item difficulty level. The average within-group correlation between the reading scores and the quiz scores was .55. Since item difficulty was varied by manipulating cueing and prompting, the relative effectiveness of the different response modes being compared became a function of cueing. The results indicated that no single form of response mode was uniquely appropriate to the learning of the kind of material used in this study. With the three item-difficulty levels used, write-in (overt) responding was found superior to covert ($P < .01$) and reading responses (not significant) only for the intermediate-difficulty level, when scores on a posttraining test were used as the criterion.

When comparisons of test scores were made for programs containing low-difficulty training items, the reading group and the covert group were superior to the overt group ($P < .01$ and $P < .05$). In time-efficiency of learning the reading group was superior at all difficulty levels to other response modes ($P < .01$). It appears that *when all the information was supplied at once*, as for the reading group, easy items were well learned. These items were not well learned by the overt group, even though they wrote out their correct responses and received feedback (Goldbeck & Briggs, 1960). A possible explanation is that there was too little challenge in the easy items for overt responding and formal feedback to become effective. When moderately difficult items were encountered, however, there may have been an increase in motivation and implicit activity associated with the effort required for response, with a concomitant increase in the value of feedback. This increase in the value of feedback for moderately difficult items appeared to occur whether the overt response was correct or incorrect during the learning trial.

The next experimental effort sought to determine whether the efficiency of learning of the reading condition found with independent frames would hold for a continuous-discourse program. A second experiment utilized continuous-discourse material that had been revised to be more difficult than in its original form and so more comparable to the intermediate-difficulty level of the first experiment. Using this one set of materials, the three response modes of the earlier experiment again were used, plus a fourth optional overt response group. (The overt group made 16% errors during learning; the option group made 10% errors plus 12% omissions of response.) The scores on a criterion test showed little difference in learning level resulting from the various response modes ($P < .20$); however, in time-efficiency of learning reading was again superior to covert responding, overt responding, and to optional overt responding ($P < .01$) (Goldbeck, Campbell, & Llewellyn, 1960). A retention test given 10 weeks after the initial test showed some drop in retention for all response modes and a significant difference among response modes ($P < .05$) in favor of the reading mode.

A special analysis of the delayed retention test data yielded evidence on another potentially significant question. The overt-response group was slightly, but not significantly, superior to the covert-, reading-, and optional-response groups only when the test used stimulus context and response terms that were identical or highly similar to those used in learning. Reading responses again were found superior to other modes of response when the retention-test items varied considerably from the learning frames in language employed and in response word required. The superiority of learning by reading when transfer responses are required suggests that the motivation to construct the response during learning interfered with use of all the relevant information presented in the frame. High motivation, when directed toward the required response, appears to result in selective responding to the materials in the frame.

Additional analyses of data from the first and second experiments have sought more detailed interpretations of the data at the frame or response levels. Pilot data have been collected on the effect of the relevance and number of response alternatives available to the subject in learning factual material.[1]

Materials in the two response-mode experiments just described contained a small amount of reading per frame, as in Skinner-type programs, but used higher difficulty levels than Skinner recommends. Results of the studies appear to justify further experimentation and theorizing concerning response-mode and feedback conditions.

Pending such further analyses, we may offer speculative comments pertaining especially to the results found by comparing the reading groups and the overt-response groups:

1. *Response Mode.* In the overt group the subject is required to produce a response; in the reading group no response is required. Two aspects of the overt-group subject's response merit investigation. One concerns the response itself; the other concerns the stimulus. On the response side, the subject undoubtedly considers various response alternatives, the nature and number of which depend upon the characteristics of the item (e.g., amount of cueing, inherent difficulty of the material, and number of relevant possible alternatives) and upon the characteristics of the subject (e.g., the number of alternatives the

[1] This study was conducted by Benjamin B. Burton and Robert A. Goldbeck. A report of results is now in preparation.

subject can consider in a short period of time and the subject's motivation).

On the stimulus side, the subject's effort to produce the correct response causes him to attend more closely to the stimulus than he might with other response modes. This attention would appear to have potential for positive as well as negative effects on learning: positive in that the subject must learn the stimulus component of the stimulus-response connection but negative in that there may be so heavy a concentration on producing a response to the stimulus that transfer to new stimulus materials would result in a decrement. (Evidence of this latter supposition is presented under *Size of Step,* below.)

2. *Feedback.* Another important difference between the reading and overt modes of response lies in the nature of the feedback. Members of the overt group received feedback by seeing the correct word after each written response. The action of the subject in writing a response and the immediately following confirmation may have created a "closure" effect in which the subject considered his task completed for that item.

In contrast, this task completion was probably absent for members of the reading group. The superiority of the reading group may have resulted from a general tendency toward better recall of incompleted tasks than of completed tasks, as first described by Zeigarnik.

It may be possible to design an effective procedure to increase the amount of time devoted by the subject to the feedback. Such a method for altering the subject's time distribution may, in itself, produce better learning.

3. *Motivation.* Differences in motivation among response modes and among feedback conditions are probable; these differences may account for the major effects of response mode and feedback variations on learning. Responding may give a subject the "set" for being evaluated (partly by transfer from testing situations) and inspire him to try harder to learn. Feedback may be motivating not only in the classical sense of reinforcement but also by giving the subject a "game-playing" set. However, the extent to which "enthusiasm for winning the game" aids learning is uncertain.

We should consider the conditions of motivation under which instructional method variables are examined. Motivation appears to play a general methodological role, as well as an explanatory role, in research in instructional methods. Thus, although reading may appear superior to other response modes when tested under the usual experimental conditions in which motivation is typically high, other response modes may be superior under conditions of low motivation. It is a matter of serious concern that most studies probably are carried out under high motivation, whereas the usual learning situations in school provide a somewhat lower level of motivation. Possibly the significant contributions of autoinstructional methods will accrue from the advantages gained under conditions of less than maximum motivation.

Size of Step

The foregoing experiments were aimed primarily toward the examination of differences among response modes, without varying size of step (e.g., amount of information per frame). The studies next to be described focus upon differences in amount to be read by the subject before he answers questions and upon the use of review questions during a single learning session.

One experiment used a lesson on the structure and functions of the United Nations. Four groups of subjects studied for two hours and were tested two days later on a 54-item factual knowledge quiz. One group read eight pages of mimeographed material in a format resembling conventional textbooks. A second group read materials in a revised textbook format which presented first an overview of topics to be covered, followed by reading materials identical to those of the first (textbook) group except that each page of prose was followed by a summary outline page. The third and fourth groups both took a small-step, constructed-response program of the Skinner type. They differed in that the third group responded with the first letter of each response word only, while the fourth group wrote complete responses.

As each subject completed his learning material, he was given multiple-choice review questions on paper that was chemically treated to confirm correct response selections immediately by a change in color. All students thus had the same amount of total learning time (two hours), but the amount of time available to each student to answer review questions varied with the time he needed to complete the basic learning materials.

For each subject a third of the material was not covered by the review questions supplied, so that analyses could be made of the learning of both reviewed and unreviewed material among the four basic instructional methods. Over-all levels of learning without review did not vary significantly among instructional methods, although mean learning time among methods varied from 20 to 70 minutes. The mimeographed textbook group was by far the most efficient in terms of time, and the fully constructed program group was the least efficient. These results were in general agreement with those of the retention test for continuous-discourse material as cited in the second experiment above (Goldbeck, Campbell, & Llewellyn, 1960). With learning time equated for all groups by the inclusion of review questions following the initial programming, we found no statistical significance for differences in criterion scores. The observed differences favored the text-plus-review group with a mean score of 65%, whereas the fully constructed program plus review produced a low mean score of 50%.

Criterion test questions were of two kinds: (1) those for which correct answers were the same as responses elicited during learning by the constructed-response programs, and (2) questions for which answers were different from program-elicited responses but which were always read in the stimulus portion of program frames. On test items for which answers were the same as program-elicited responses, both of the constructed-response program groups evidenced superior learning $(P < .15)$. Conversely, when test answers were different from program-elicited responses, the level of learning by constructed-response program groups was inferior $(P < .10)$. The major portion of the foregoing two effects can be attributed to the interaction of the fully constructed-response programs and the elicited-nonelicited response dichotomy. The fully constructed program group gave correct test answers 54% of the time when the answers were the same as those given during Skinner-type program learning. (A score of 54% correct is a higher level of learning than it would appear. Testing was conducted two days after the learning session, and each item required a written recall type of response to questions read aloud to the group.) The percentage of correct answers dropped to only 27 when test answers were different from those elicited during the learning program. The difference between elicited and nonelicited effects was highly significant $(P < .001)$. These results confirm a dictum of those preparing constructed-response programs, which can be paraphrased thus: "State learning objectives as specific criterion behaviors and elicit each behavior during training." We might now add a corollary: "If you employ a Skinner-type program, do not expect even a moderate level of learning of program content which is not elicited during training." But note carefully that when *no* responses are elicited, as in a straight reading condition, learning levels and efficiency are very favorable.

The textbook reading groups achieved a 38% level of learning for items not elicited by the Skinner programs. It is appropriate to ask why the reading material in the Skinner-type programs was learned less well (27%), even though it was presented far more redundantly than in the text. It was found that about one fourth of the difference in test items correct between text and constructed-program learning of nonelicited materials was associated with what we have termed "program carryovers." Such carryovers are program-elicited responses that are applied to the wrong test question. (These are similar to "overt intrusions" in rote learning.) It would seem almost as if each constructed-program subject had developed a repertoire of program-elicited responses that could be evoked not only by an appropriate stimulus context (54% of the time) but also by an incorrect stimulus which may have been subjectively similar to the correct one. If this is the case, the solution to the "carryover" problem may lie in training for more precise stimulus discrimination.

It should be stressed that the low level of retention for nonelicited response materials is not simply a theoretical problem that can be solved by elicitation of all criterion responses during training. The learning of United Nations material in this study is a case in point: if all important responses had been elicited by the experimental fully constructed program, learning time would have been increased from 70 minutes to some 175 minutes. When contrasted to the 20 minutes required by the textbook reading group to reach an equivalent level of learning, practical considerations of learning efficiency cannot be ignored.

The multiple-choice review questions that were made available to each subject when he completed his basic materials were quite similar to the self-scoring "chemo card" reported by Peterson (1931). They also were generally similar in function to the self-instructional devices developed by Pressey (1927; 1932; 1950) in that a correct response had to be made and recognized before a student could go on to the next question (called by Thorndike the "retained situation").

Multiple-choice review questions did increase scores on test items having answers that were the same as the correct answers in the response portion of the multiple-choice questions. This effect was evidenced for all instructional method groups and was highly significant ($P < .001$). (These effects applied equally to program-elicited and nonprogram-elicited response learning within any of the four instructional-method groups.) The percentage of correct test answers was higher for reviewed than nonreviewed items by 28% for the text group and by 10% for the constructed-response program group. The amount of increased learning due to review for each of the four instructional-method groups ranked perfectly with the amount of time that was available to each group for review. Review time varied from a high of 75 minutes for the text group to a low of 28 minutes for the fully constructed response group.

The multiple-choice review questions also enhanced the learning of responses that were not directly elicited by review but that were read in the stimulus portion of review questions $(P < .01)$. Review was found to be as effective for test answers not elicited during review as for review-elicited answers $(F < 1.0)$. The text group subjects did show some advantage of review-elicited responses to the extent that all subjects in this group showed superior learning of responses elicited during review. In general, however, our results indicate that it does not matter much whether information to be learned by review questions appears in the stem of the question or as a response choice. By contrast, it is necessary to assign criterion behavior in the response portion of constructed-response program frames.

A further study now in process will examine variations in the text-plus-review-question format. In order to determine optimum size of step for this material, the total text will be divided into 1, 8, and 18 steps, with each step followed by multiple-choice questions. Also, the number of questions will be varied for each size of step. The results should produce a more precise indication than that given in the experiment just described of the optimum study condition for such material. Still further study is needed of the structure of materials in order that generalization of results can be specified for defined dimensions or categories of material. Such dimensions may involve deductive versus inductive arrangement of material or amount of stress on rules versus examples.

Individual Differences

Two general methods have been proposed whereby individual differences among students are taken into account by automated programs. First, one may employ a linear program that requires all students in a group to read the same sequence of materials and to respond by the same mode to all questions posed. Time to complete the program is allowed to vary, since each student sets his own pace. Skinner has argued that even if some students know some of the material before taking the program, or if some need less redundancy than others to acquire the new learning, these fortunate students may go quickly through the program and will benefit from the "overlearning" provided.

A second approach appears to represent a more versatile mode of adjustment to individual differences. Parallel, branching, or bypassing programs may be responsive to variations in prior knowledge and ability to learn and may offer corresponding variations in material presented and in mode of responding and amount of review. By direct adjustment to differences in prior knowledge, branching may excuse the student from studying again that which he already knows. This second approach probably reflects less confidence that there is one ideal sequence of material that can be prescribed for all to follow. Individuals are also, perhaps, permitted to differ in more relevant ways than are contemplated by designers of single-track programs. Thus the selection of sequences for each student may be a complex function of prior knowledge, rate of learning new material, and mode of learning suitable for the individual.

Although branching may be less rigid or more efficient than a linear program, the former method also requires more information about student needs. This knowledge may be obtained in either of two ways, depending upon one's choice of experimental or programming strategy. On the one hand, one may take a theoretical or conceptual approach whereby one first hypothesizes the nature or source of individual difference that would lead individual A to profit more from program A than from program B. Then measurements may be taken to verify the hypotheses before normal application is made. The greater the number of proven relevant sources of individual differences, the more parallel programs there are to write or the more complex the branching program becomes. If most individuals have unique profiles of combinations of different degrees of the various dimensions of differences, the adjustment becomes still more complicated.

An alternative strategy is to design grossly different parallel programs or flexible branching-bypassing programs to determine first whether individuals actually use the program variations made available. If they do not, the effort seems wasted; if they do, one can next try to determine why different people take different routes to the goal and whether these individual routes yield increased learning or greater time-efficiency of learning over a linear program.

We have made limited efforts to employ both the theoretical strategy and the empirical strategy with nonlinear programs. In one study we hypothesized that some individuals would learn best by heavy, direct prompting, whereas others would learn best by more subtle, indirect cueing techniques (Briggs, 1960). We failed to find clear evidence to support the hypothesis, and the slight trends we did find could as easily have been attributed to differences among the several subject matters presented as to the experimental variation in cueing. Next we hypothesized that an option to make or not to make an overt response, depending on the subject's own subjective confidence of being right, would allow each individual to make fewer overt errors during learning and would thus result in higher criterion scores due to the option to respond. This hypothesis was not supported. Groups required to respond did make more overt errors during learning, but they nevertheless scored as well as the option groups on the criterion.

A third effort used a bypass program in which subjects who responded correctly to the first half of a frame, which contained a rather condensed statement of the material, were permitted to skip the second half of the frame, which contained more detail. A second group was required to respond to both halves of each frame; that is, no bypassing was permitted. A third group was given only the first half of each frame. On posttest scores in one school the bypass group did as well as the no-bypass group and took much less time to complete the lesson. This result encouraged us greatly, but, to our consternation, when the experiment was repeated in a second school, the bypass and no-bypass groups did no better than the short-form group. The school-by-learning-method interaction in test scores was significant; a possible explanation for this interaction lies in motivation differences between the two schools.

Present plans call for repeating the experiment in other schools and for further modifying both the language of the program and the bypass technique in a search for a bypass method useful in teaching the same lesson to subjects covering a wide age range.

In our experiments in individual differences we identified program characteristics that could be varied, rather than first assessing personal characteristics of the individual as a basis for developing varied program characteristics. We suggest that research employing both kinds of starting point may be fruitful. Various sidelights to the major results presented above and further details regarding these experiments appear elsewhere (Campbell, 1961).

Summary

In general we have found no evidence to support the widely held belief that programs must consist of very easy frames and must require overt written responses. Under the experimental conditions reported, we find learning level to be a function of an interaction between item difficulty and mode of response. (Much of the data reported are based on covariance analysis, as we find predictor variables to correlate with criterion scores more highly than in many other studies reporting programming research.)

In terms of time-efficiency of learning, we find reading conditions generally superior, whether small or large segments of information are presented as a frame or unit. When posttraining test scores are used as the criterion, we find reading conditions of learning to be superior to overt responding conditions, especially when the language of the test item and the required answer are not identical to the language of the learning frame and to the response required there. In some respects, therefore, a reading program results in better transfer than a program requiring overt responding. Conversely, if all criterion items are in the program and if the responses are elicited by the same language in the program or in the stem of the test item, a Skinner-type responding program is superior.

Under the experimental conditions employed, subjects read units as long as eight pages with time-efficiency superior to, and learning levels equal to, a more time-consuming program requiring responses. If the subject is required to give implicit responses to blanks in frames, or to supply the first letter only to a constructed response, his learning efficiency falls at a level between straight reading and normal constructed-response conditions.

Errors made during learning, when corrective feedback is invariably supplied, do not clearly detract from the criterion performance. Evidence suggests that feedback may be more important in determining learning level when the feedback follows wrong responses than when it follows correct responses. The sets of alternatives considered by the subject before answering difficult questions during learning may interact with the requirement to respond and with feedback effects. Size of the set of alternatives implicitly considered and relative strengths among the alternatives appear to be factors in our obtained interaction of item difficulty and mode of response.

Confirmation following a correct response may actually detract from retention test score. A form of "closure" may, in effect, cause the student to dismiss the item from further consideration, much as a completed task is recalled less well than an incompleted task, as first reported by Zeigarnik. High motivation caused by the requirement to respond and to view the feedback term may or may not effect such a "closure," depending possibly upon the difficulty of responding.

Bypassing, as a method of adjusting to individual differences among learners, appears to be a promising learning condition, especially from the viewpoint of time economy. The value in terms of learning level is less clear. The size of learning difference found for bypass versus linear conditions in our research is still not great enough to support operational recommendations. In future research we will seek techniques for the development of a program that will be successful not only for a given age group but for students of wide age range, thus avoiding repetition of lessons over several school years.

REFERENCES

Briggs, L. J. *A survey of cueing methods in education and automated programs.* Pittsburgh: American Institute for Research, May 1960. (AFOSR-TN-60-286; AIR-314-61-IR-106)

Campbell, V. N. *Adjusting self-instruction programs to individual differences: studies of cueing, responding and bypassing.* San Mateo, California: American Institute for Research, July 1961. (AIR-C41-7/61-SR)

Crowder, N. A. Automatic tutoring by means of intrinsic programing. In E. H. Galanter (Ed.), *Automatic teaching: the state of the art.* New York: Wiley, 1959. Pp. 109–116.

Goldbeck, R. A. *The effect of response mode and learning material difficulty on automated instruction.* Santa Barbara, California: American Institute for Research, September 1960. (AIR-328-60-IR-124)

Goldbeck, R. A., & Briggs, L. J. *An analysis of response mode and feedback factors in automated instruction.* Santa Barbara, California: American Institute for Research, November 1960. (AIR-328-60-IR-133)

Goldbeck, R. A., Campbell, V. N., & Llewellyn, Joan E. *Further experimental evidence on response modes in automated instruction.* Santa Barbara, California: American Institute for Research, December 1960. (AIR-328-60-IR-132)

Peterson, J. C. The value of guidance in reading for information. *Trans. Kansas Acad. Sci.,* 1931, **34.**

Pressey, S. L. A machine for automatic teaching of drill material. *School and Society,* 1927, **25,** 549–552.

Pressey, S. L. A third and fourth contribution toward the coming "industrial revolution" in education. *School and Society,* 1932, **36,** 668–672.

Pressey, S. L. Development and appraisal of devices providing immediate automatic scoring of objective tests and concomitant self-instruction. *J. Psychol.,* 1950, **29,** 417–447.

Skinner, B. F. Teaching machines. *Science,* 1958, **128,** 969–977.

Teaching science and mathematics by autoinstruction in the primary grades: an experimental strategy in curriculum development

EVAN R. KEISLAR and JOHN D. McNEIL

University of California, Los Angeles

In the opening chapter of this book Dr. Carter rightly contends that the relevance of automation to education depends upon whether automation can be used to achieve educational goals. It follows that those who accept the challenge of automation in education must concern themselves with the goals of education. Without an examined methodology for determining proper instructional objectives, those preparing autoinstructional materials have no way of demonstrating that their efforts are truly contributing to education. In fact, their very successes in changing the learner's behavior may be miseducative.

Lack of a long-range policy will result in failure to realize the true potentialities of programmed instruction for improvement in educational methodology. A wide variety of scattered exploratory studies is to be expected and even desired in a field as new as programmed instruction. But if, in haste to introduce programs into the schools,

These investigations were made possible by a grant from the Hughes Aircraft Company and by a contract under the Cooperative Research Program of the U. S. Office of Education (No. 1090) entitled "Abilities of First Grade Pupils to Learn Mathematics in Terms of Algebraic Structures by Means of Teaching Machines." Appreciation is expressed for the generous cooperation of the administrative staff and teachers of the California public schools in Santa Monica and West Los Angeles where the studies reported in this chapter were conducted.

considerable time and money are spent developing miscellaneous programs of many kinds at all grade levels, we may unfortunately thrust upon the schools a patchwork curriculum. The consumers, in this case the schools, will be left in a welter of confusion, since the available programs must be fitted into an over-all curriculum within which the schools operate.

Another inherent feature of programmed instruction is that it represents an investment in production time and money far greater than that required for textbooks and the usual courses of study. Minor revisions in frames or short frame sequences are already considered an important part of program maintenance; however, once a program is introduced in the schools, there may understandably be considerable resistance on the part of publishing companies and schools to change to a new sequence throughout the grades. Consequently, unless we are careful, current developments may freeze an educational content that is already to be questioned on many grounds. We cannot afford to have programmed instruction teach, no matter how efficiently, an invalid curriculum.

We have often spoken of the serious weakness, for some purposes, of programs that are only one or two hours long. But, in the context of educational planning, programs that are only one or two *semesters* long are also likely to be inadequate. We must give thought to programs or sequences that encompass many grades. Such programs cannot be prepared casually; they must be preceded by a vast amount of study and careful experimental strategy.

The work of the School Mathematics Study Group (Begle, 1958) is an excellent example of the preliminary study that is required. Here a completely new curriculum is being developed and programmed from the first through the twelfth grades. However, many school systems have a policy of revising the curriculum at the high school level and then working downward. This policy has a serious drawback, which may be encountered by the SMSG. A course of study, and even carefully programmed materials, may be prepared for higher grade levels; but, if it is found that younger students learn the content easily, albeit in a different mode of presentation, the materials prepared for later grades may become immediately obsolete.

The Physical Science Study Committee (1959), for instance, has carefully prepared materials for the high school level. These costly materials may later require drastic revision if it is demonstrated that junior high pupils readily learn wave theory and other topics considered to be too advanced for them and if junior high materials are prepared in light of this finding.

As another example, a currently popular programmed textbook in English mechanics and grammar, designed for the junior high level, may be found utterly inappropriate when improved methods of teaching and a completely new content based on the contribution of modern linguistics are introduced into the elementary school.

Selecting Curriculum Content

The practice of revising school curriculum with little regard for what can or should be taught in the early years may be understood historically. A major function of the schools has been to prepare students for higher education. The colleges and universities have more or less independently arrived at decisions concerning the appropriate content for their students. Often the curriculum at lower levels has been developed in the light of such higher educational requirements rather than in consideration of what can be taught efficiently to children in the lower grades.

One could well argue that a broad total approach to the curriculum from the first grade through college should be adopted. In this way, topics could be more appropriately ordered in terms of subject-matter organization and of the abilities of students, optimizing transfer from one grade level to succeeding levels. Now that we can introduce more efficient methods of instruction at any grade, we can no longer afford the luxury of uneconomical instruction resulting from a faulty sequence of topics and the unnecessary deferment of important content. In fact, a basic reorganization of the topics throughout the total school curriculum, a change which might be made possible by the new instructional technology, may yet prove to be a more important contribution of programmed instruction to the schools than increased efficiency in teaching the present content.

Key concepts in academic disciplines might profitably be introduced early in the life of a school child. A principle or assumption that is regarded as basic in a subject field may also be most useful for learning this subject, hence should be acquired by the learner at the earliest possible time. It should not be postponed simply because it is assumed to be complex and difficult to teach. It may well be possible, with the newer methods of instruction becoming available, to teach the topic in an efficient manner before the child has acquired interfering notions or habits of thinking that may later have to be unlearned.

In determining the appropriate content or instructional objectives for any grade level, a variety of questions must be asked.

1. Is the proposed objective something for which agencies other than the school can or should be responsible?

2. Is it something that the child acquires even without systematic and deliberate instruction?

3. Will it facilitate, both directly and indirectly, learning in later grades?

4. Will it enable the learner to use his experiences outside the school in a more educative fashion?

5. Is it economical to teach, in terms of the resources of the school and its personnel and their abilities?

6. Will it increase the student's ability to generate new hypotheses and to conceptualize alternatives and their consequences?

7. Can it be taught efficiently to the child, considering the child's abilities and interests?

It was to this last question that the studies summarized in this paper were directed. An attempt was made to explore the possibilities of teaching primary-grade children basic concepts in the fields of physical science and mathematics. In physics, for example, the principles of molecular movement are fundamental. In one study, therefore, a three-week program was prepared to develop in primary-grade pupils an understanding of molecular movement for the explanation of a few restricted physical phenomena. In mathematics it appeared desirable to have students understand basic principles whose logical interrelationships constitute algebraic structures. Hence a pilot program of 15 weeks' duration was constructed for first-grade pupils to determine the feasibility of an autoinstructional curriculum that would teach mathematics in terms of structure.

Instructional Procedures

A prototype model of the Videosonic Teaching Machine (Fig. 1) developed by Hughes Aircraft Company was used for these investigations. Slides were projected on a viewing plate at the front of the machine while the child listened through earphones to a tape recording. By pressing one of three buttons, each of which represented a

Fig. 1. Videosonic Teaching Machine.

different picture on the screen, the child indicated his answer to a question contained in the recording.

After each question the tape recorder stopped and the pupil responded. If he was correct, a green light went on beside the button pressed, and the tape recorder started to play again. When required by the program, the child was given a word or two of approval along with an explanation as to why he was correct. A new slide was automatically presented and the procedure repeated. If the child selected the wrong answer, no green light appeared. The child then pushed a yellow button to permit a second attempt. The program advanced only when the child gave the correct answer.

The programs prepared for use in this machine necessarily consisted of multiple-choice frames. This is not, however, an illustration of the undesirable situation in which machines place undue constraints upon the programmer (as compared with programmed textbooks). For pupils in the primary grades, where reading abilities are still undeveloped, this teaching machine gave the programmer a vast amount of freedom in that he was able to use recorded speech as he desired. The flexibility of programming thus afforded certainly offset some of the restrictions placed on response mode. Parenthetically, it should be noted that the inclusion of a variety of constructed responses is envisioned in newer models of the Videosonic Teaching Machine.

A Study in Teaching Physical Science

In the first of these investigations the possibility of teaching children an abstract scientific language was explored. The topics of evaporation and condensation of water were treated in terms of the movement of molecules, the relation of their speed to the properties of attraction, hence the relation of temperature to changes from a liquid to a gaseous state and vice versa (Keislar & McNeil, 1961a).

In this program children were taught to distinguish among the three states of matter in terms of molecular movement. Molecules were represented as dots or circles. Vectors were used to represent speed and direction in these still pictures, and children readily learned to interpret schematic drawings in terms of "hot" or "cold," where such a comparison was possible. The topic of "attraction" proved to be a particularly difficult one and was inadequately taught. The children were given many examples of the ways in which purely mechanical operations of molecules may be used in talking about physical phenomena of evaporation and condensation.

The program in physical science was given to approximately 100 children in the first, second, and third grades. Children arrived from their classes at 20-minute intervals throughout the school day for a period of three weeks. They responded to about 35 frames each day, spending 10 to 20 minutes daily at this task. Screens were placed between the children to reduce social distractions. Children returned to their classes as soon as they completed each day's lesson. The number of errors each child made each day was recorded.

Since the objective was to find out how much the children understood, the criterion used to assess the child's learning was a test of transfer. This posttest consisted of multiple-choice items that were different from the frames in the program, plus an individual standardized interview in which the child was asked questions about physical phenomena.

The results indicated that most of the children interviewed could, to a limited extent at least, use the words describing molecular movement to explain certain phenomena of evaporation and condensation. Although differences between an experimental group receiving the instruction and an uninstructed control group were clear and significant, it is more rewarding to study individual items. For example, most of the children were able to demonstrate, by holding a tennis ball in each hand, how molecules of a solid move differently from those of a liquid. When shown a glass of ice water and asked why the outside of the glass was wet, they were able to give answers which, although usually incomplete, were correct as far as they went.

As would be expected on such a transfer test, there was a wide range of individual differences (McNeil & Keislar, 1961a). Some children demonstrated unusual comprehension, whereas others apparently had learned little. Although performance was clearly related to both mental age and grade level, the usual overlapping between the grades was obtained. Boys were found to do significantly better than girls, even though they were matched in terms of mental age and in terms of a pretest of initial competence in this subject. This finding of a difference despite pretest matching is of interest because under ordinary classroom conditions it is sometimes argued that boys are superior only because they are given preferential treatment by the teacher in the topic of science.

A Study in Modes of Presentation and Response

Using the three-week program in science, a special study in modes of presentation of the program was undertaken with approximately 300 children in the primary grades (Keislar & McNeil, 1961b; McNeil & Keislar, 1961b). Subjects were divided into five groups. Children in two of the groups were taught individually by teaching machines. In two other groups children received instruction in group settings, in which the program and commentary were presented as pupils sat in a classroom, 12 to 15 at a time. Children in a control group also came each day but were taught mathematics instead of science. All subjects came at 20-minute intervals from their regular classrooms to special rooms for their instruction.

The children in the first two groups (those who were taught individually) composed (1) an overt response group who were required to answer by pressing a button to indicate their choices and (2) a nonovert response group who merely watched and listened as the program was individually presented to them. The program for the nonovert group included a five-second pause at the end of each question. With this exception, and the difference in mode of response, the two groups were treated in identical fashion.

Our comparison of these two groups differs from other studies of overt responses (Goldbeck, 1960; Suppes & Ginsberg, 1960) in that with our multiple-choice items the overt response of pressing buttons was not the response being tested on the posttest. Rather, it was assumed that each child was making certain implicit responses to the items and that these implicit responses constituted the learned behavior which acted as a mediator permitting transfer on the posttest. It was assumed that both the overt response and the nonovert response groups would make implicit responses. But, since the overt responders were differentially reinforced for their answers, it was believed that they would be more "motivated"; they would be more likely to make the appropriate implicit behavior than the nonovert response group who received reinforcement regardless of what they did.

The results showed no significant difference; there was less than one point difference between the groups on the posttest, an amount that was much less than the standard error. The study was replicated in another school with the same results. If further replications continue to reveal no difference of practical importance, a possible explanation may be that the science program alone is effective in getting the nonovert response group to make the appropriate implicit responses. In other words, children pay attention and "think through" the problems even though they do not have to commit themselves overtly. Furthermore, since they can always wait to see the right answer, members of the nonovert response group are less likely to make incorrect responses, hence experience less interference with the correct response.

For the third and fourth groups (those who were taught in classes of 12 to 15), the slides in the program were projected on a large screen, with the correct answer identified by a green sticker, while the program was played on a tape recorder in the room. Conditions were similar to those that exist when audiostrip films are shown in regular classrooms. To make the class setting realistic, the research assistant was instructed to be sure that these children did not distract each other by talk or other disturbances. Subjects in one of these classroom-setting groups heard the tape recording in question form, as did the individually instructed children; in the other group all questions were rephrased and presented as statements. There was no difference in the effect of these two classroom presentations on pupil achievement.

On the posttest, as illustrated in Fig. 2, each of the two classroom groups made scores 17 points above chance, whereas the two individually taught groups, the overt response and the nonovert response, had scores 21 and 20 points, respectively, above chance. The control group made a score nearly nine points above chance. A highly significant variance ratio (F) was found for these five groups; the two audiostrip film groups differed significantly from the two individually taught groups. It appears that individual instruction, whether requiring an overt response or not, was superior to instruction in which the children observed and listened in a group setting to the same program as an audiostrip film. It is not necessarily true, however, that an improved filmstrip on this subject would be inferior to the program using teaching machines.

Children who received individual teaching-machine instruction were significantly more favorable toward both the subject matter and the

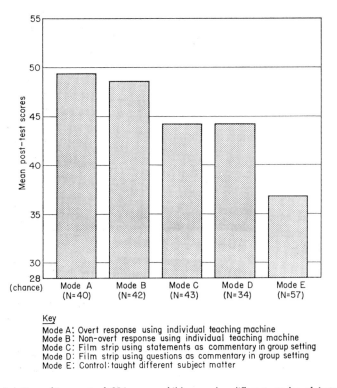

Key
Mode A: Overt response using individual teaching machine
Mode B: Non-overt response using individual teaching machine
Mode C: Film strip using statements as commentary in group setting
Mode D: Film strip using questions as commentary in group setting
Mode E: Control: taught different subject matter

Fig. 2. *Relative achievement of 216 young children under different modes of instructional presentation and response.*

instructional procedures they encountered than the children who were shown the audiostrip film in the classroom setting.

A Study in Teaching Mathematics

In another investigation the ability of first-grade children to learn mathematics in terms of algebraic structures was explored. Mr. Robert C. Crawford, as full-time subject-matter consultant, was given responsibility for directing the study and was solely responsible for preparing the program. This instructional unit was designed to develop in students an understanding of algebraic structures and of certain basic principles of mathematics, such as the commutative law, the associative law, and the distributive law, especially as they relate to the process of addition. At the same time, the children were expected to learn the common addition and subtraction facts in arithmetic.

The instruction consisted of a 15-week autoinstructional program with a total of approximately 1350 frames. Cuisenaire Blocks, used to represent algebraic quantities, played an important role in the instruction. Children at the beginning of the program manipulated the colored blocks without reference to number. Later, the same types of instructional frames were presented with numbers placed on the blocks corresponding to the length of the block in centimeters. The frames were then presented in black and white so that color would not be variable; the child responded primarily to length and number. Later in the program the child was shown the numbers alone and was required to answer without the use of blocks.

An important characteristic of the program was that it attempted to have the child discover the selected basic principles for himself by giving him a variety of illustrations of each principle. Nowhere in the program was the principle called directly to his attention.

The only concrete illustration given of the principles and arithmetical relationships consisted of the lengths of the blocks. Children learned to find for themselves the sum of two numbers; they did not learn this by counting but presumably by manipulating blocks that were arbitrarily labeled with certain numbers. The program included neither applications from everyday life nor illustrations using any other materials. The symbols "plus," "minus," "greater than," and "smaller than" and equality and multiplication signs were introduced entirely with reference to block manipulation.

This instructional program, therefore, eliminated concrete illustrations in which extraneous factors were likely to distract the learner from the abstract relationships to be learned. It was intended to help the child acquire a structure of such relationships. The structure would constitute an abstract and simple model that might later be applied, but it was first necessary for the child to develop a comprehension of the pattern.

The experimental program was given to 136 first-grade children in two schools. In school A, where six teaching machines were available in a small separate room, children from three first-grade classes were instructed individually. Six children at a time appeared at 20-minute intervals during the day and returned to their classes as soon as they were finished. In this school these pupils were also given the conventional course in arithmetic with their regular classroom teachers.

Counters were provided in school A to keep a record of the total number of errors each child made daily. To discourage guessing, these counters were placed beside each teaching device and were made to register one point for each *correct* first attempt per frame. If the child's first attempt was not correct, the counter never registered, even though on subsequent tries he did get the frame right. This procedure seemed to have a marked effect on many children. They were found to wait longer before making their first response and to pay more attention to the total scores they made each day. In fact, some competition developed between the children, as demonstrated by the fact that they compared scores on occasion as they left the room. No systematic attempt was made, however, to study the effect of informing the child of his total scores each day in this fashion.

In school B children from two classes were instructed in groups of 8 to 10 at a time. For this purpose, a single teaching machine projected slides on a screen before all the children. Each child listened to the commentary through earphones. Each child had his own response panel and indicated his answer by selecting one of three buttons. A red light appeared for the wrong answer and a green one for the correct one. When the last child in the group had given the correct answer, all lights were turned out and a new frame was presented. Children from school B who were in the experimental group were not given any other instruction in mathematics.

No differences were found in learning performance between children in school A and those in school B; consequently, these two schools are considered together in subsequent discussion.

Difficulty level varied widely among the lessons, with error rates ranging from 11% to 53%. The average rate was 31% for all except the first few lessons. Since the multiple-choice program allows students to answer many items correctly by chance, the higher error scores were approximately at chance level. Although some subjects' error rates were as low as 15%, many children found the program quite difficult, as indicated by error rates of 40% and 50%. In many instances children appeared to be guessing on frame after frame.

The use of Cuisenaire Blocks in the mathematics program illus- trates the possibility of combining a teaching-machine program or a programmed instruction course with other devices. In the case of the mathematics program, children found the correct answer before they registered it. The correct block fitted and the incorrect block did not. Consequently, the child's reinforcements came directly from his own manipulations rather than by having the correct answer arbi- trarily supplied. The child was less dependent upon the "authority" of the programmer; he could see for himself that he was correct.

The effectiveness of the mathematics program was evaluated by comparing the performance of the experimental subjects with that of two control groups, one at the first-grade level and the other at the fourth grade. These control groups had received only a conventional course in arithmetic with no special attention to algebraic structures. In addition to group tests, the criterion included an individual test given to each child in the experimental and control groups by an interviewer. In the most important part of the individual test, devel- oped by Mr. Crawford and Miss Natalie Wilson, pupils were given plastic symbols, numbers, and letters in various combinations; they were asked to build, by arranging these objects on the table, as many true mathematical statements, or "stories," as they could think of. Pupils were scored in terms of the number of correct statements they were able to compose; no points were subtracted for wrong statements. On this individual test the experimental group not only scored signifi- cantly higher than a control first-grade group which received conven- tional instruction in arithmetic but did almost as well as the average of a fourth-grade control group.

These results should be interpreted in light of the fact that sig- nificant differences were found between the scores assigned by dif- ferent interviewers and the fact that some interviewers were used for the experimental group but not for the control. Furthermore, the questions asked used a language and materials with which only the experimental group was familiar. The control groups may have per- formed relatively poorly simply because they had not had an adequate opportunity to become acquainted with features of the testing situation that were somewhat extraneous to the understanding of basic principles.

In a group test prepared by Dr. Rodney Skager, formerly a student in the Department of Psychology at U.C.L.A., the experimental group was significantly superior to the first-grade control on an arithmetic test; this test required the selection of a number that fell between two other numbers. On other tests, requiring the conventional adding and subtracting of numbers, the experimental group was not inferior to the first-grade control.

In another group test children were required to rewrite certain algebraic statements in a different form, in which only the letters were to be inserted. For example, the statement "$T + H = U$" was to be rewritten (commuted) in a box that appeared as follows:

$$\square + \quad = \square$$

Although the experimental group was significantly superior on one of these items, the first-grade control group did at least as well on the remaining ones. It appears that the program must include frames giving practice in this kind of generalizing.

The mathematics program needs considerable revision because it has a fairly high difficulty level and limited transfer effects. But, it is significant that for most of the children there was no marked loss of the eagerness with which they came each day, even though the program was difficult and required daily attendance for 15 weeks. The program is a bold and imaginative one that should be extensively explored.

Conclusion

We have attempted to show that activities in the field of autoinstruction must be guided, at least in part, by a long-range strategy that considers the existing state of knowledge in all disciplines. This strategy should also consider the abilities of the learner, under conditions made possible by developments in instructional methodology, to acquire and use new knowledge. Programs that are based on the content of existing textbooks and courses of study are likely to be invalidated and to block overdue revisions in the total school curriculum. Our long-range strategy will require programmers to work closely with a corps of specialists drawn from many disciplines.

Fundamental to the accomplishment of our long-range goals is experimentation to determine not only the most efficient methods by which topics may be taught at a given grade level but also the optimum sequence of topics within a subject field. Since the content in later grades depends upon what children have previously learned, experiments in curriculum construction must begin at the primary-grade level, as illustrated by the exploratory studies reviewed in this report.

Although these exploratory studies in teaching principles of science and mathematics considered certain programming variables, the value of the investigations lies in suggesting ways of ordering and presenting content for young children. There is no convincing evidence that the children mastered the instructions presented, but the results are promising enough to warrant serious study of the teaching of basic subject-matter principles in the primary grades. We must learn more about what can be taught efficiently to young children before automated instruction can realize its full potentialities for the total school curriculum.

REFERENCES

Begle, E. G. School Mathematics Work Group. *Mathematics Teacher,* 1958, **51,** 616–618.

Goldbeck, R. A. *The effect of response mode and learning material difficulty on automated instruction.* Santa Barbara, California: American Institute for Research, September 1960. (AIR-328-60-IR-124)

Keislar, E. R., & McNeil, J. D. Teaching scientific theory to first-grade pupils by auto-instructional device. *Harvard Educational Review,* 1961a, **31**(1), 73–83.

Keislar, E. R., & McNeil, J. D. Comparison of two response modes in an auto-instructional program with children in the primary grades. Paper read at Amer. Psychol. Assoc., New York, September 1961b.

McNeil, J. D., & Keislar, E. R. Individual differences and effectiveness of auto-instruction at the primary grade level. *California Journal of Educational Research,* 1961a, **12,** 160–164.

McNeil, J. D., & Keislar, E. R. Questions versus statements in the learning of young children. Paper read at Educ. Res. Assoc., March 1961b.

Physical Science Study Committee. A symposium: the Physical Science Study Committee. *Harvard Educational Review,* 1959, **29**(1), 1–36.

Suppes, P., & Ginsberg, R. *Application of a stimulus sampling model to children's concept formation of binary numbers, with and without an overt connection response.* Institute for Mathematical Studies in Social Studies, Stanford University, December 1960. (Technical Report No. 35)

Research in programmed learning

ARNOLD ROE

University of California, Los Angeles

> It was six men of Industan
> To learning much inclined
> Who went to see the elephant
> (Though all of them were blind)
> That each by observation
> Might satisfy his mind.
> —John G. Saxe

This poem goes on to describe how one of the blind men touched the tail and thought the elephant was very like a rope; another touched a leg and thought the elephant was very like a tree; one touched the ear and thought the elephant was very like a fan; and so on.

An analogy can be made between the experiments being conducted on programmed instruction and the investigations of the elephant by the blind men. One person investigates here, another investigates there, yet the sum does not add up to a description of the strange phenomenon of learning. It is evident to anyone who has tried to organize an investigation on programmed learning that he touches only a limited area of the subject and then probably on the surface only.

Why is this so? It certainly appears more desirable to step back and get a whole, or integrated, view of the teaching-learning process and then, knowing where each part fits into the whole, to examine the parts in detail. Possibly the reason that the total picture has eluded investigators is that they have not yet developed the perceptual means for viewing an extremely complex, multivariate dynamic domain. They look at only a limited range of a limited number of variables.

The experimenter who wishes to investigate a limited number of variables encounters many problems. First, he must decide *which* variables to investigate. Edward Fry,[1] in his classification of variables in programmed learning, lists 212 items. However, since no overview is available, there is no rationale for choosing the variables that might describe the salient features of the domain. The choice of variables, then, is largely a matter of personal preference or current popular interest. However, the choice of any one variable immediately gives rise to the suspicion that this variable may interact strongly with other variables. For example, assume that an experimenter is interested in the response-mode variable or, more specifically, the role of overt and covert responses in learning. Some of the variables that may possibly interact with the chosen variable are subject-matter characteristics (artistic, mechanical, language, psychomotor, etc.); individual differences (age-maturity, fatigue, aural-visual preference, etc.); presentation media (visual, auditory, etc.); response media for the overt responses (written, spoken, manipulative); response form (composed, multiple-choice, etc.); length of program; size of steps; and so on. Not only could each of these variables interact with the chosen variable, but many of them could interact among themselves.

A few further examples of interaction among variables may be cited: an experimenter who wishes to examine the possible interaction of age with the response-mode variable may be confronted with the problem of preparing different versions of the programmed material, each best suited to a particular age level, thereby introducing a program variable; or an examination of the possible interaction of the response form (e.g., multiple-choice versus composed response) again introduces the program variable, for, if program items are prepared in composed-response format and the multiple-choice format is obtained by substituting a choice of responses for a blank space, then multiple-choice items may have been cast into an unnatural context. However, if we write two separate programs, each best suited to its response mode, then we may have incorporated subtle, though substantive, changes in the subject content.

These are but a few illustrations of the problems involved in choosing the variables for an experiment. The choice seems to be between a limited variable experiment, with the attendant danger that the excluded variables could modify the experimental conclusions, or multivariable experiments of such scope that the time, number of

[1] Fry, E. *Teaching machine programming.* New York: McGraw-Hill, in press.

subjects, and financial resources involved are enough to stagger the imagination. Neither choice is attractive.

Another serious problem facing the experimenter who examines the teaching-learning process or, for that matter, any process involving human behavior, is that of mensuration. Current experimental procedures, which demand that observations be expressed in quantitative form, were developed in the physical sciences, where man's great triumph has been the increasing precision with which he can make his measurements. The same precision of measurement does not exist in the human behavioral sciences.

For example, consider the problem of measuring student performance after exposure to some experimentally controlled set of stimuli. For the sake of illustration, assume that the measuring instrument is a written test. The first question concerns the validity of the test. Does it measure the kind of performance that we say it does and is this performance in any way related to the controlled set of stimuli to which the student has been exposed? Probably most experimenters, even though they generalize by putting "tag" names on the "thing" they are examining, realize that they are getting only a performance response on each of the specific components (questions) that make up the test. Since test items seldom include the complete set of stimulus-response items to which the student had been previously exposed, but rather some sampling of these prior items, a subjective assessment is made of the transformation to obtain a validity number.

Another question that arises concerns test reliability. One common procedure for finding reliability is the split-half method, which requires checking the consistency of responses to similar paired items. However, this method is not without its dangers in learning experiments. If the paired items are made very similar (or identical), the student may change his performance on the second of the similar items as a result of his experience with the first. And in verbal performance, unless the two paired items are identical, there is always the danger that the paired items do not measure the same thing.

Assuming that validity and reliability measures are obtained, what use is made of these measures? They are used, in a subjective fashion, to discredit completely the experimental findings, or the experimental data are accepted as recorded, and thereafter the validity and reliability measures are ignored in subsequent analyses. Presumably, if the continuous scale on which the validity and reliability measures are stated has any meaning, it should not be necessary to make an accept-or-reject judgment but rather to use these measures to increase the error variance of the test scores. (Preferably, reliability test data should be used to form a separate dimension in an analysis of variance.) Such a procedure would undoubtedly add to the difficulty in finding statistically significant differences in teaching-learning experiments.

Selection of subjects for a teaching-learning experiment may also present a problem. The first temptation is to use students who are completely naïve about the subject content, until one realizes that complete naïveté is the exception rather than the rule in the common nonexperimental learning situations. Since most learning situations build on prior student experiences and entail extending the student's behavioral repertoire, an experimental procedure that imitated these circumstances would require measuring the behavioral repertoire of the student at both the beginning and the end of the experiment. However, the very presence of the pretest can have an effect on the student's performance, both during the experiment and during the posttest. Also, if the pretest is the same as the posttest, it may be difficult to distinguish between the learning that takes place during the pretest and that which occurs during the experiment. On the other hand, if different pretests and posttests are used, no simple subtraction of pre- from posttest scores can be made; then one must decide what scaling factor to assign to the pretest scores when using them to adjust the posttest scores (e.g., in analysis of covariance).

Another interesting problem is that of the duration of the experiment. In short-term experiments the experimenter has more opportunity to control the subjects' environment and behavior than in long-term experiments. However, the short-term experiment may not have predictive value for longer term, less controlled teaching-learning situations. To illustrate this, I cite the study in which one group of students was given an accurate and complete lecture while another group was given an inaccurate, incomplete lecture covering the same topic.[2] Both groups were given the same test immediately after the lectures, and the first group scored significantly higher than the second group. Had the matter ended there, in what could be called a short-term study, the conclusion would have been that the accurate lecture method was better than the inaccurate lecture method. However, the same procedure was continued with each group for an entire semester, with the added factor that both groups had uncontrolled re-

---

[2] Batteau, D. W. The effect of "good" versus "bad" lectures on student performance. Unpublished paper. Study conducted at Bray Laboratory, Tufts University, Medford, Mass.

course to notes and reference books. At the end of the semester the results were reversed: the group that had heard the inaccurate lectures scored higher on the final examination than the group that had heard the accurate lectures. I use this illustration not to advocate use of inaccurate course material but rather to indicate that it is difficult to control all the variables influencing student behavior in long-term experiments. Other conclusions can be drawn from this illustration, not the least of which is that motivation plays a large role in learning. Yet we know next to nothing about how to measure or manipulate this admittedly important variable.

None of the individual problems mentioned above, or those which were not mentioned, is completely unsolvable. However, attempting to solve one problem often makes the solution of another more difficult, so that data in human learning experiments are generally stated in quantitative terms with a relative precision that belies the underlying uncertainty in the measuring scales or testing procedures. All these conclusions are well known, but I have restated them here because, taken all together, they seem to add up to a strong indictment against the methodology currently employed in the experimental studies of human behavior. I cannot believe that the ultimate solution lies in acquiring precision in experiments through the use of artificial circumstances (such as the nonsense syllables used in paired associate tasks); for, although such antiseptic experimental methods may be more likely to yield statistically significant results, they are less likely to yield socially significant results.

The amount of human effort expended in the development of the behavioral sciences has been monumental compared to the contributions to human welfare resulting therefrom. I can anticipate the same thing about to happen in the area of programmed learning. Insignificant experiments can proliferate where we have not yet defined a measure of merit with which to gauge the relative importance of results. What, indeed, is the import of changing a person's performance level from 70% to 80% or even 100%? Perhaps in some industrial situations it may be possible to translate an increase in performance into dollar terms, but in the general school situation it becomes more difficult to assess such a change. Possibly we could assess change on a national scale if, for example, we could estimate the effect on the national economy of having high school students graduate one year sooner than they do now. We could then decide how much to spend in exploring and implementing a change in educational procedures. At present we have no such measure of merit, nor have we a way to define the efficiency of the teaching-learning process. In programmed learning crude, arbitrary attempts have been made to state efficiency in terms of a simple relationship between programming effort, time required for learning, and the level of student performance. Worse still is the experimenter who merely states such results as learning time and performance levels, with the attitude that whoever wishes to use these results later in a practical situation will find the weighting factors to use with each variable. This attitude ignores the fact that the very procedure adopted for the experiment has created an implicit relationship between the learning-time and level-of-performance variables.

We can continue to skirt these questions of methodology by conducting small-scale experiments that avoid the problem areas outlined above, but I do not believe we can make substantial advances in education until we face up to the problems, understand their implications, and boldly search for new means of solving them. If we recognize the lack of precision in our measurements, then we should look for a strategy of experimentation that minimizes the importance of any decision based on the results of a given experiment; reduces the amount of data gathering and computation involved in any given experiment; permits shorter cycle times between experiments; and allows rapid convergence on a practical, if not optimum, final solution of the problems under consideration. I have suggested one such strategy elsewhere [3] and look forward to hearing of other new approaches.

To summarize, current research efforts in programmed learning follow the traditional physical-science approach of stating a theory, specifying a model, and testing a hypothesis. However, when dealing with human learning behavior, criterion measures are weak; the number of variables that can be examined at one time is limited; the major performance measures—learning time and test scores—have not been completely separated nor completely combined; and an adequate rationale for specifying the efficiency of the teaching-learning process is lacking. It is not surprising, therefore, to find very little of statistical or social significance emerging from even the most elaborately controlled and analyzed experiments.

The traditional approach to experiments would be fruitful if examination of the learning situation yielded a simple set of laws. How-

[3] Roe, A., Lyman, J., & Moon, H. A dynamic statistical approach to the control of human behavior. In S. Margulies & L. Eigen (Eds.), *Programmed instruction: applications to industry and the armed forces.* New York: Wiley, in press.

ever, no such simple set of laws is in view. Rather, this approach may uncover a large number of restricted rules, each adequate for a specific set of circumstances. If no broad principles are disclosed, then the major problem will be how to use the large number of restricted rules in a workable teaching system. If we are to use the results of a multitude of traditional experiments in an on-going teaching system, it seems likely from a logistical point of view that digital computers will play an important role. The same vital role will be played by computers if some new dynamic procedure for simultaneously investigating and manipulating the teaching-learning process is evolved.

Behavior theory and the automation of instruction

DONALD A. COOK

Basic Systems, Inc.

The rapid advance of machine technology in the data-processing sphere is opening a widening set of possibilities for the automation of instruction. Since these possibilities may soon appear to be limitless in scope, it is of interest to consider whether there may be guideposts helpful in focusing the exploration of this new area. It is the purpose of this chapter to suggest that the study of behavior itself can act as such a guidepost and to give examples of issues wherein our understanding of the nature of behavior may both constrain and stimulate developments in the technology of automated instruction.

Let me make clear that the notion of a science of behavior means more than the use of careful techniques for investigating claims *about* behavior. Experimental studies, employing matched control groups and complex statistical methods, can be applied to any set of claims—dignified as "hypotheses"—no matter how outlandish or even appealing. *But it is the claims themselves that count.* Do they come from an account of behavior which is sound and tenable in its own right? A science of behavior should not merely help us check claims; it should also help us *generate* those claims. As such a science of behavior develops, it will shape our expectations and emphases in the automation of instruction.

At the outset an important distinction must be made between *pedagogy* and *curricular administration*. By pedagogy I mean those aspects of instructional design that concern the interaction between the individual learner and the subject matter he is learning. By curricular administration I mean the adaptation of the pedagogical enterprise to large-scale instruction and to the individual differences which a sizable population always offers the educator. Machine technology will play an important role in both aspects of education, and these aspects may even interact in important ways, as we shall see below. But in thinking about new possibilities of machine design, it is important to be clear whether one's purpose is pedagogical or administrative. It is my belief that pedagogy should always come first, that pedagogical decisions should govern administrative decisions, and that behavioral science will find its greatest use in this primary area. Let us consider some examples.

The Active Response

Most current approaches to programmed instruction incorporate the principle that the learner should make active responses at frequent intervals. Yet the exact form of the response is open to controversy, and even the very requirement has been brought under question. The studies so far available are not decisive on this issue. I think one reason for this may be that most of these studies employ rather brief program sequences—often not more than 100 frames—and further make their comparisons immediately after the program has been completed, so that the long-term effects upon retention, or differences therein, are not assessed. It is perhaps not surprising that exposure to a single page of text, four Crowderian frames with multiple-choice questions, or 30 brief "Skinnerian" frames requiring constructed responses should be indistinguishable in their effects immediately after the experiment.

Classical data in the field of psychology emphasize the importance of active participation and suggest certain broad parameters which govern the probable importance of the active response. It is crucial to remember here that "covert" responses cannot be made at all unless the organism has a prior history of making that response in overt form. Therefore one way of estimating the importance of active responses in a given program is to assess the prior history of the organism in the emission of the behavior under consideration. These points are well illustrated in an early study by A. I. Gates (1917). This study investigated some of the parameters which govern the advantage of recitation over reading in memorizing material. In all cases recall measures were higher when a greater proportion of learning time was spent in recitation. But the slope of this function varied with other factors. It was steeper for nonsense materials than for meaningful passages, and it was steeper for younger than for older subjects. In other words, where learners with already-established verbal repertoires attack material whose organization taps the structural properties of those repertoires, then the role of the active response may be minimal.

Such findings suggest that teaching machines be built in which the requirement (for active responses) could be in force for younger subjects, or with poorly organized ("rote") material, or in cases in which new responses (such as vocabulary) are being established. For *any* kind of material, active responses should perhaps be called for occasionally. If the demand were made intermittently—on an unpredictable schedule—it might help ensure that the intervening covert responses were brought to full strength, frame by frame, even though they were not individually recorded.

The functional specifications of such a machine are illustrated in Fig. 1. In the first instructional cycle a unit of instruction, S_1, is presented. (This occurs at the point marked "S_1" in Fig. 1.) In the presence of S_1 the learner thinks of the required answer covertly at the point marked $(R_c)_1$. When ready, he presses an advance button at R_{A_1}, and the feedback panel gives the correct answer at S_{F_1}, with S_1 still in view. The learner presses the advance button at R_{A_2}, which brings S_2 to view. Thus the first cycle is concluded without the demand for an overt response. In the second cycle the learner thinks of his answer $(R_c)_2$ and advances with R_{A_3}. The monitor demands a written response at D (say by a flashing light or sign), which the learner makes on the response tape at R_w. S_2 remains in view. R_{A_4} then brings S_{F_2}, with S_2 and R_w both in view (though R_w may move under a window). Then, after comparison, R_{A_5} eliminates S_2 and R_w, bringing S_3 into view. Thus the second cycle requires an overt response.

Demands can be scheduled according to an empirically determined pattern, in which the average density may reflect the maturity of the student and the nature of the material. Their spacing can be random (say Poisson distribution), so that each frame will be taken seriously by the student. Demand density can be varied from early to late segments of a program, becoming less frequent, for example, as a student's covert behavior becomes better established. It is quite possible that sequences of demands can be designed which will be effective in establishing habits of clear and explicit thinking. The demand schedule can be coded independently of the program and thus be

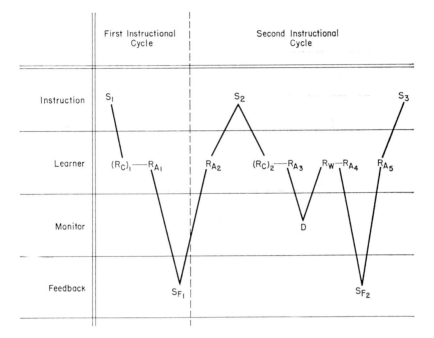

Fig. 1. Two instructional cycles with optional demand for overt response.

tailored to the student rather than tied to the program. Of course, it would also be potentially possible, in a machine in which error or rate records were kept, to tie the demand schedule to properties of the learner's progress through the program.

The Instructional Cycle

Various automatic approaches to instruction embody variations in the sequence of events making up the instructional cycle. The question arises, then, whether knowledge from the study of behavior dictates any considerations about the design of these events.

Programming which has come to be known as "Skinnerian" adheres to a characteristic sequence, as illustrated in Fig. 2a. The instructional increment is presented at S, the learner composes or constructs a response at R, and then the feedback is given at F. This complete cycle, enclosed in the rectangle, is rarely violated. The choice-point at B illustrates that branching is perfectly feasible with such a pro-

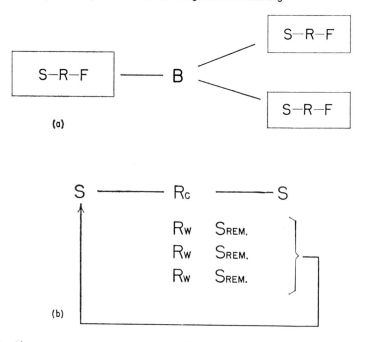

Fig. 2.   *The sequence of events in constructed response (a), and multiple-choice selected response programming (b).*

gram but that the choice is made *outside* the instructional cycle. The decision to branch may be governed in many ways, as we shall see below.

The sequence of events in the kind of program described by Crowder is shown in Fig. 2b.   After the instructional increment, the learner must select an answer to a question from several alternatives.   The correct choice moves him on to the next frame, whereas a wrong choice moves him to a remedial frame, then back to the instructional frame to try again.   (Intervening frames may be more numerous, with more complex alternatives presented.   The path from remedial frames may go directly to subsequent frames without return.   But the sequence shown is the most frequent and exhibits the essential properties I want to stress here).

Both styles of programming make provision for frequent student participation and both deliver frequent evaluations.   These common characteristics emphasize the explicative or accounting features of programming and hardly require much theory of behavior.   Theoretical issues arise in the design of the material and in the expectations the methods give rise to. Multiple-choice selected-response programming has been criticized on the basis of several behavioral notions. One is that the active response requirement ensures better learning and retention; this point has been discussed above. Another is that the correct response selection may emerge, not because it is strong, but merely because the false ones have been eliminated. A third is that a student who makes a correct choice through guesswork—and reducing the likelihood of this would require a great increase in wasteful wrong alternatives—is thereby deprived of cautionary instruction and may fell its ill effects later in the program; such protection against future error—so goes the argument—might well be incorporated into the main program for all to learn from. A final argument, made forcefully by Skinner (1961), is that the inspection of wrong choices plausible enough to be worthy of inclusion may disrupt learning by the same processes being used to build it up.

Each of these separate points deserves experimental attention. Experimental comparisons of method variables have thus far been indecisive, primarily for the reason cited earlier: short sequences have been employed, and postprogram measures have been inadequate. Even clearcut results in such studies would not tease out the relevance of the issues listed above. I have mentioned these issues because they represent unsolved questions of pedagogy which have been bypassed in the design of automatic teaching systems that are administratively attractive.

Constructed-response programming offers the prospect that these pedagogical issues will be taken seriously. This is so because the response of such programming to errors is to improve the program. In the face of a multiple-choice program, the pedagogical programmer would be interested in data on *which* wrong alternatives are in fact being chosen. Those that are not chosen should be eliminated from the program, whereas those that are should be studied to suggest ways of rewriting the main sequence so that errors do not occur.

Branching

It should be clear from the foregoing discussion, and by reference to Fig. 2a, that branching in instructional programs is not contingent upon the use of multiple-choice items. This confusion may have arisen in part because of the administrative appeal of the selection

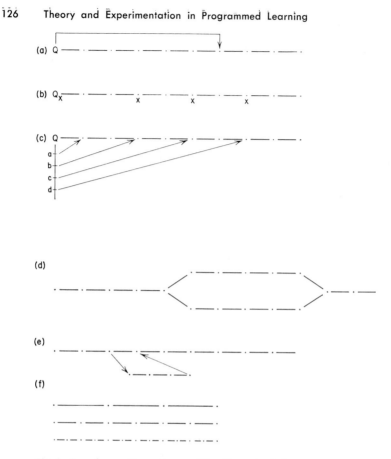

Fig. 3. Some forms of branching possible with constructed response programs.

technique, since it permits automatic scoring. Automatic scoring of constructed-response programs awaits the solution of two difficult problems. One is optical character recognition (or equivalent thereof for various response modes) and the other is a problem of assessing the semantic equivalence of comparable utterances or phrases.

It is nonetheless possible, and not premature, to indicate some of the branching possibilities inherent in the use of constructed-response programs. A number of these are shown in Fig. 3. In all sections of this figure the solid circles represent complete instructional cycles—instruction, response, feedback—and the branching choices are outside the cycles. The first example (*a*) illustrates a simple "express stop," wherein a diagnostic frame *Q* advances well-prepared learners to later stages of a program. A variant, which might be called "distributed express stopping," is shown in (*b*). Here a passing score on the diagnostic frame Q_x directs the learner to skip all subsequent frames designated in a certain way (marked with an *x* in the diagram). Such a technique would be useful, for example, where the main program taught both basic computer operation and programming techniques in an integrated manner but where some students were already familiar with the first topic.

The principle of express-stopping is shown in a more complex example in (*c*), where a diagnostic routine controls a series of "graded entry points." The basic episode in an optional branch is illustrated in (*d*). The decision to branch could be based on the need to specialize or the wish to amplify coverage of a subject. In the latter case the more detailed routine might not return to the main sequence.

A remedial branch is shown in (*e*). The principle is similar to that of the express-stop, except that the decision can be based on errors rather than a diagnostic frame.

The need for a branch, however, is not usually the property of a single frame. A more satisfactory approach would be a track system, such as is shown in (*f*). Every learner might start in the center (medium) track. If his errors exceed a critical rate, he is switched to the lower track, where interframe step size is smaller. If error rate is low, the switch is to the next higher track. Any switch could be reversible over a fairly short-range sample of frames. This would be an administrative decision, but the design does not lock-step the student so that falsely imposed "individual differences" are multiplied and stratified.

A totally different approach to individual differences, which still respects the integrity of the instructional cycle, is shown in Fig. 4. Here each successive layer provides additional "clueing" or prompting *before* a response is made. The learner exposes himself to as much of this material as he needs to be confident of his response. The rapid learner moves rapidly through the frames at level 1, while others dip down into deeper frames. Here again, each frame is independent, so that the learner is not administratively frozen into one level of presentation.

A more intricate elaboration of this approach, designed by Kent Aldershof (1961) has recently come to my attention. As in Fig. 4, frames are shingled in groups of four. But they are bound so that lifting frame 1 not only exposes the frame below it but also the top frame of the *next* set. He finds the answer to frame 1 on the hitherto

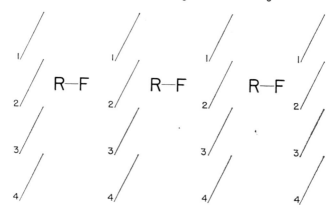

Fig. 4. "Clueing" in depth, or "internal" branching.

covered portion of frame 2, and after seeing it he makes a choice. If his response is correct, he can go directly to frame 1 of the second set. If he answered incorrectly or is unsure of his grasp, he can study frame 2 of the first set and then lift it to expose frame 3, and so on. Turning pages always carries unused frames away, so that each new set is encountered afresh at the top. Aldershof's discussion of the possible applications of this method are most suggestive and should convince machine designers of the utility of models that will handle these contingencies.

In concluding, I would like to emphasize that my examples have been merely illustrative. Their purpose has been to suggest that there are many possible directions in the automation of instruction but that each of these has pedagogical implications for the fate of the individual learner. If programmed instruction in automated forms is to fulfill its promise, it must indeed make contributions to the problems of large-scale administration and individual differences, but it must do so in a manner that holds instructional design for the individual to be the heart of the matter of teaching.

REFERENCES

Aldershof, K. L. *A new format for programmed instruction.* International Business Machines, General Products Division, Development Laboratory, Endicott, New York, 1961.
Gates, A. I. Recitation as a factor in memorizing. *Arch. Psychol.,* 1917, **6,** No. 40.
Skinner, B. F. *Cumulative record* (enlarged edition). New York: Appleton-Century-Crofts, 1961.

Adaptive teaching machines

JOHN SENDERS

Minneapolis-Honeywell Regulator Company

When I was a child I had an early predecessor of the teaching machine. It was a small box into which you could insert cards containing questions. It would ask you, for example, to select the name of the longest river in the world; if you answered correctly it gave you a buzz (reinforcer).

We have come a long way from these early games, but I feel that we have not made proper use of available models in nature to direct our efforts in developing new teaching machines.

The situation in automated teaching is similar to that which would exist if one tried to deduce laws of astronomy on the basis of what he could observe inside a cave, without looking at solar systems and stars.

We have a model in nature for automated teaching: the human teacher. So far as I can determine, however, none of the participants of this conference has attempted to examine this model and to analyze its behavior. It is surprising to me that we have ignored such a source of useful naturalistic information.

I recently remarked to a dean of the University of Minnesota that schools of education are institutions for programming people; I am not sure that the dean was particularly pleased with this designation. Nevertheless, the student of education either learns how to teach or learns the subject matter that is to be taught. (There is, of course, much controversy as to the proper relationship between these two goals.)

Teachers are, I think, adaptive teaching machines. By adaptive I mean that they learn things both in their programming period in school and after they become teachers. Some of them become very good teachers; some of them are not so good.

We should ask whether it is possible to examine the behavior of teachers, either individually or in groups, and to learn the differences between the good and the bad teacher in terms that will enable us to duplicate the desired functions in a nonbiological system. The University of Minnesota has conducted research of the kind I believe is appropriate to the field of automated teaching. This research concerned intraclassroom interaction—who says what and when; what the teacher does; when he does it and why.

A teaching machine which is not adaptive—which is not, to some extent, a self-organizing learning machine—can be considered only a limited channel of communication between a teacher (who may not necessarily be a good one) and a student.

Closed-loop teaching systems have been a topic of recent discussion. As an illustration of such a system, we may note the work of Dr. Licklider (described in another chapter of this book), whom I would consider a good teacher of German. By the use of a machine that introduces artificial constraints on the form and set of permissible student responses, he has made himself a fair teacher of German. (Admittedly, with this machine he can teach a number of students simultaneously.) I believe, however, that Dr. Licklider could do better by himself in face-to-face interaction with the student. This last conjecture is also suggested by Dr. Licklider's observation that the human engineering of his machine's input-output system is one of the most important variables in determining the machine's effectiveness.

Recently there has been discussion of something called the "teachable moment" for each child. According to this concept, brief periods exist when a student is particularly receptive to instruction—when information can be poured or pounded into his possibly reluctant head. This notion suggests that the continuous, closed-loop relationship discussed in this conference is not a full representation of the real student-teacher relationship. It suggests, rather, that the teacher must be constantly alert to the existence of the "teachable moments."

Before conducting research on automated instruction, we should resolve one fundamental question: are we interested primarily in investigating systems for improving *learning* or in studying and improving teaching? There is a difference between learning theory and something which I shall call "training theory."

In the development of a *learning* theory you put an organism into an environment which you control, allowing perhaps one variable to vary, and you measure performance as a function of time or trials.

The result is a set of learning curves from which you derive "laws of learning."

In *training* theory, our paradigm might be a situation in which we desire to maximize the rate of assimilation of information or the rate of elimination of errors. The appropriate experiment might be to manipulate the environment in a multidimensional way, so as to maximize the slope of the performance curve as a function of time or trials.

In our own research program we began with the paradigm of the training theory. Our *conceptual* model was a gigantic system having under its control *all* the environmental variables—those that are known to affect the rate of learning and those about which nothing is presently known. We would apply this hypothetical system to a million identical twins, so that when we finished ruining 250,000 of them we would know exactly how to teach the remaining students.

In actual fact, of course, we used no such gigantic system and no such sample of students. Instead, we chose a motor skills task, used 12 subjects, and manipulated only two variables. A motor task was chosen for several reasons: (1) the ease of specification of the behavior to be learned; (2) the practicability of the task and of its applications; (3) the strong mathematical theories of skilled behavior that are available; (4) the ease of measurement of level of performance; and (5) my own personal predilection.

The student's ultimate task was to fly an aircraft, but the immediate training task was to execute a series of prescribed switching activities in a manner depending on his performance on the previous trial. I felt that this kind of training was important because it helped the student to learn to manipulate his instructional environment.[1]

In our motor tasks training we used a computer merely as a channel of communication between an "instructor" (the training device) and a student. The student served as a decision maker, operating under the constraints of an established program.

Our experimental hypothesis was that a *certain error rate is necessary for learning skills;* that is, if no errors are made, there will probably be little improvement in skill. We reasoned that if one wishes

---

[1] The relevance of such training can probably be illustrated by a story—perhaps apocryphal—about an *F-86-D* flight simulator that was found surprisingly effective. Upon investigation it was discovered that the sergeant who ran the trainer turned off target maneuvers during the early stages of training. This allowed the student time to learn how to run the training machine, after which he could concentrate on target motions.

to improve his game of tennis or chess he will normally avoid playing with someone poorer than himself. At the other extreme, if errors are made all the time (i.e., if the input-output relationship to be controlled is essentially random), then there is no improvement in skill level.

It was reasonable to assume that there is at least one—possibly important—optimal error rate between the two extremes. We used three levels of error rate in our study and hoped to find one that was better than the other two.

Two modes of operation were used. In the first mode the problem difficulty level was increased whenever the error rate dropped below a certain level; problem difficulty was *decreased* whenever the error rate rose above another prescribed level. The second mode *never* allowed problem difficulty to be decreased; it could only be increased.

The effectiveness of the training was measured on a standard transfer task. I will not attempt to give the full results but will comment briefly on one finding of interest. Subjects who studied under a relatively easy error criterion, and for whom difficulty level only increased, had a "training curve" that was essentially a linear increase in performance. By contrast, a control group who used the transfer task throughout, and who studied this task assiduously, had a negatively accelerated curve that fell below the levels reached by all the progressively trained groups.

In a second experiment, somewhat similar to Licklider's work in German (see Licklider's chapter in this book) we taught the language of the Morse code. Morse was selected because of the available research data on the effectiveness of different instructional methods and on performance norms for a variety of populations.

It is hard to find people who want to learn Morse code these days, but we were able to locate a troop of Boy Scouts who were interested in this activity. (An added advantage of using Boy Scouts is that they are likely to cover a fairly representative range of intelligence or ability.)

The results of our study showed a striking interaction between measured intelligence and the effectiveness of various training methods that we used. I believe that this interaction represents an *important* research area that should be studied before too many teaching machines are used.

We should also study the effect on teaching performance of progressively limiting the communication between a good teacher and his student; this would give us information about nonadaptive teaching machines, which create just such restrictions.

In summary, I feel that the only true teaching machine is an adaptive (learning) device; such a device is a teacher, rather than merely a communication channel for a teacher. A communication channel may be useful for multiplying the efficiency of a good teacher, but its value depends on our being able to describe the relevant characteristics of such a teacher. When we have determined these characteristics, we may be able to build a machine that could learn to be a good teacher.

I once heard a person express the belief that a learning machine was something that "learned people how to do things." The mistake has a kernel of truth.

Some theoretical and practical problems in programmed instruction

A. A. LUMSDAINE
University of California, Los Angeles

In presuming to discuss both theoretical and practical issues in a single chapter one makes an implicit assumption that the two are related. This relationship does not, of course, apply in all cases; a number of practical issues in the design and use of programmed instruction can be discussed without reference to theory. Some of these important practical issues, discussed elsewhere (cf. Lumsdaine, 1962a), include those involved in assessing instructional outcomes for purposes of "quality control," needs for improvement in the definition of instructional objectives, use of empirical programming techniques in relation to mass instructional media, and the allocation of research and development resources to meet educational requirements of this nation and of the rest of the world.

Problems in which theory and practice *are* closely related lie partly in certain interactions between theoretically oriented research efforts and practically oriented development efforts; such interactions are discussed in the second part of this chapter. More immediately, how-

In addition to his position at the University of California, the author serves as Adviser on Educational Media to the American Institute for Research. Part of the preparation of this chapter was accomplished in connection with a research project conducted by A.I.R. for the Office of Naval Reseearch under Contract No. Nonr-3077(00). Other aspects of the points of view here expressed reflect outgrowths of research conducted at A.I.R. under Air Force sponsorship and at A.I.R. and U.C.L.A. under sponsorship of the U. S. Office of Education. The specific interpretations made here are the responsibility of the author and do not necessarily reflect the views of his colleagues or of sponsoring agencies.

ever, we should consider the role played by theoretical orientation both in guiding the selection of hypotheses for experimental test and in determining foci of effort in practical development work. With respect to the latter role, we might contend that the principal justification for conceptual or theoretical development is its potential utility in guiding and reducing the amount of sheer trial and error in practical endeavor. At least this kind of pragmatism seems more worthy of respect than an attempt, which one cannot help feeling is sometimes in evidence, to dress a programming enterprise in theoretical trappings merely as a prestige symbol, to enhance its intellectual dignity or to impress customers with its "scientific" status.

Let us, then, accept as a point of departure the dictum (as phrased, I believe, by Kurt Lewin) that "nothing is as practical as a good theory." We may consider briefly some of the requirements which such a theory must satisfy in the field of programmed instruction if it is to serve as a useful guide to practice. In terms of our pragmatic orientation, a "good" theory in the present context is one that helpfully describes, and can serve as a guide to, the process of instructional programming.

Since this book is primarily concerned with the application of digital computers to automated instruction, I should comment here on the fact that most of the following discussion is more directly applicable to linear than to branching instruction. The two obvious potential fields of computer application are in the generation of program sequences and in the regulation of branching or variable sequences governed by some form of feedback from the students' response; the latter field seems at present to represent the more dominant interest. On the other hand, most of the programs currently being constructed, and certainly most of those that purport to be based on a systematic theory of instruction, appear to be linear or nonbranching sequences. Without disputing the evident needs for branching in a program that would cope most efficiently with individual differences in aptitude, interest, and prior competence, it can be contended that the theoretical problems involved in the linear program have a certain primacy in that branching programs can be thought of as variations on an essentially linear sequence of development that is needed to progress from zero initial competence to a desired terminal level of capability. At the present time, indeed, I believe that linear programs should almost invariably be constructed first, even if branching is later to be introduced, since this seems the only way to assure that all necessary aspects of competence will be provided for. In addition, it is in the context of the linear program sequence that some central differences in theoretical assumptions seem to need most immediate resolution.

Two of the more central theoretical problems arising in programmed instruction concern the role of student response and the appropriateness of reinforcement theory as a guide to programming. The first of these has been discussed elsewhere, both in relation to analysis of differences between "Skinner-type" and "Crowder-type" programs (Lumsdaine, 1960a, 1961a), and in more general terms (cf. Lumsdaine, 1961b, especially the concluding chapter). In brief, two of the more important distinguishable roles of student response are (1) affording direct practice through which learning is affected (which tends to be stressed in the rationale for Skinner-type programs) and (2) that of testing or discrimination (which is primarily of interest as a basis for some form of program variation, as in Crowder's programs or in other forms of branching—including, of course, branching mediated by a computer). An important, though often neglected, further role of overt response is its function in regulating or controlling the student's implicit responding—for example, requiring suitably selected overt responses in order to insure that the student reads the context in which they occur. A further function theoretically served by the student's response concerns assumptions about the role of reinforcement as a requirement for learning and sometimes may involve the assumption that reinforcement operates selectively with particular reference to overt responses, as distinguished from imp'icit responses such as those involved in reading. The latter role leads us directly to the question of the status of the reinforcement concept as a variable in programmed instruction.

Reinforcement Theory and Instructional Programming

In considering theoretical problems in the field of programmed instruction it is important to have a clear picture of what the existing state of theory does and does not provide as a guide to practical decisions in the construction of programs. One rather widely espoused point of view is that the theoretical substructure for a technology of instruction has already been largely developed in the behavioral laboratory and waits only to be applied in specific practical instances. The particular kind of theory for which this claim is commonly made is based primarily on the study of differential reinforcement as a technique for shaping behavioral repertoires in lower organisms, though very similar techniques have also been applied in creative research for the development of behavioral repertoires in humans ranging from young children to college professors.

I question very seriously whether theories placing primacy on the manipulation of reinforcement provide an adequate or even a very useful theoretical model for the development of programs of instruction in many academic or technical subject matters. In doing so, I do not in the least intend to belittle the major contribution which has been made by the intensive study of reinforcement in the laboratory nor to question the readily demonstrable fact that very remarkable repertoires of behavior can be developed by the manipulation of reinforcement contingencies. Neither am I sympathetic to any hyper-humanist position which would contend that men (and children) are so different phylogenetically from rats or pigeons that no science of behavior based on experimental study and shaping of the latter's behavior could possibly have much to offer in the understanding of complex ideational processes in human beings. On the contrary, I see no intrinsic reason why the experimental study of reinforcement techniques for shaping the behavioral repertoire of a rat should not offer very useful hypotheses or insights on how similar problems of response shaping can be managed in training, for example, the language habits of children or the social behavior of corporation executives. (In fact, I am even willing to concede the converse notion that insights on how to train your dog may be derived from observing how differential reinforcement can be made to "work" with humans.) In short, I think that the skillful use of differential reinforcement and the manipulation of reinforcement schedules represent an invaluable asset for many educational purposes.

Nevertheless, I am very much dissatisfied with reinforcement concepts as a guide to the instructional programmer; my dissatisfaction reflects in large part the fact that manipulation of reinforcement contingencies does not seem to be what even the most ardently Skinnerian programmers actually *do* when they start writing the frames of a program for an academic or technical subject. It is true that they try to select response patterns that they believe should be reinforced (in the sense of being strengthened or made more probable, at least) and to get relevant responses elicited in an appropriate context. But I think that what preoccupies the programmer's attention—and I believe rightly so—is the manipulation of prompting cues, not the manipulation of reward schedules. I think this will be evident on self-examination by any unbiased observer of his own behavior in starting to compose the frames of a program. (Those who would maintain otherwise are, I submit, simply not unbiased observers!) I think this emphasis on prompting cues is also evident in any of the several papers (e.g., Skinner, 1958; Klaus, 1961) that have sought to describe the programming process or offer rules for its conduct. Skinner (e.g., 1961) has also recognized explicitly the prevalence of situations in academic/technical instruction in which we can short-cut the process of waiting for appropriate response elements to appear and then shaping these up by differential reinforcement; however, this emphasis seems to have been largely ignored by some of his followers in their representation of reinforcement as the theoretical cornerstone of verbal programming.

The "Ruleg" system of Homme, Glaser, and Evans [1] conspicuously uses statements of principles or examples as cues or prompts for the completion of incomplete further statements of a rule or example; other less formalized procedures for eliciting desired responses, in contexts that progressively approximate a desired context for the appearance of a response, similarly depend primarily on the manipulation of prompts. This manipulation involves first the judicious and often ingenious introduction of the prompts and then their gradual withdrawal ("fading" or "vanishing"). Thus, as Zeaman (1959) has suggested, the appropriate theoretical model or paradigm here would appear to be that of classical conditioning through simple temporal contiguity of cue and response (with a deliberate effort being made to get the desired response to occur in the stimulus-context, which will become the proper signal for its subsequent elicitation) rather than one of operant conditioning situations in which attention is focused on the reinforcing effect of a reward that comes after the response has been made.

The reason for the importance of the manipulation of cues is simply that for a very wide range of responses appropriate for academic subject matters we already have at the outset of a program sequence an adequate unconditional stimulus (UCS); that is, we have an adequate way to elicit most of the desired responses whenever required—for example, if need be, by simply having the learner copy any given verbal response. The problem is not to identify the right response or to get it to occur but to attach it to the right stimulus context. This attachment is brought about by causing the response (through suitable prompting) to occur in the desired context and by subsequently van-

[1] See Evans, Homme, & Glaser (1960) and Homme & Glaser (1959).

ishing out the prompts. The fact that the student now learns to emit the response in the new desired context seems clearly to be most parsimoniously accounted for through the principle of conditioning by temporal contiguity—as most notably formulated and elaborated by Edwin R. Guthrie (1935). This scheme of instruction, like the manipulation of reinforcements in animal or child training, indisputably "works"; in various elaborations it can be seen operating in any so-called Skinner-type program through the sometimes obvious, sometimes quite subtle introduction of prompts or cues (of which ingenuity reveals an enormous variety of forms), followed by their measured withdrawal.

It is important to note that such a repertoire of suitable prompts (or varieties of UCS) is *not* so readily available for some other important classes of learning situations. This is notably true in animal training—where we have no way to convey a rich variety of instructions to the learner—and it is evidently true also in the training of a considerable range of human skills where no effective prompt or UCS is available that will dependably elicit the desired response in preference to competing, less adequate responses. Examples of such skills are readily found in the articulation of new phonemes in second-language learning, in perfecting a serve in tennis or a vibrato in playing a stringed instrument, and in many kinds of social proficiencies. Here instructions to the learner are effective only in getting out a response that may be a very rough approximation of what is desired; we can, by instruction, only get the response in "the right ball park." Beyond that there is no discriminative cue at our command initially; we can only wait for the right response (or a progressively closer approximation of it) to occur and then reinforce it.

Among the most important classes of responses for which we have no dependable UCS—that is, responses that we are not able to call out at will—are those of "paying attention" and of keeping at the task of studying. These ill-defined response classes are clearly propaedeutic to the elicitation of substantive responses that will mediate the subject-matter learning only if the student keeps working at the task of study or learning. Accordingly, I believe that one of the most relevant applications of reinforcement contingencies in academic programming is with respect to this heuristic attentional requirement. However, the experimental situations in which external controls are imposed, so that all subjects are marshaled through a program, are not ones in which such effects of variations in efficacy of reinforcement are very likely to be observed. Edwards (1956) has suggested some interesting possibilities in this area which, so far as I am aware, have not been followed up experimentally.

For the very wide class of responses that *can* be elicited by instruction (or by prompting, etc.), the question whether some observed or postulated reinforcement is necessary for acquisition is neither vital nor highly relevant. One reason for its irrelevance, as noted above, is that this question does not command much attention in the programming of academic subjects. Another reason is that it was long ago shown (notably by Hilgard & Marquis, 1940) that Guthrie's formulation of the principle of association by contiguity and the Thorndikian (or Skinnerian) principle of "effect" or reinforcement can each be logically derived from the other. To do so it is only necessary to note that the effect of an effective reward introduced into any situation inevitably changes the situation, so that the last response made before reinforcement is also simply the last response made (in that exact situation). If this be granted, the position that attention to cueing factors in much academic programming is more pertinent than attention to reinforcement contingencies need not become the focus of theoretical controversy; the act of learning can be thought of as being describable in either set of terms, and the object becomes, for a given class of learning situations, to work in terms of the descriptive aspects that are more helpful in managing that kind of learning situation. I think it is particularly desirable, in the context of this book, to recognize the very wide range of learning situations in which the prompting (or if you like, classical conditioning) facet provides the more useful perspective, because such a perspective, if recognized, may lead to rather different approaches to the use of computers in program mediation than a perspective that considers primarily the manipulation of reinforcement and/or response consequences. The importance of taking a classical or prompting perspective may be especially great, since many computer engineers and computer programmers (as well as the builders of artificial intelligence systems and models) appear to have a cybernetic orientation that already conduces to a reinforcement/feedback approach. The reinforcement/feedback orientation may be partly inevitable as long as attention is focused on adaptive learning without emphasis on the *guidance* of learning through *instruction*. But it is indeed the business of instruction to provide such forms of guidance (by prompting and related cueing techniques) that shortcut or bypass the need for much pure trial-and-error learning, hence reduce the need for corrective feedback.

In any case, I believe that one of the important problems of theory is to specify more precisely the conditions under which attention to the variation of reinforcement contingencies by the programmer of instruction really furnishes a useful guide to programming certain forms of behavior. A second problem is to formulate extensions of the general notions of prompting and vanishing that will afford more precise suggestions of the ways in which prompts can be most effectively introduced and withdrawn in various kinds of instructional programs. Here one suspects that two directions of inquiry might prove fruitful. The first direction would be an intensive analysis and classification of the prompting devices and techniques that appear most appropriate to various categories in an adequate taxonomy of the competencies involved in various subject matters. (Both of these taxonomies still remain to be developed.)

The second form of inquiry would be to develop ways of predicting, or knowing how to adjust, two or three important gradients. The first of these gradients is obviously the "vanishing" gradient over a sequence of frames in a program; the goal is to study the factors that govern the rate at which prompts can most efficiently be withdrawn. Here one can at present, perhaps, do little more than suggest that empirical inquiry could be guided by the general concept (Lumsdaine, 1959) that the strength of prompting cues used at any point in time should be just enough, but no stronger than is required to elicit the correct response.

A second, and related, theoretical gradient is an intraframe gradient involving the possibility, at least in principle, of progressively increasing prompt strength within a frame from zero to the point at which each student is able to respond. Exploratory experimentation by Angell & Lumsdaine (1961b), Israel (1960), and Guthrie & Lumsdaine (1961) suggests that evolving a satisfactory way of doing this might require instrumentation with considerable versatility; this is one of the places in which experimentation with computer-mediated program variation might be of considerable interest.

The third gradient concerns the frequency of reintroduction of previous material, or spacing and form of review sequences. In order to determine this pattern, we must consider the *testing* function of student responses (discussed earlier in distinction to the practice function of responses). Two theoretical or conceptual notions might be invoked to guide and reduce the amount of trial and error in empirical determination of review patterns. The two notions, though differently stated, perhaps reflect a common dynamic. One represents an application of reinforcement scheduling in which, at successive stages of training, the frequency of reinforcement can be progressively decreased so that the behavior in question continues in strength even after long periods of nonreinforcement. By analogy, at least, this suggests progressively greater increases in the intervals at which any given concept or skill-unit is reviewed. The second theoretical approach, which leads to the same general prediction, represents an extension of the notion of vanishing; in this extension it is the cue-effect of immediately, shortly, or more remotely preceding frames that is "vanished." At present I see little basis for preferring one of these conceptualizations over the other. Nevertheless, the application of the knowledge gained from the study of reinforcement schedules seems potentially more promising to me for the prediction of optimal review patterns than (as in programs dealing with academic or technical subjects) for the initial development of the capabilities required in most academic and technical learning. This predictive application, however, remains to be made in any systematic way, and it is possible that here too the use of a computer-mediated program might prove useful. One thing that might transcend the capabilities of a noncomputerized system, for example, would be the introduction of review for one concept on a basis that would be influenced by the needed frequency of review shown by the student during a given session for review of other related concepts or facts. The computer-stored information might be thought of as a shifting parameter, something like an alertness index or retentivity quotient.

A word might be added here concerning another aspect of the relationship between the prompting and the reinforcement or confirmation elements in an instructional sequence. Findings obtained by Cook & Kendler (1956) and subsequently reconfirmed by Cook (1958) in paired-associate learning indicate that when a prompting procedure is pitted against a no-prompting confirmation procedure the prompting procedure is superior. This finding, however, cannot necessarily be interpreted as directly in support of the above-elaborated recommendation for attention to prompting as opposed to reinforcement factors in academic/technical programming. One reason is that the Cook and Kendler studies were limited to paired-associate materials. A further reason is that the role of the confirmation procedure in these experiments was clearly not limited to a rewardlike reinforcement function; rather, it served also an informational or cue function. The same dual function is served by revelation of the correct response in most Skinner-type constructed-answer programs.

Shifting the focus from prompting-confirmation to the use of pure prompting versus mixed prompted and unprompted trials, Angell &

Lumsdaine (1960) obtained evidence supporting the notion that a mixture of prompted and unprompted trials is more effective than exclusive use of prompted trials (a prediction predicated on the same S-R contiguity principles that underlie the rationale for "vanishing" of prompts).

A more recent experiment reported by Angell & Lumsdaine (1961a) demonstrated that when adequate prompting is provided variations in the kind of confirmation or feedback given are much less important than when less prompting is provided. Similarly, a number of observers of programmed learning behavior have noted informally that in a well-cued program students may tend to ignore or bypass the confirmation or correction subframe. On logical grounds, furthermore, it is evident that showing the student the correct answer after he has responded involves more than a reward function of *post hoc* reinforcement. Specifically, the correction panel affords a cue or prompt for a further response, generally at an implicit or covert level, rather than merely strengthening the practice effect of the response already made. This fact is of particular importance when the student's first response has been in error; he can now supersede his incorrect response with the correct one. In any case, the immediate feedback providing confirmation or correction in instructional programs cannot be equated theoretically to any simple conception of reinforcement in the sense of reward.

The foregoing discussion has been concerned primarily with the applicability of one central theoretical concept to the programming of academic or technical subject matter, as opposed to its applicability in strengthening various operant forms of behavior (i.e., behavior not readily elicited by already identified and available cues). The major goals of this discussion have been twofold: first, to enter a plea for a change in emphasis from S-R reinforcement theory to S-R contiguity theory as an underlying rationale for programmed instruction in academic subject matters; and, second, to illustrate a more general argument for gauging the utility of a theoretical point of view in terms of its operational relevance in the practical job of program construction.

Theoretical and Practical Objectives of Research and Development

The other aspect of the relation between theory and practice which I should like to discuss involves some distinctions between the nature and purposes of *research* as opposed to *development* (or of more "basic" as opposed to more "applied" research efforts). Considerable confusion and wasted effort can arise when their purposes and potential outcomes are not clearly differentiated. The two kinds of effort are not antithetical; indeed, as Melton (1959) and others have persuasively argued, they can and should be mutually supportive. Both are useful in the development of a science and technology of instruction. But they do differ fundamentally in terms of purpose and of the kinds of outcome that each may be expected to generate. Basically, these two kinds of outcome are (1) increases in generalizable knowledge based on experimental tests of theoretically stated hypotheses and (2) the generation of effective instructional products. A third important kind of outcome, frequently identified as a unique product of "exploratory" laboratory research, is the generation of new hypotheses and of ideas for new instructional techniques.

It can well be argued that such new hypotheses find a more congenial atmosphere for development in exploratory research that is not fully committed in advance to the testing of preformulated hypotheses. However, it appears that they may also arise, not uncommonly, as by-products based on informal observation made in the course of conducting more formal experiments and also in the context of work on applied development projects. Thus, as an alternative to providing separately funded projects for purely exploratory research, it would be interesting to budget a sizable uncommitted fund as a reserve pool; this pool could provide for exploratory follow-up of hypotheses and new techniques suggested in the course of more structured projects.

Formal experimentation to test hypotheses has come in for considerable criticism from some of those who propose greater emphasis on unstructured exploratory research. Yet the formally controlled experiment, organized specifically for the test of a particular hypothesis is, if not the only way, at least the most dependable way to test hypotheses about instructional variables or processes and to rule out alternative explanations of observed effects (including, of course, the alternative "null" explanation that they are explainable on the basis of chance factors). The sterility of much of the formal experimentation on instructional media is not to be denied; however, in my opinion the weakness lies primarily not in the rationale of experimental comparison per se but in certain faults in the conduct of particular experiments. Conspicuous among these faults are the unsophisticated, nontheoretically oriented way in which independent variables are often defined or implemented and the lack of adequate standards for assuring the sensitivity or power of experimental comparisons.

The latter weakness obscures the effects of potent sources of variation in a welter of statistically nonsignificant differences. These multitudinous differences often stem from a variety of technical shortcomings, most of which reflect the premature conduct of formal experiments prior to adequate preliminary experimentation. One of the main shortcomings is reliance on inadequately sensitive criterion measuring instruments. It is easy to find instances in which a No Significant Difference finding is reported along with evidence that any likely difference between experimental treatments would be concealed by ceiling effects in the criterion test. These and related instances could have been avoided by adequate development and preliminary tryout of the criterion instrument.

Inadequate sensitivity of experimental comparisons may also result from poor control of the independent variables; this loss of control in turn may be caused by insufficient spadework prior to formal experimentation. The effective operation of most experimentally manipulated variables requires an extensive debugging process and skill in constructing experimental materials that potently exemplify the operation of these variables. A common violation of these requirements is found in premature demonstration experiments that are intended to show the value of a new general "method," before the materials presumed to exemplify the method have been subjected to sufficient development and refinement. However, the same fault is often apparent where a more specific hypothesis about a particular instructional factor is presumably being tested.

The other major class of weaknesses in the conduct of formal experiments—unsophisticated definition of the independent variables—requires a little more elaboration. For this purpose it is convenient to distinguish several rough categories of experimentation. These may be regarded as representing successive stages of sophistication in the definition of experimental variables and in the testing of hypotheses concerning them.[2]

Global Assessment Studies

The first stage represents an over-all evaluative assessment of a program. The effects of the program may be gauged either absolutely,

[2] For amplification of these or closely related distinctions among classes of experimentation and of some of the arguments summarized here concerning their defensibility, see Hovland, Lumsdaine, & Sheffield (1949, Chapter 1), and Lumsdaine (1960b, 1962b).

against some set of norms or in comparison with some alternative "method" of instruction. This kind of evaluative experiment is, in any case, a "global" assessment of effects achieved, without experimental variation of specific factors that could reveal what particular aspects of the program were responsible for these effects. Such an "experiment" may be conducted for one of three general reasons, one of which is entirely legitimate, one of dubious justifiability, and one, in my opinion, generally indefensible. The legitimate purpose is achieved when the effects of two preliminary versions of a program are measured as a step in program development; the purpose is the frankly technological one of product improvement, and there is no pretense at generalization of results to represent a "method" presumed to be exemplified by the program. The second, and more dubious, purpose is to conduct a field test or demonstration of the effects of a completed program in a practical field setting. Often the intent here is at least partly propagandistic—to demonstrate the merits of a particular program to potential users—and little other use is made of the data. The utility, if any, of the findings of such a field test is likely to depend largely on how good the program actually turns out to be, and this in turn is likely to be proportional to the amount of care that has been expended in developing the program. Such demonstrational experiments are particularly subject to criticism when insufficient preliminary effort has been made to develop a program of maximum effectiveness. At the present state of the art this prior spadework largely involves the empirical evaluation and improvement of preliminary forms; the response data afforded by small-step linear programs are peculiarly useful for this process.

The third purpose of global assessment studies is based on the erroneous supposition that the effects of a particular program can be considered representative of a general method or approach; this goal often involves a comparison of a "new" approach—for example, programmed instruction or use of instructional television—with a "control" group presumed to represent "conventional instruction." As was long ago pointed out by Hovland, Lumsdaine, & Sheffield (1949), such a comparison is generally indefensible because the things compared—the "new" method, the "conventional" method, or (usually) both—are not defined in a way that permits reproducibility or generalization.[3]

Unlike global assessment studies, experimental attempts to relate instructional effects to the operation of specified factors can potentially

[3] See also references cited in preceding footnote.

contribute to the development of a science of instruction comprising a set of testable propositions about reproducible factors in program design or use. The extent to which such a potential contribution is realized depends on the way in which the experimental variables are defined and manipulated.

Comparison of Grossly Defined Program Features

A second category, representing only a limited advance in level of sophistication, is one in which gross descriptive features of program format or instrumentation are manipulated in unitary form—for example, experiments comparing a branching versus a nonbranching program, multiple-choice versus constructed responses, or some form of smaller versus larger instructional "step-size." Such manipulation seems unlikely to yield generalizable findings or to contribute to a science of programming. The effectiveness of such gross features generally depends on *how* they are implemented; one form of branching may be effective, another form ineffective. Thus greater precision in describing the experimental factors in reproducible terms is required. Even rather exhaustive description of a particular experimental feature—though representing an advance in sophistication and specific reproducibility—is, however, likely to generate finding of very limited generality, applicable only to program uses nearly identical to those employed in the experiment.

Studies of Greater Sophistication

Further categories of research more useful to the development of a science of programming would seem to require three additional aspects of sophistication. One of these relates to the terms in which the variables are defined, one to the form of the proposition that is subjected to experimental test, and one to the purpose for which the test is conducted. I believe that the experiments which are most useful scientifically will define variables in terms of theoretically conceived factors rather than in terms descriptive only of physical features; that they will state contingent rather than absolute generalizations (expressing the predicted effects of one factor in relation to other factors with which, on theoretical grounds, it may be expected to interact); and that they will seek not so much to demonstrate the importance of specific program features per se as to test specific implications of a more general theoretical hypothesis.

Research of the type just described is as difficult as it is important, partly because of its mutual interdependence on theory development; not only is such experimentation essential for successful (i.e., ultimately practical) theory development, but, conversely, the extent to which it can be formulated is limited by the existing prior state of theory. It is not surprising that few examples are still to be found within the field of research on instruction or complex human learning; perhaps the clearest examples to date are not in the current literature of programmed instruction but in experiments on learning from demonstrational films (e.g., Maccoby & Sheffield, 1958, 1961; Sheffield & Maccoby, 1961) and in experiments on persuasive communication (e.g., Hovland, Lumsdaine, & Sheffield, 1949, Chapter 8).

Of particular importance to the development of a science of programmed instruction are experiments (of the last category listed above) which involve contingent predictions that take into account interactions of programming variables with task and learner characteristics. The limitations of currently available schemata for providing a functional taxonomy of these classes of variables suggest that an advanced science of programming—as distinguished from useful empirical technology—will probably require much time. I think its development will, however, be slowed, rather than expedited, by any failure to recognize the need for this science—for example, by contenting ourselves with the illusion that the necessary theoretical developments already exist.

In conclusion I should like to add a few words about the role of computers in the development of a science and technology of instruction. I have at most a very cautious optimism about the role computers are likely to play in the near future, other than for processing experimental data, in the development of instructional science. (Even their use as highly efficient data processors may have liabilities as well as assets because their very capabilities may tempt us into designing gargantuan multifactor experiments that manipulate a multiplicity of theoretically ill-defined, hence ultimately unimportant, variables.) The principal basis for this restraint is that the level of theoretical sophistication now available is not commensurate with the adequate use of computer capabilities; I doubt that we can write the necessary computer programs until we have progressed further toward satisfactory definition of relevant subject-matter variables and learner characteristics. Naturally I hope I am mistaken in this supposition and that the next symposium will so indicate. One of the uses of computers which I believe might most likely contribute to an improvement in definition of variables would be to employ them as simulation devices for the reproduction of teacher and learner behavior in tutorial sequences, somewhat as Newell, Shaw, & Simon (1958) have done in the study of problem solving. I certainly consider this a high-risk venture with little assurance of success, but it appears to be worth investigation.

With respect to more immediately practicable applications of computers for implementing programming variables as now conceived, I am tempted to be somewhat more optimistic. Whether the capabilities of the computer in using stored information to mediate branching sequences will be worth the cost, however, seems to me to depend on two considerations. The first of these relates to computer engineering and economics, on which I am not competent to comment. The second consideration is the empirical question of how much variance in achievement will be accounted for by relatively subtle variations that require computers rather than simpler devices. A compelling argument for devoting computer facilities to such empirical research is that there is no other way to determine whether their capabilities are worthwhile. But, although some ardent souls are devoting themselves to this enterprise, I sincerely hope that the glamour of computers will not prove so universally captivating that other avenues to the further development of programming art and science, using less complex instrumentation, will fail to be adequately explored.

REFERENCES

* Note: Many of the references listed below have been reproduced or abstracted in A. A. Lumsdaine & R. Glaser (Eds.), *Teaching machines and programmed learning: a source book*. Washington, D. C.: National Education Association. For brevity of notation these references are designated by the letters *TMPL*.

Angell, D., & Lumsdaine, A. A. *Prompted plus unprompted trials versus prompted trials alone in paired-associate learning*. Pittsburgh: American Institute for Research, 1960. (AFOSR-TN-60-808) Research Report AIR-314-60-IR-129.

Angell, D., & Lumsdaine, A. A. *The effects of prompting trials and partial-correction procedures on learning by anticipation*. San Mateo, California: American Institute for Research, 1961a. (AFOSR-1343) Research Report AIR-C14-9/61-SR5.

Angell, D., & Lumsdaine, A. A. *A study of subject-controlled partial cueing in paired-associate learning*. San Mateo, California: American Institute for Research, 1961b. (AFOSR-1342) Research Report AIR-C14-9/61-SR4.

Cook, J. O. Supplementary report: Processes underlying learning a single paired-associate item. *J. exp. Psychol.*, 1958, **56**, 455. (Also in *TMPL,** pp. 601–602.)

Cook, J. O., & Kendler, T. S. A theoretical model to explain some paired-associate learning data. In G. Finch and F. Cameron (Eds.), *Symposium on Air Force human engineering, personnel, and training research.* Washington, D. C.: National Academy of Sciences—National Research Council, 1956. (Also abstracted in *TMPL,** pp. 602–604.)

Edwards, W. D. *Skinner's teaching machines.* Unpublished Laboratory Note, Air Force Personnel Training Research Center (mimeo.), May 1956. (Also abstracted in *TMPL,** pp. 611–614.)

Evans, J., Homme, L. E., & Glaser, R. *The Ruleg (rule-example) system for the construction of learning programs.* A report prepared under the Cooperative Research Program of the United States Office of Education at the Department of Psychology, University of Pittsburgh, 1960. (Also abstratced in *TMPL,** pp. 619–620.)

Guthrie, E. R. *The psychology of learning.* New York: Harper, 1935.

Guthrie, P. M., & Lumsdaine, A. A. *Some effects of graduated partial cueing on the learning of paired-associates.* San Mateo, California: American Institute for Research, 1961 (AFOSR-1341) Research Report AIR-C14-9/61-SR3.

Hilgard, E. R., & Marquis, D. G. *Conditioning and learning.* New York: Appleton-Century-Crofts, 1940. (2nd ed., 1961.)

Homme, L. E., & Glaser, R. Problems in programming verbal learning sequences. Paper read at Amer. Psychol. Assoc., Cincinnati, September 1959. (Also in *TMPL,** pp. 486–496.)

Hovland, C. I., Lumsdaine, A. A., & Sheffield, F. D. *Experiments on mass communication.* Princeton: Princeton University Press, 1949.

Israel, M. L. Variably blurred prompting: I. Methodology and application to the analysis of paired-associate learning. *J. Psychol.*, 1960, **50**, 43–52. (Also abstracted in *TMPL,** pp. 643–644.)

Klaus, D. J. The art of auto-instructional programming. *Audiovisual Communication Review*, 1961, **9**, 130–142.

Lumsdaine, A. A. Some issues concerning devices and programs for automated learning, 1959. (In *TMPL,** pp. 517–539.)

Lumsdaine, A. A. The development of teaching machines and programmed self-instruction. In *New teaching aids for the American classroom.* Stanford University, California: Institute for Communication Research, 1960a. Pp. 136–173.

Lumsdaine, A. A. Graphic aids, models and mockups, as tools for individual and classroom instruction. In G. Finch (Ed.), *Symposium on educational and training media,* Washington, D. C.: National Academy of Sciences—National Research Council, 1960b.

Lumsdaine, A. A. Some differences in approach to the programming of instruction. In J. P. Lysaught (Ed.), *Programmed learning: evolving principles and industrial applications.* Ann Arbor, Michigan: Foundation for Research on Human Behavior, 1961a. Pp. 37–52.

Lumsdaine, A. A. (Ed.) *Student response in programmed instruction: a symposium.* Washington, D. C.: National Academy of Sciences—National Research Council, 1961b, in press.

Lumsdaine, A. A. Improving the quality of instruction through programmed learning. In *Proceedings of the twenty-sixth conference of the Educational*

Records Bureau and the American Council of Education. New York: Educational Records Bureau, 1962a, in press.

Lumsdaine, A. A.   Instruments and media of instruction.   In N. L. Gage (Ed.), *Handbook on research on teaching.*   Washington, D. C.: American Educational Research Association, National Education Association, 1962b, in press.

Maccoby, N., & Sheffield, F. D.   Theory and experimental research on the teaching of complex sequential procedures by alternate demonstration and practice. In G. Finch & F. Cameron (Eds.), *Symposium on Air Force human engineering, personnel, and training research.*   Washington, D. C.: National Academy of Sciences—National Research Council, 1958.   Publication No. 516.

Maccoby, N., & Sheffield, F. D.   Optimum methods of combining practice with filmed demonstration in teaching complex response sequences. III. Summary and interpretation.   In A. A. Lumsdaine (Ed.), *Student response in programmed instruction: a symposium.*   Washington, D. C.: National Academy of Sciences— National Research Council, 1961, in press.

Melton, A. W.   The science of learning and the technology of educational methods.   *Harvard Educational Review.*   1959, **29**, 96–106.   (Also abstracted in *TMPL,** pp. 658–660.)

Newell, A., Shaw, J. C., & Simon, H. A.   Elements of a theory of human problem solving.   *Psychol. Rev.,* 1958, **65**, 151–166.

Sheffield, F. D., & Maccoby, N.   Summary and interpretation of research on organizational principles in constructing filmed demonstrations.   In A. A. Lumsdaine (Ed.), *Student response in programmed instruction: a symposium.*   Washington, D. C.: National Academy of Sciences—National Research Council, 1961, in press.

Skinner, B. F.   Teaching machines.   *Science,* 1958, **128**, 969–977.   (Also in *TMPL,** pp. 137–158.)

Skinner, B. F.   Learning theory and future research.   In J. P. Lysaught (Ed.), *Programmed learning: evolving principles and industrial applications.*   Ann Arbor, Michigan: Foundation for Research on Human Behavior, 1961.

Zeaman, D.   Skinner's theory of teaching machines.   In E. H. Galanter (Ed.), *Automatic teaching: the state of the art.*   New York: Wiley, 1959.

PART II

Computer-Based

Instructional

Systems

Potential uses of computers as teaching machines

JOSEPH W. RIGNEY

University of Southern California, Los Angeles

We Americans seem to have unlimited faith that the machine will save us from whatever dilemma—personal, social, or national—that we find ourselves in at any particular time. Of all the machines upon which we lavish this childish faith, probably the digital computer is most frequently regarded as a *deus ex machina,* or perhaps we should say a *machina ex machina.* Apparently, it has proved to be such a powerful slave that we now wish to endow it with an attribute formerly peculiar to living organisms, the ability to learn. Anyone who has attended recent computer conferences has observed this anthropomorphic pre-occupation, and some elder statesmen amongst the scientists have solemnly tried to foresee the implications of all this, one being that the slave may learn to turn on its master. I find it hard to become concerned about this possibility—we long ago were enslaved by machines, as anyone knows who tries to maintain a household full of mass-produced gadgets and two cars in the garage. One more cold-hearted master will not make a significant difference.

But this conference does mark a significant shift in recent interest—from trying to get computers to learn to trying to make teachers out of them. It was, of course, inevitable that American thinking should run in this direction. We are told hourly that we are in the midst of an educational crisis. Our educational system did not let us meet the ultimate criterion of an advanced culture—which evidently is to put things into orbit first.

The preparation of this paper was supported by the Personnel and Training Branch of the Office of Naval Research, under Contract NONR-228(02).

It was predictable that people with computers and people with teaching machines would get together. The idea of a computer as a teaching machine has too much fascination for it to be otherwise.

This chapter is concerned with one characteristic of the digital computer as a teaching machine—its interactive capacity in relation to individual differences in learning. This may not be the most valuable characteristic of a computer. After all, the well-known data-processing capabilities of the digital computer might indeed be used in the educational system, just as they are being used so successfully in science, business, and industry. A central computer might control banks of teaching machines presenting linear programs and do all the work attendant on sequencing program frames, recording responses, and accumulating student records. These seem to be relatively simple matters of applying what already is known about automating similar operations.

However, the interactive capacity afforded by a computer with suitable input-output equipment is really a new tool not heretofore available to the researcher studying learning nor, of course, to the educator. It is, at least superficially, an attractive notion that a computer can be programmed to interact dynamically with one or more students. Various possibilities for the content of this interaction have been suggested by a number of people. Discussions by Ramo (1957) and by Coulson & Silberman (1959) are germane. The use of this particular capability in a practical educational or training environment, however, does appear to be a long way in the future. There are many questions that have to be answered and many problems that have to be solved. And, despite its superficial attractiveness, no one really has gone far enough down this road to know whether the practical gains would be worthwhile.

The interactive capacity of the computer, in response to individual differences, may be applied in a variety of ways. Initial interactions between a student and a computer can be used to determine the pattern of subsequent communications. The computer may dominate the interaction—that is, it may contain the general rules which determine the communication pattern on the basis of information obtained from the students. Or, the student may dominate the interaction. In the latter case the student controls the general rules and determines what next to ask of the computer. In either case all desired variations in the interactive sequences must be provided for, in advance, in the computer program and in the other information stored in the computer.

There are two types of individual differences for which the computer's interactive capacity must make allowances. Individuals may differ among themselves at any one time (the traditional among-subjects differences), or each individual may change over a period of time (the traditional within-subject differences).

It is the objective of this chapter to examine three types of learning environments in which man-computer interaction has been, or could be, used. Two of these environments are discussed only briefly. The third, programmed verbal learning, is examined in more detail.

Interactive Capacity and Individual Differences in Learning

Team Training in Game Situations

Computers have already been used, of course, to facilitate learning. The most extensive experience with them has been in connection with very complex group training, either in war gaming or in tactical environments. Here the objective is realistic simulation of environmental events, and the interactions are primarily between the group being trained and these events. The effects of an individual's responses to stimulus material often are intermixed with the reactions of other individuals. Although group performance measures are possible, individual knowledge-of-results usually is not supplied. As Hall (1957) noted, individual responses correlate imperfectly with informative feedback, which Hall therefore called "socially confounded feedback."

In some cases team training has sought to capitalize on individual differences among members of a particular team by letting the team evolve more or less original methods of dealing with the simulated events. Thus there might be many subtle differences among teams after training, and the effectiveness of each team would depend upon maintaining group membership intact. In other cases team members are taught standard roles, resulting in groups that use more or less standard procedures.

This is such a complicated learning situation that no one has discovered all the interactive relationships that may hold among individuals and between individuals and environmental events. The System Development Corporation is, of course, concerned with this situation on a day-to-day basis, at a practical working level, and unquestionably has done the most work with it. Also, some early observations of interactive relationships were made by Bryan and associates (1956) in connection with Combat Information Centers. Subsequently, Dunlap's Operational Sequence Diagrams (Brooks, 1960) and similar human engineering techniques have been applied to the analysis of weapon systems operation. These have yielded good descriptive information, but all the subtleties of man-man and man-machine interactions are difficult to capture by these approaches and certainly cannot be rigorously explored. Glanser & Glaser (1959, 1961) reviewed theoretical and experimental studies of group structure and of the effects of different structures on various performance measures. One of their final conclusions was that (1961, p. 26) "there is still a major need for a system to order the data already obtained and to direct further work on the effects of group structure. . . ."

Therefore, rather than manipulate all interactions in a controlled fashion, the systems trainer generally must be satisfied with an attempt to evoke representative interactions by doing realistic simulation. That it nevertheless is important to identify and control these interactions is demonstrated by recent research on team training by Egerman, Klaus, & Glaser (1961). These investigators found that for some levels of proficiency and for what they called a "redundant team" socially confounded feedback actually may result in group performance decrement as training is continued.

Although computers were used to facilitate learning first in these team-training situations, their principal roles here have been, and remain, those of problem generators and simulators rather than as teaching machines.

Advanced Technical and Professional Training

A second potential application of interactive capacity is in advanced technical and professional training for the individual. This application is seen as an outgrowth of information retrieval techniques. A member of any profession is in danger of being buried under the literature of his field, and automation of information retrieval may be his only salvation. But, beyond this, in teaching such diverse activities as research planning or trouble shooting of a large electronic system, learning could be facilitated by what Licklider (1960) called "man-computer symbiosis." At this level of achievement the individual must learn to be self-programming. Different individuals, with different talents and interests, will approach a research problem or a trouble-shooting problem in different ways, yet all may achieve the same goals.

The individual needs to learn how to direct and organize his own activities. Somewhere earlier in his training he presumably has passed the spoon-feeding stage. Therefore, he probably should control the interaction with the computer, which becomes an inanimate assistant performing a variety of routine tasks for him, including pure information retrieval functions. Licklider (1960) has discussed this as computer participation in real-time thinking and problem solving and described some of the technical obstacles to achieving this at present.

There is a thin line between performance and learning, and one cannot always say when a professional or a technician is doing one and not the other. For example, for a number of years our group has been interested in electronics trouble shooting, both as a form of problem solving and as a technical training requirement. One of the difficulties associated with training people to trouble shoot is that there is no unique solution route for locating a malfunction. The technician has to accumulate enough symptom information to permit him to make an informed guess about the source of the trouble. Within reasonable limits, the sequence of moves by which he accumulates this information is not crucial, as long as he has some guiding strategy in mind.

A certain amount of trouble-shooting training, with certain levels of technicians and with relatively simple equipment, can be accomplished by using only one of the possible optimal sequences for each problem. However, for very large systems and for more advanced training, this approach probably is too limited. The technician needs to learn to program his own sequences, and he also needs assistance in handling the sheer mass of information that describes the system. He has a severe information retrieval problem with conventional printed handbooks. Much of his time can be spent in searching through these for the one schematic or the one paragraph he needs. We believe he could also use assistance in interpreting the symptom information he collects. Technicians find it relatively easy to take readings at test points but relatively difficult to extract all the useful trouble-shooting information these contain (Rigney et al., 1961a & b). To a limited extent, at least, a computer might be programmed to store sequences of test readings as they are inserted by the technician and to assist in the interpretation of these readings by presenting logical diagnostic possibilities based either on circuit design or on problem histories. Man-computer task sharing in such trouble shooting could be used to facilitate learning; beyond this, such task sharing might provide a useful approach to automatic checkout equipment, since it would be more likely to utilize the technician's talents appropriately than current approaches erroneously oriented toward removing him altogether from the system.

Programmed Learning

A third area of application of the computer's interactive capacity is in individual verbal learning, using teaching-machine programs. This area, like the others, will obviously require much research. Despite the attractive (or unattractive, depending on your profession) prospects of automating the school, someone should first go a long way further down this road at a research and development level.

At this point we should examine some of the issues involved and the problems that will have to be solved. These are discussed under two headings: (1) the interactive model and its requirements and (2) transfer value of current information about individual differences and learning for implementing this model.

The following discussion is based on the assumption that the objective of the computer-controlled teaching machine will be to deal more satisfactorily with individual differences in learning. It is also assumed that reasonably homogeneous groups will be involved and that each individual will be learning the same subject matter.

The Interactive Model and Its Requirements. A computer can be programmed to use a student's earlier responses as the basis for determination of subsequent presentations to the student. This idea occurs more or less spontaneously wherever computers are considered in the same context with teaching machines. Such an application is analogous to the use of computers for real-time process control in industry, although in the case of instruction we do not know much about the process we are trying to control. There are two related approaches to achieving this control. One might begin the process in the same way for everyone and let it continue until one observes signs that it is getting out of bounds. Then some action could be taken to bring it back within the desired limits. This approach is called "remedial sequencing." Or one might attempt to predict the optimal conditions to maintain the process within limits for each individual. This is called "predicted sequencing."

Remedial sequencing seems to be the approach with which investigators have started. The method begins with some linear program which presumably would be satisfactory for some proportion of a group but not for all of it. Hence branching criteria are built into the computer program, which controls sequencing of the material and records and analyzes selected aspects of the student's responses. When the criteria indicate it is necessary, the student is branched away from the linear program into a remedial loop. But he is always brought back to the linear program and, in fact, would never leave it if analysis of his responses indicated it was not necessary. Coulson & Silberman (1961) have been doing extensive experimentation with this variation.

The second variation, predicted sequencing, would not necessarily be based upon a linear program. Except by coincidence, each student would normally have a different program for learning the subject matter. Predicted sequencing would attempt to predict the one best path for each individual to follow from measures of each individual's characteristics. Initially, differences between individuals would determine the selection, but this would be modified later on the basis of measured changes within the individual. Pure predicted sequencing undoubtedly requires much more precise knowledge of relationships between individual differences and learning than we now have.

Clearly these two approaches are not mutually exclusive. Present-day remedial branching programs take the student back over the same material or transfer him to some new sequence. In either case a prediction is at least implicit that the postbranching sequence will be effective. But, since prediction is not very likely to be perfect, some provision must be made for further remedial branching to get the process back within limits. Both approaches could be built into the same program since the basic procedural requirements are the same, as shown in Fig. 1.

The cycle depicted in Fig. 1 would be repeated as many times as necessary to achieve the desired control. Conceivably, it could be

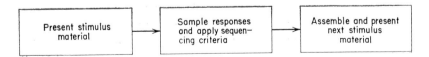

Fig. 1. The basic interactive cycle.

repeated for each recorded response, or it could occur only once per lesson.

Implementation of the basic interactive cycle implies a number of requirements. First, the initial stimulus material must be appropriate. For remedial sequencing this is a relatively small problem, since everyone starts at the same place. For predicted sequencing the initial materials might be concerned with several kinds of measures, such as prior experience, aptitudes, including intelligence, learning abilities, attitudes and motivation, or samples of the possible arrangements and sequences of material to be learned. Of these, a measure of prior experience is most directly related to the arrangement of subsequent program material.

In some military and industrial training situations groups simply cannot be homogeneous with respect to prior experience. For example, the personnel in a certain Navy programmer school vary considerably in terms of mathematics background and experience. This variation is likely to be predictive of their ability and motivation to work through a linear program in Boolean algebra. A linear program designed for individuals with a poor mathematics background bores those students who are more sophisticated mathematically. Yet all students need to learn the subject. Here the transfer of specific knowledge is less important than the acquisition of attitudes and techniques.

Although the use of variations in relevant achievement for predicting student abilities and needs might be fairly simple, the connections between intelligence, aptitudes, attitudes, motivation, or learning abilities and the optimum arrangement of subject matter certainly are more tenuous.

A second requirement of the interactive cycle is that responses measured must be reliable. If the test frame or other stimulus material could be repeated, would the subject give the same response or response pattern? Obviously it is not easy to test this in learning studies. But no one should expect the single response to a single frame to be a reliable indicator. What would be the subject's response to that frame again? If it were an easy frame, both responses should be correct. If very difficult, both might be incorrect, and so on. The four possible patterns for each frame given twice are shown in Table 1.

Some data from a recent experiment in which each of 107 frames in a lesson was presented twice to each of 41 subjects are shown at the bottom of Table 1. Table entries show the mean number of subjects per frame with a particular response pattern. One would not predict this distribution from a knowledge of trial 1 alone. One cannot assume

TABLE 1   POSSIBLE RESPONSE PATTERNS PER SUBJECT PER FRAME ON TWO
TRIALS AND DISTRIBUTION OF ACTUAL RESPONSES, 41 SUBJECTS, 107 FRAMES

	A	B	C	D
Trial 1	Right	Wrong	Wrong	Right
Trial 2	Right	Right	Wrong	Wrong
Means per frame	30.84	5.41	2.77	1.95
(S.D.)	(6.08)	(4.27)	(3.25)	(1.91)

that if a frame is missed once it necessarily would or would not be missed again; nor can one be certain that if it were not missed once it would not be missed on a subsequent trial. There is more than one reason either for missing or for not missing a frame. Branch-points for remedial branching should probably be based on performance on concepts rather than on individual frames; they should utilize response patterns rather than single responses, unless special frames, such as self-appraisal items, are used.

A third requirement of the cycle is that the branching or sequencing criteria be valid. If the student is not doing well with a linear program, presumably he should be branched to a remedial loop. But what kind of loop? In the case of predicted sequencing, what is the optimum arrangement suggested by the test? There must be some way to establish predictive relationships between responses to test material and kinds of remedial loops or subject-matter arrangements. Common sense suggests that a high error rate on frames dealing with a particular concept means the student is not learning that concept. But what next? Should the frames be repeated, should a different approach be tried, or should a new topic be temporarily introduced? There is little in error rate, or response latency, per se, to help decide among these possibilities. For example, do increasing latencies mean that the student is finding the subject matter increasingly difficult, is he becoming bored, or has he simply changed response sets? Nor does analysis of the contents of a one- or two-word response to a frame hold much more promise. A good teacher often can infer what has gone awry from listening to successive responses of a student, but to do so he uses much more knowledge of the situation and of the student than is contained in these immediate responses. The teacher is also likely to ask probing questions suggested by this broader context of information. Special self-appraisal items might be devised to simulate this technique, as has been done by Coulson & Silberman (1961).

A fourth requirement of the cycle is a battery of effective remedial or predicted sequences. What are the different approaches to teaching something? When not concerned with methods as independent variables, learning studies often have relied upon repetition of the stimulus material; practice and drill are familiar educational techniques. Repetition in the form of restated review, or disguised among new frames, is a standard ingredient of linear programs. It also would seem to be the simplest thing to do after remedial branching.

Although sheer repetition is boring, it could decrease between-subject differences within very limited learning objectives. The following data illustrate this (Table 2). Three groups were classified by Otis mental test scores. Each group worked through the same linear program twice. With two trials, the dullest group's mean approached that of the bright group for one trial. But note that the bright group could go on and learn much more while the dull group was taking the second trial. It is probable that reports of no correlation between intelligence-test scores and programmed-learning criterion-test scores merely mean that the brighter individuals were held back by the material.

"Common sense" provides some ideas for effective remedial and predicted sequences, involving adjustments based on relationships between the material to be learned and measures of such things as reading comprehension, vocabulary level, intelligence, special aptitudes, and motivation and attitudes. For example, the computer program might adjust word and sentence difficulty in the frames to student

TABLE 2   MEAN ERROR SCORES FOR THREE INTELLIGENCE LEVELS ON EACH OF TWO REPETITIONS OF A BOOLEAN ALGEBRA PROGRAM LESSON (107 FRAMES)

	Otis (20 min. form)		Trial 1		Trial 2		Abso-lute Gain	Percent-age Gain
	Range	Mdn.	Errors	S.D.	Errors	S.D.		
Low IQ (n = 10)	30–41	38	27.70	18.33	17.70	14.67	10.00	36.10
Average IQ (n = 12)	42–47	45	27.83	12.72	17.75	5.90	10.08	36.22
High IQ (n = 18)	48–70	53	12.44	7.54	4.06	3.29	8.38	67.36

differences in verbal comprehension. Or the frames-per-concept ratio might be adjusted to differences in intelligence. In any case the necessary predictive relationships and the effectiveness of particular kinds of sequences would have to be established by research.

Implications of Current Information About Individual Differences and Learning. This section raises the question of the transfer value of the literature about individual differences and learning to automated instruction. It is discouraging to think that research with the objective of applying interactive capacity of individual differences will have to start with a clean slate or cannot be related or integrated in any way with what has been done with individual differences and learning in the past. Yet there undeniably are methodological barriers involved.

The traditional approaches have recently been discussed by Cronbach (1957), Gulliksen (1961), and Estes (1960). They are part of the broader streams of experimental and correlational psychology which Cronbach characterized as having become, to a large extent, two separate rivers. Unfortunately, knowledge about learning comes from one stream and information about individual differences comes from the other. Thus, when one looks to learning studies for information bearing on individual differences in learning, one finds a preoccupation with group means. As Cronbach put it (1957, p. 674),

Individual differences have been an annoyance rather than a challenge to the experimenter. His goal is to control behavior, and variations within treatments is proof that he has not succeeded. Individual variation is cast into that outer darkness known as "error variance." For reasons both statistical and philosophical, error variance is to be reduced by any possible device. You turn to animals of a cheap and short-lived species, so that you can use subjects with controlled heredity and controlled experience. You select human subjects from a narrow subculture. You decorticate your subject by cutting neurons or by giving him an environment so meaningless that his unique responses disappear. You increase the number of cases to obtain stable averages, or you reduce N to 1, as Skinner does. But whatever your device, your goal in the experimental tradition is to get these embarrassing differential variables out of sight.

Estes pointed out the disadvantages of single-minded concentration on group learning curves and analyzed a series of what he called miniature experiments in which he found that these curves obscure important individual learning effects of an all-or-none nature. They also obscure the individual's learning curve. To the extent that this curve differs from the group curve, the latter is not a useful substitute. In fact, the traditional approach to the study of learning has not been especially concerned either with individual learning curves or with the possibility of there being different learning abilities.

What of the information that is available in the correlational stream? There certainly is no dearth of data about individual differences, expressed in terms of scores on tests or of factors extracted from score intercorrelations. There are well-known attempts to organize these descriptions into patterns or structures, Guilford's (1961) structure of the intellect being a notable example. There are the large-scale uses of tests of achievement or aptitude by educational institutions to predict some aspect of academic success. And, more or less midway between the two streams, there are the intriguing studies in which the experimental and correlational approaches have been merged to yield information about interrelationships between individual differences and learning and to study different learning abilities and different learning curves.

Probably none of the specific data in these studies is directly transferable to automated instruction. Nor is it possible in this chapter to survey this vast literature in any adequate way. However, there are some thought-provoking conclusions that occur from a perusal of it, which have implications for anyone who wishes to do on-line remedial or predicted sequencing with a computer.

1. There are surprisingly broad ranges of intelligence and achievement in any one grade level in many, and probably most, schools. Cook (1959) summarized several studies of the range of mental age and found that it tends to increase with grade level. He concluded that in the typical school, by the sixth grade, 2% of the pupils will have mental ages of less than 8 years and 2% will have mental ages of more than 16 years. The high school teacher will find a range of 8 to 10 years in mental age at each grade level.

The ranges of achievement for the areas of reading comprehension, vocabulary, the mechanics of English, composition, science, geography, and history were similarly wide. In fact, Cook pointed out that since the beginning of the educational movement no fact had been more frequently revealed—or ignored—than the great variability in the achievement of pupils in the same grade.

The interactive capacity of the computer-controlled teaching machine would certainly seem to have plenty of individual differences as raw material. However, some of Cook's conclusions concerning how conventional teaching procedures influence individual differences are also thought provoking.

Do conventional procedures make individuals more alike or less alike with respect to a given ability? Is the variability of a class increased or decreased by good teaching? Although Cook found the research on this question somewhat difficult to interpret, he concluded that when the responses to be learned are simple and the goals are so limited that a high proportion of the group can achieve a criterion of mastery during the period of learning the variability of the group decreases. However, if the task is more complicated and the goals are unlimited, so that the most capable members of the group can proceed at their own speed, the variability of the group is increased.

In other words, the idea that groups can be made more homogeneous in a given achievement area through effective teaching implies limited educational objectives with respect to the complexity of the learning and also with respect to the amount of simple learning. A number of things may be done to accommodate to the less able student. Rote factual learning can be emphasized, textbooks can be written down, and curriculum materials can be selected for mastery by at least 80% of the students. The teacher's time may be devoted almost exclusively to the slower learners. When this is done, it is not surprising that pupils with the lowest initial scores make the greatest progress or that a negative relationship is found between initial scores and gain or between gain and intelligence.

2. There is evidence for the existence of several different learning abilities. It probably would be unsafe to assume otherwise. The two studies by Stake (1958) and Allison (1960), among others, suggest this. Allison factor analyzed 13 learning situations with 29 reference variables; he used for each learning task two measures: a rate parameter (average rate of learning) and a curvature parameter (was learning faster during first or second half of the situation?).

Allison interpreted seven learning parameter factors: verbal conceptual learning, that is, learning the relationships among words; spatial-conceptual learning, learning relationships among spatial configurations; mechanical-motor learning, learning mechanical principles and psychomotor skills; three rote learning factors, two independent of sensory modality, the third in learning of simple spatial material; and early versus late learning, derived from the curvature parameter for situations which involve learning spatial material.

If further investigations confirm and identify different kinds of learning, it may be that in the future learning tests which measure such factors can be used as predictors for different arrangements of the same subject matter.

3. There is evidence of different kinds of learning curves. Tucker (1960) applied factor analytical techniques to probability learning data and found, for the more complicated of two situations, that three different learning curves were needed to explain the data. One was negatively accelerated and two had inflected S-shapes. Different subjects had different weighted combinations of these curves. Tucker concluded that mean learning curves are appropriate only for a limited class of special cases.

This suggests that the development of within-subject differences can vary from subject to subject. If, for example, some subjects are early learners, some medium learners, and some late learners, the arrangement of subject matter for them might have to take this into account.

4. There is evidence that aptitude patterns shift as learning progresses. Here the work of Fleishman & Hempel (1954) is instructive. Although they were concerned with psychomotor rather than verbal learning, there is no reason to believe that the same general tendency would not be true of verbal learning. They found that the percentage of variance represented by each of nine factors gradually shifted through eight stages of practice. Spatial relations, for example, became less important and rate of movement more important in the later stages of practice. During the first stages of practice, "nonmotor" factors contributed 46.1% of the variance, whereas three "motor" factors contributed but 29.5%. However, by the final stage of practice, nonmotor factors accounted for only 10.5% of the variance, whereas motor factors accounted for 74.5%.

These studies by Fleishman and Hempel suggest clearly that the pattern of abilities involved in learning changes as learning progresses. Evidently, subjects call upon different combinations of abilities at different stages of learning. This has implications for the interactive model. A particular arrangement for material that would be optimum at one point in learning might not be very good at another point.

Summary and Conclusions

The use of interactive capacity to deal with individual differences in learning has potentialities in at least three types of learning environments. However, its application to this problem in any of these environments is in relatively crude stages.

Although technologically possible, the development of man-computer interactions that will adjust the presentation of the material to be learned to individual capabilities and requirements depends upon a suitable background of psychological information for guidance. At the present time there appears to be much of this information that is suggestive of directions to take and of problems that will arise. However, it is likely that investigators trying to use this new tool for instruction will have to develop their own specific methodology and their own fund of research experience within the broader context of traditional studies of individual differences in learning. They will need at least the following:

1. A systematic classification of individual differences upon which to base predictions. Guilford's structure of the intellect is an example of a classification of this sort, although it is not necessarily being recommended in its present unfinished form.

2. A systematic classification of ways of presenting subject matter. Psychologists working in this area now evidently have faith that different combinations of organizational and procedural variables can produce an effective battery of different kinds of presentations of the same material. However, no one has had time to go very far in this direction.

3. A body of information about interrelationships between (1) and (2). People have had much experience in attempting differential prediction of what subject-matter area a student should go into, based on aptitude and achievement measures. But there evidently is little information about relationships between these measures and different ways of presenting the same subject matter.

REFERENCES

Allison, R. B., Jr. *Learning parameters and human abilities.* Princeton, New Jersey: Educational Testing Service, May 1960.

Brooks, F. A. Operational sequence diagrams. *IRE Trans. on Human Factors in Electronics*, 1960, **HFE-1**, 33–34.

Bryan, G. L., Rigney, J. W., Orr, W. K., & Svenson, D. W. *An analysis of destroyer CIC officer duties in anti-submarine operations.* Los Angeles: University of Southern California, Electronics Personnel Res. Group, February 1956. (Tech. Rep. 16, CONFIDENTIAL)

Cook, W. W. The functions of measurement in the facilities of learning. In E. F. Lindquist (Ed.), *Educational measurement.* Washington, D. C.: American Council on Education, 1959. Pp. 3–46.

Coulson, J. E., & Silberman, H. F. *Proposal for extension of automated teaching projects*. Santa Monica, California: System Development Corp., July 1959. (Field note)

Coulson, J. E., & Silberman, H. F. Automated teaching and individual differences. *Audiovisual Communication Review*, 1961, **9**, 5–15.

Cronbach, L. J. The two disciplines of scientific psychology. *Amer. Psychologist*, 1957, **12**, 671–684.

Egerman, K., Klaus, D. J., & Glaser, R. Decremental effects of reinforcement in teams with redundant members. Paper read at Amer. Psychol. Assn., New York, September 1961.

Estes, W. J. Learning theory and the new "mental chemistry." *Psychol. Rev.*, 1960, **67**, 207–223.

Fleishman, E. A., & Hempel, W. E. Changes in factor structure of a complex psychomotor test as a function of practice. *Psychometrika*, 1954, **19**, 239–252.

Glanser, M., & Glaser, R. Techniques for the study of group structure and behavior: I. Analysis of structure. *Psychol. Bull.*, 1959, **56**, 317–332.

Glanser, M., & Glaser, R. Techniques for the study of group structure and behavior: II. Empirical studies of the effects of structure in small groups. *Psychol. Bull.*, 1961, **58**, 1–27.

Guilford, J. P. Factorial angles to psychology. *Psychol. Rev.*, 1961, **68**, 1–20.

Gulliksen, H. Measurement of learning and mental abilities. *Psychometrika*, 1961, **26**, 93–107.

Hall, R. L. Group performance under feedback that confounds responses of group members. *Sociometry*, 1957, **20**, 297–305.

Licklider, J. C. R. Man-computer symbiosis. *IRE Trans. on Human Factors in Electronics*, 1960, **HFE-1**, 4–11.

Ramo, S. A new technique of education. *Engn. & Sci.*, 1957, **21**, 17–22.

Rigney, J. W., Schuster, D. H., Budnoff, I. J., & Runyan, T. L. Analysis of fault-location behavior in electronic equipment. *IRE Trans. on Human Factors in Electronics*, 1961a, **HFE-2**, 84–87.

Rigney, J. W., Schuster, D. H., Budnoff, I. J., & Runyan, T. L. *Field evaluation of a trouble-shooting training package*. Los Angeles: University of Southern California, Electronics Personnel Res. Group, April 1961b. (Tech. Rep. 32)

Stake, R. E. *Learning parameters, aptitudes, and achievement*. Princeton, New Jersey: Educational Testing Service, June 1958.

Tucker, L. R. *Determination of generalized learning curves by factor analysis*. Princeton, New Jersey: Educational Testing Service, July 1960.

On conversational interaction

WILLIAM R. UTTAL

International Business Machines

Consider the differences in the behavior of a student in a lecture hall as contrasted with the same student engaged in a conversation. The difference in the pattern of responses may be traced to the nature of the feedback which exists in each of these situations. In servoanalytical terms, the first case would be described as an "open loop" system, whereas the second is a "closed loop" mechanism with extensive feedback.

In the last 20 years we have seen the evolution of servo-control systems leading continuously to more highly sophisticated forms of feedback to accomplish specific control or search functions. Yet, in the highly analogous situation of human learning, little has been done in 4000 years to increase the quantity of feedback. In fact, as the imbalance between the numbers of students and available teachers has

The present IBM Research Computer Teaching Machine Project was preceded by a pioneering experiment of IBM Research in teaching binary arithmetic. Although the present work does not derive specifically from the earlier study, which was conducted by Dr. G. J. Rath and Dr. Nancy Anderson (1959), the imaginative feasibility study by Rath and Anderson provided encouragement and stimulation for our work.

The appearance of a single author's name in a chapter such as this does not, in fact, represent the totality of contributors. Such a project requires the contributions of many people in such diversified activities as programming, computer engineering, psychology, and lexicography. Specifically, I should like to acknowledge the contributions of Dr. W. J. Koppitz, Mrs. Marilyn Charap, Mrs. Lenore Selfridge, Mr. C. A. Dickinson, and Miss Louella Cook, all of whom are staff members at the IBM Research Center, and Mr. Ralph Grubb and Mr. John Lasco of The King's College, Briarcliff Manor, New York.

increased, the amount of feedback has been reduced. The master-disciple, or tutorial, relationship is becoming increasingly rare as great classrooms are filled to overflowing with "open loop" students. (The major exceptions to this general statement have been the training techniques in motor-skill tracking, which is in the strictest sense a servo system.)

Today, however, we have the opportunity to bring back a large degree of interaction to the instructional process. Technology now enables us to provide individualized instruction to large groups by the use of powerful logical machines. The success of teaching machines will depend largely, I believe, on the degree to which they provide feedback to the student and are responsive to the student's learning needs. The desired relationship between student and teaching machine may be termed "conversational interaction," by analogy with the relationship between a student and a human tutor. Many of the "general principles" of learning that have been proposed during the recent enthusiastic acceptance of the teaching-machine concept seem rather to be special cases of the "superprinciple" of conversational interaction.

I should like to suggest that the differences between the simple linear programmed educational device and the computer-controlled methods of automated instruction are not mere differences of methodology but rest on substantially different foundations. With highly individualized instruction and completely flexible branching, it is entirely possible to adjust the education process to each student's needs and abilities and thus accelerate the trend away from the "survival of the mediocre" in our current educational structure. Fully automated education will represent not merely a set of new teaching methods but, rather, a major sociological revolution.

The important fact to remember is that the *human tutor is a superb teaching mechanism*. The highly adaptable nature of the conversational interaction found in the tutorial process is apparently a very effective means of imparting information. Those of us who share the enthusiasm for computer-based teaching machines do so because a computer allows us not only to simulate all other classes of teaching machines but also to approach full simulation of the human tutorial process. In this sense a computer represents the only research tool that does not limit our imagination and creativity.

Obviously, it will not be possible to simulate human conversation fully in the immediate future. Input-output mechanisms are generally inadequate. Specifically, no adequate speech input device exists.

Furthermore, the logical power of a computer, although extensive, still is not on the level of the complex interpretations and similarity recognitions at which people excel. It is a fundamental restriction that no computer program can now satisfactorily handle generalized verbal inputs but requires well-ordered input sentences.

The specific requirements of a computer for teaching-machine research are somewhat different than those for the usual scientific calculation, just as the problem itself is different. Because of the real-time nature of teaching-machine research, only moderate speed is required for a considerable number of students. The storage of material of almost textbook quantities requires unusually large and accessible memories. But these requirements are within the limits of present technology. It is at the interface between the students and the computer that most current engineering problems arise. Adequate terminal devices must be made available. It is becoming increasingly clear that different course materials require different kinds of terminals. Furthermore, reliability considerations may develop somewhat differently than in ordinary scientific calculation. We would all certainly be willing to put up with minor errors, such as occasional missing display bits, if we could balance this loss with a comparable decrease in the possibility of a catastrophic machine failure that might leave a large class of students entirely inactive.

I discuss the relevant computer parameters now only to indicate how very well our needs have been met by a not-so-exotic vacuum tube computer—the IBM 650 RAMAC. Our computer installation is pictured in Fig. 1. The 650 has a basic add time of 0.7 millisecond, which we feel will be more than adequate for our current experimental program.

The 650 system has a number of auxiliary features which suit it very well for teaching-machine research. A large random-access disk file capable of storing 6 million digits of information with a maximum of 0.8 second access time provides the necessary bulk storage for dictionaries and text material. The system also has a large number of input-output features including magnetic tape and punched cards. Most significant, though, is its ability to handle 20 special terminal devices known as inquiry stations (or as teaching stations). These teaching stations are computer-controlled typewriters on which the student may also type his response. Our attitude towards typewriter input-output is still ambivalent. On the one hand, the typewriter is available, reliable, and rewards precision; on the other hand, it requires a rather slow and somewhat unnatural response mode.

Fig. 1. Partial view of the computer installation.

The purpose of the IBM Research Computer Teaching Machine Project is to carry out preliminary fundamental investigations in computer-controlled human learning. We are interested in the almost unspecifiable complexity of a system in which many students are interacting with a computer. Our initial approach has been the empirical one so eloquently championed by Dr. James Holland in an earlier chapter of this volume. Later, when we know our way through the many combinations of variables, we shall investigate selected combinations.

Research of this kind is badly needed. Many of the recent controversies concerning automated education are quite artificial and in many instances based upon specialized interests, educational background, or available instrumentation rather than conflicting experimental results. It is clear that the problems of computer-controlled education are complex and multivariate. Yet all too often we see the psychologist stating flatly that the sequence of instructions represents the entirety of the problem or the engineer specifying the components of a complex system completely unbounded by psychological constraints. Certainly the engineering, the psychological, and the computer language-programming factors are all strongly interacting variables that cannot be separated without a substantial loss of creative effectiveness.

This chapter describes our preliminary experiences in implementing computer-controlled teaching machine experiments. By discussing the challenges we have faced and some of the modest successes we have achieved, I hope to illustrate the multifaceted nature of this problem area.

I shall discuss individually the three courses which make up our current curriculum:

1. Stenotypy [1] (organized by W. R. Uttal)
2. Psychological Statistics (organized by R. Grubb)
3. German Reading (organized by W. J. Koppitz)

This particular mix of course materials was suggested by our desire to cover three distinct areas of associative learning. Stenotypy represents a highly idealized and extremely well-ordered subject matter in which associations are developed between verbal materials and the motor skills of multiple-press keyboards. The second course, statistics, was less well ordered than the other two in that it is difficult to define exactly what associations are being made in learning the mathematical concepts involved. The third course, German Reading, contains a well-ordered set of materials requiring the student to make associations between two verbal sets: the German and English vocabulary and a set of syntactical rules.

One of the first problems encountered was the presentation of bulk text material to the student. Extensive computer-controlled output typing is prohibitively time consuming and may, under some conditions, tie up the entire computer system. Our expedient in the statistics and German courses was to provide the student with a loose-leaf textbook. The computer directed the student to the appropriate page containing the necessary information and then interrogated and further instructed him. These texts were originally intended to be used in place of a complex photographic projection system, but they fulfilled our needs so well that we have begun to think of them in a more permanent sense. A book can be an excellent teaching mechanism.

Before I deal with the details of our curriculum, I would like to emphasize the preliminary nature of all of our results. Our flow

[1] The Stenotypy Teaching Machine Project was partly supported by the Air Research and Development Command Rome Air Development Center, Griffiss Air Force Base, New York, under contract AF 30(602)-2466.

charts change almost hourly, and this chapter should, therefore, be treated as an interim progress report.

Stenotypy

Course Description

Stenotypy is a machine shorthand method that uses a special-purpose keyboard and printing machine. Ordinarily, spoken words are transcribed into the device phonetically—a syllable at a time—by means of multiple-press keying operation. In addition, there is an elaborate list of abbreviations for many words to increase the input rate. As can be seen in Fig. 2, there are only 23 keys on the steno keyboard, yet two sets of consonants, one initial and one final set, as well as a set of vowels, are represented. Thus some alphabetic or phonetic characters are represented by the simultaneous depression of a number of keys. An expert stenotypist can enter as many as 280 words per minute with a 95% retranscription accuracy.

The course was designed to cover the "theory" of stenotypy, which usually involves the first three months of training. It was simplified by concentrating on teaching the input keying and ignoring retran-

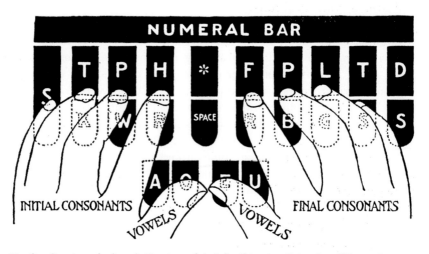

Fig. 2. Stenotype keyboard (Courtesy of LaSalle Extension University, Chicago Stenotypy Handbook).

Fig. 3. Stenotype teaching terminal.

scription, a task for which another computer is being developed. We also chose to teach from visually displayed alphabetic information rather than audio signals, even though stenotypy is primarily a means of recording the spoken word. This use of visual displays is consistent with the use of textbooks in almost all elementary "steno" instruction.

Instrumentation

Since there was no stenographic input to the standard IBM 650, a special input-output device was designed and constructed. The teaching terminal (shown in Fig. 3) was connected to one of the three input-output buffers that are usually used to match the electronic calculating speed of the computer to the speed of the electromechanical card-handling and printing mechanisms. This buffer allows the computer to continue calculating at high speeds even though an input-output operation has not yet been completed.

The alphabetic characters displayed to the student are formed by electroluminescent alphanumeric characters. A set of cue lights, geometrically identical to the steno keyboard, is also included in the display. The alphabetic characters are arranged in two registers: one composed of 20 characters for the display of the word to be encoded and the second composed of eight characters that are used for the display of syllabication or abbreviations.

Four levels of coding can be manipulated in the investigation: the word itself, the abbreviation, the cue lights, and the parameters of the subject's keypress responses.

Immediately in front of the student is a stenotype keyboard which has been modified so that each key depression enters a bit of information into the computer memory. Thus the pattern of keys depressed for any stimulus can be compared with the correct answer stored in the computer. The "feel" of the keyboard is not altered by this added circuitry because of the mechanical advantage afforded by the keylever construction. In addition to specifying what information is to be entered into the computer, the keyboard also controls the time at which the entry is made. Reaction time (that is, the interval from the appearance of the display to the time all the keys are released at the completion of the keystroke) can therefore be measured. We are presently installing a real-time addressable clock that will allow reaction times to be measured to the nearest one hundredth of a second, with only a few milliseconds uncertainty.

The subject is instructed to respond as soon as possible after presentation of the display, and knowledge of results is available to him within ¾ of a second. This feedback usually takes the form of the word "correct" or "wrong" appearing in the upper 20-character register.

A small auxiliary control panel allows the student to identify himself and ask for prompts or rest periods. A further control unit provides the necessary sequence of voltages to simulate the usual card punch and reader and to decode the two-decimal-digit-per-character output of the 650 into the 14-bit binary code for the electroluminescent character generators.

The Program

The computer program for the stenotype teaching machine consists of a number of subroutines for various bookkeeping and control functions. We shall describe only the core program, which actually controls the logic of the branching decisions made during the student's progress.

In general, the interaction between the student and the teaching machine is characterized by the following series of operations:

1. The word to be encoded is presented to the student. According to his record of experiences with this word, it might be with the appropriate abbreviation and/or cue lights.

2. The student keys his response into the keyboard. When he has released all keys, the information is entered into the computer.

3. The computer evaluates his answer and indicates whether he is correct or incorrect.

4. A new item is presented to the student or the same item is repeated, as determined by the branching logic that is programmed into the computer.

5. After a number of these items have been presented, a lesson is considered complete, and the student is queried to determine if he wants to continue. During that inquiry the computer assembles a new set of items from the list of new problems or from the problems that have been answered correctly, as well as items from the "error buckets" (a set of memory locations that store the addresses of items that have been missed a given number of times). The ratio of the items from the various sources is controlled by a variable criterion register so that it is possible to manipulate such parameters as the ratio of the number of review items to the number of new items.

The flow chart in Fig. 4 describes the central part of the teaching routine. There are two distinct major levels of branching and a large number of secondary choice points. The first set of decisions determines the nature of each new exercise that is to be assembled from the student's history. At the present time the student's history is recorded by the formation of the error buckets. New items are also fed as required into the lesson assembly routine from one further source of items—the master dictionary.

The second set of decisions includes those made during the lesson concerning each item. The details of this branching procedure may be seen in Fig. 4. Because of the variable nature of each student's responses and the decision logic, students will proceed through an enormous number of different sequences. The only main stem through which all students pass is the transition from one major area of study material to the next.

Another exceedingly important block on the flow chart is that por-

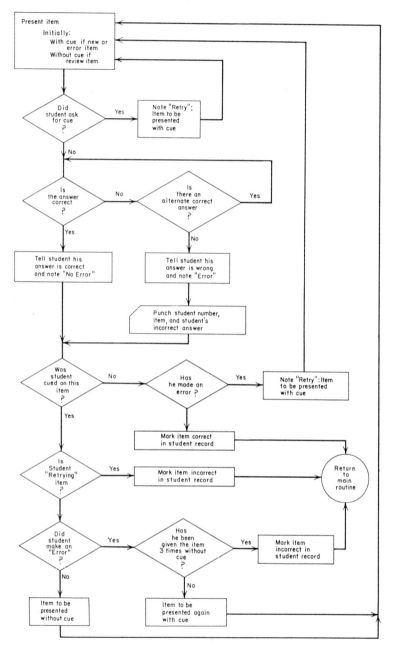

Fig. 4. Flow chart of the decision logic in the core of the stenotype program.

tion indicating the recording of incorrect answers. By use of this permanent record it is possible to classify the type of errors a student is making and to provide special remedial material during a later lesson assembly. In the near future we plan to do this error analysis automatically for immediate modification of the sequence of problems.

Another major portion of the program is a special dictionary of stenotypy that was prepared for this teaching machine. This dictionary contains the word to be encoded, any abbreviations, and the correct keypress code. To teach another similar code (e.g., stenotypy for a foreign language), one would merely have to prepare another dictionary instead of reprogramming the entire course. Such flexibility, which is also an asset of our language course, suggests that programming costs may in some instances be substantially reduced for related classes of materials.

We have not yet used a large enough sample of students to draw firm generalizations about this form of teaching, nor have we completed any specific experiments isolating a single learning variable. We have, however, confirmed the enormous motivational strength of the conversational interaction between the student and the reacting machine, and our results so far suggest that the student will learn at an accelerated rate compared to the usual classroom training methods.

Psychological Statistics

Course Description

The descriptive statistics program is intended to be the equivalent of an ordinary one-semester course and to cover material through analysis of variance and the Chi-square test. The statistics course is not so highly idealized and reduced as the stenotypy and German Reading courses; therefore, a very elaborate textbook is required. This specialized textbook is based on a series of protocol studies carried out at The King's College by Mr. Ralph Grubb.

In the statistics course the computer acts primarily as a mentor for problem-solving sessions. The program directs the student through the text and does not permit him to proceed until he has completely satisfied the programmed performance criterion on the related problem session. Unlike the stenotypy course, there is a main instructional trunk through which the student progresses, branching to successively more elaborate explanations only when remedial material or prompts are required.

Instrumentation

The standard IBM 838 inquiry station, a computer-controlled input-output typewriter, is used as the basic teaching terminal. Certain special requirements of the teaching process made it necessary to add a number of improvements to the machine. Computer-controlled carriage return, tabulation, and color control were added. On the standard machine there is but one button that enters a typed answer into the computer. We added a set of five buttons that not only allow information to be entered but also permit requests to be made for prompting, rest period, or dictionary assistance. (The teaching terminal is shown in Fig. 5.) Inquiry stations are connected in two series to the computer through the 652 control unit. Each series is inde-

Fig. 5. Computer-controlled typewriter teaching station.

pendent of the other and also of the central processing unit. Only a single typewriter in each series, however, may be active at any one time. Depending upon the queuing requirements of each course, this may be found to be a major handicap. Even though the calculation speed of the computer is adequate for many teaching stations, the interlocking of the terminals would prevent more than a modest number of students from being simultaneously active. Our current engineering plans include an attack upon this obstacle. (The stenotypy console and other similar devices operate through separate input-output buffers and are completely independent of this restriction.)

A standard feature of the inquiry control unit in the 652 is an automatic queuing device that gives priority to the students in order of their request for access to the computer.

The Program

The general pattern of interaction between the student, the statistics textbook, and the computer is characterized by the following series of operations:

1. The computer directs the student to read a numbered paragraph in his text. At the end of the paragraph there is a code number(s) addressing a relevant problem(s) in the computer memory.

2. The student keys the code number into the computer and the problem is presented to him by computer-controlled typing. The current course includes mostly constructed answer problems, but there are also some multiple-choice items.

3. The student answers the problem and, depending upon his answer, the machine directs him to a new text page or to progressive levels of remedial material.

4. After sufficient remedial training the student is returned by the computer to the text for additional instruction.

Once again let us pay specific attention to the branching core of the statistics program and ignore the many bookkeeping functions.

The statistics core program differs from the stenotypy core in having a main trunk along which all students are led. The flow chart in Fig. 6 details the branching logic. Figure 7 shows the basic logic underlying the various decisions indicated on the flow chart.

A student who is having trouble with a certain problem would be directed to increasingly elaborate remedial levels until finally, if he still does not understand the concept involved, the machine would direct him back to some preliminary portion of the course. Ultimately we hope to have the student's incorrect answer analyzed automatically by the computer; the computer would then guide him to the prerequisite material specifically needed. This additional training perhaps might come from another section of the computer-stored curriculum and not from the statistics course itself.

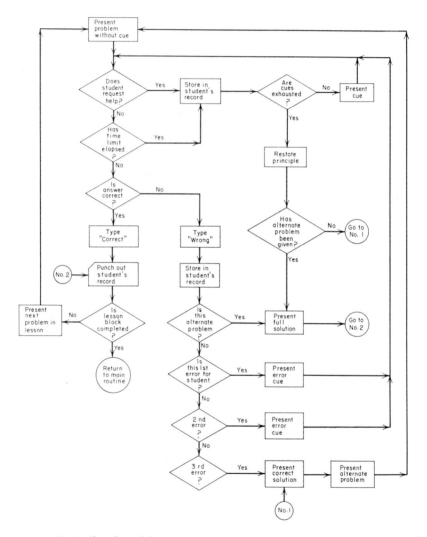

Fig. 6. Flow chart of the decision logic in the core of the statistics program.

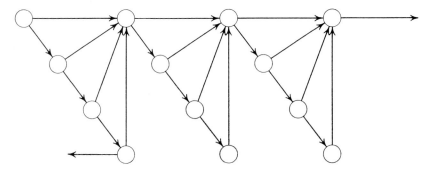

Fig. 7. Pattern of item sequence alternatives for statistics program.

When a student successfully completes an item, he is returned to the main instructional trunk for the next item.

Branching sequences in this course do not approximate the complexity found in the stenotypy course because the sequence of items in statistics is predetermined by the author of the text. In stenotypy and German the sequence is much more a function of the student's responses and experiences. The difference between the two types of material is a fundamental one and, we feel, is related to the "orderliness" of the subject material. Orderliness is probably best measured by the number of possible correct responses. For example, in stenotypy a stimulus word may be associated with only one correct response —a specific simultaneous depression of a particular set of keys. In a philosophy course, however, one might be faced with the question, "What is love?" The number of combinations of different words that can be used to answer this question (to somebody's satisfaction) is enormous; therefore this question would be considered poorly ordered. It is our feeling that the earliest successes with computerized teaching machines will be with well-ordered material such as those we have used.

German Reading

Course Description

Our language effort, a reading course in elementary German, is designed to approximate a one-semester college course. A special textbook has been prepared in which each paragraph is numbered and followed by references to the computer-controlled exercises.

Based upon the criterion of the number of possible responses, it appears that the degree of order of the German course is somewhat less than the stenotypy course but greater than the statistics course. A main instructional trunk is specified by the textbook, but the selection rules are flexible enough to allow various vocabulary items to be reviewed or introduced at any time. Vocabulary and syntax are both included within the course.

An unusual feature of the German teaching program is the stored automatic dictionary. A student may ask the computer for a dictionary definition of an unknown word or verb table at any time if the item is within the limits of the course vocabulary.

Instrumentation

The modified 838 inquiry station described for the statistics course is also used for the German reading course. Special German characters (such as the umlaut) are made available as necessary by changing type bars.

The Program

The sequence of instructional items presented to the student is a function of the design of the textbook as well as of the student's record. In the German course the student reads the text until he comes to one of two types of interrogatory material. Spaced throughout the text are questions that serve to check the student's progress and guarantee mastery of the text material. Upon arriving at such a question, the student types the answer into the computer along with the appropriate question number. The computer evaluates and reinforces his answer, allowing him to go on to new information or back to review information.

This question-and-answer method is an auxiliary aid designed to regulate the student's speed so that he does not skim any important reading material. Figure 8 shows the major branching logic, which controls the manipulations of a set of tutorial exercises.

A student answers each item as it is presented to him. In the event of an error, the student is given the correct answer and the item is

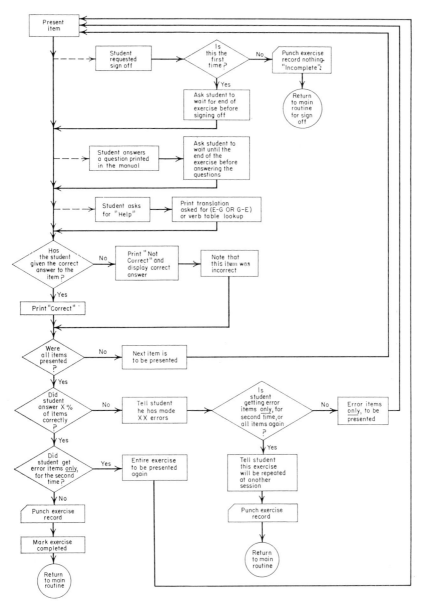

Fig. 8. Flow chart of the decision logic in the core of the German reading program.

coded for later representation. Error items are reviewed immediately afterward, and the student does not leave the exercise until he has completed the entire list of items by achieving a programmed criterion.

The most important characteristic of the flow charts of all three courses is that they are relatively simple, yet they represent extremely complicated sets of possible sequences of student progress. A relatively short stored program read into the computer may, by adapting itself to the student's needs, represent instructional material of almost infinite variety.

Conclusion

All three courses in our current curriculum are in early stages of development, and I report them here more in the sense of what *can* be done with computer teaching machines than what *should* be done. It would be very satisfying now to report specific experimental results and draw universal conclusions. Unfortunately, we may not be able to do this for many years to come. One has only to look at the history of conventional education techniques to realize the complicated nature of the problems. Yet it is entirely conceivable that a satisfactory theoretical and experimental foundation for teaching machines may not be laid down until long after such machines are contributing substantially to our educational system.

Those of us who have worked with computer simulation of biological processes learned quite early that a computer has another asset beyond its ability to handle large numbers of equations at high speed. The requirements for precise specification of the program (or model) mean that a detailed look must be taken at the process under investigation. Many qualitative models do not stand up well under this scrutiny, and it seems that the sole reason for their early success has been their very superficiality.

Our educational system also needs a detailed examination. The automated instruction movement, if nothing else, has been an additional stimulus for the educator to reflect on his own teaching methods. I am sure there has been no other time in world history when so many scholars were attending to the problems of mass education. In retrospect one wonders how so little attention could have been paid to programming course materials in the past. Dr. Pressey states in a recent article, "Almost any reasonable method involving pupil activity and adjustment to individual differences will show gains." [2] Such a basic and elegant concept seems to have taken a long time to be established. [3]

It should be possible to expand these gains greatly; to do so, however, will require exploiting every possible dimension of the learning experience.

Our major experiences to date can be summarized as follows:

1. Computer teaching is feasible. We have been delighted at the ease with which some of the rules of learning have been embodied and with the broad applicability of computer-based teaching machines to many different types of material.

2. The major engineering difficulty lies in the input-output systems. Buffered and multiplexed terminals are badly needed. The calculating speed of modern computers appears to be adequate for the simultaneous operation of many students, and this number will increase if a few special instructions particular to the teaching-machine problem are made available.

3. The modifiable stored program of the computer has great implications for ease of organizing a curriculum. We may expect some computer programs to be used for several different course materials by simply utilizing different dictionary and problem lists. The use of automatic assembly programs to prepare lesson plans is a distinct possibility.

4. Automatic error analysis and the simultaneous use of the computer as a research data processor suggest the possibility of automatic updating and modification of curricula. This learning aspect of the teaching machine is probably the most important long-range consideration in modern education.

5. Branching logics may be tentatively dichotomized into these categories: (a) *Fully Branched* courses in which the sequence of events is fully student-determined and (b) *Main Trunk* courses in which the

[2] Pressey, S. L. Certain major psycho-educational issues appearing in the conference on teaching machines. In E. Galanter (Ed.), *Automatic teaching*. New York: Wiley, 1959. Pp. 187–198.

[3] My colleague, Miss Louella Cook, recently reported the results of an experiment carried out in a public school. This experiment evaluated a particular automatic arithmetic tutor. The results of the study are not germane to this issue (the machine-taught class showed twice the improvements in achievement tests compared to control groups) but the interesting result was that two of our control classes did not show any significant difference between pre- and posttests after several months of classwork. Do we know very much about our schools?

student is directed along a specific sequence, branching only for remedial or special training.

6. The nature of the branching logic is a manifestation of the type of course material. A taxonomy is required that will allow comparison of two courses on the basis of their logical similarities rather than content. The measure of orderliness is tentatively defined as the number of possible correct answers to a given question. Clearly, teaching machines will have their earliest successes with well-ordered materials such as stenotypy, languages, and problem sessions in the physical sciences and mathematics.

7. The excellent motivational properties of a conversationally inter-acting tutor, mechanical or human, must not be minimized. Probably the most misinterpreted and oft-quoted result in the history of psy-chological research is the so-called "Hawthorne Effect." The results of that famous experiment were less a demonstration of the confound-ing of a neat experimental design than a demonstration of the magnifi-cent adaptiveness of the human organism to a challenging environment and of the effectiveness of motivation on human performance.

A computer-based laboratory for research and development in education

JOHN E. COULSON

System Development Corporation

System Development Corporation began its experimentation with variable-sequence methods of automated instruction in 1959. In the initial experiment (Coulson & Silberman, 1960) autoinstructional frames were presented to students by human experimenters operating behind wooden screens. Independent variables were student response mode (multiple-choice versus constructed-response), item step size, and method of item sequence control. Dependent variables were required training time and student acquisition of subject matter, as measured by a post-training criterion test. Subjects were junior college students, and the subject matter was introductory psychology.

In this first experiment the independent variable of most significance to the present report was the method of item sequence control. For one group of students the sequence of items was completely fixed. The experimenter behind the screen merely presented each item in turn through a window in the screen and caused the student to receive appropriate knowledge of results for the student's answers to questions in the items.

Each member of the second group, called the "branching group," received a different sequence of items, depending on his performance in the lesson. The form of branching used for the second group was necessarily simple. A student who correctly answered the first question on a particular topic was not given the remaining items on that same topic.

Branching students were found to require significantly less training time than fixed-sequence students but did not differ significantly on the criterion measure. Thus results were interpreted to favor the branching procedure.

Our analysis of the initial experiment indicated the effectiveness of branching methods in autoinstruction but also revealed a definite need for more efficient means of sequence control if the full potentials of branching were to be explored. Experimenters operating the manual equipment were barely able to manage even the simplest types of sequence modifications during the experiment without introducing undesirable delays. Clearly, more automatic methods of presentation and control were required for more complex forms of branching.

Experimental Computer-Based Instructional System

In early 1960 SDC developed an experimental autoinstructional system designed for maximal flexibility as a research tool. This system, which taught one student at a time, used a Bendix G-15 computer as the central unit (see Fig. 1). Instructions prepared by the lesson designer were read into the computer in the form of punched paper tape.

Lesson materials were displayed to the student by a random-access slide projector operating under computer control (Fig. 2). This projector held as many as 600 35-mm slides, each of which contained one instructional item.

It projected these slides in any sequence directed by the computer. The student answered multiple-choice questions contained in the items by pressing appropriate keys on an electric typewriter (Fig. 3), which was also connected to the G-15. He could be given immediate knowledge of results in messages typewritten under computer control. If longer messages were required, as for clarification of the student's errors, additional slides could be used.

The goal of flexible-sequence programming, or branching, is to ensure that each student receive the sequence of instructional materials and the type of reinforcement, or knowledge of results, that will lead him to most efficient learning. The brighter student is allowed to move rapidly from one topic to the next, whereas slower students are given the extra review they require to meet the specified performance level.

Successful branching depends on the accuracy with which the student's needs and capabilities can be diagnosed. The computer's excel-

Fig. 1. *Experimental computer-based instructional system. Computer is shown at left, student station at right.*

Fig. 2. *Random-access slide projector used for presentation of instructional materials.*

for this function has not yet been proven in the context of automated instruction, there is reason to believe that it would be an important consideration in applications over an extended period of time, where student interest might otherwise lag. However, it is likely that occasional questions would serve this purpose as well as questions in every item.

c. Answers given by students to questions contained in the lesson serve a major role in lesson quality control. They provide the means by which the lesson designer is able to determine that the items teach what they are intended to teach.

d. In a branching procedure student responses to questions provide an important criterion for determining the student's learning needs. For this function, however, it is not necessary to include questions in all items. We have found it inefficient to use the same item for both informational and diagnostic purposes. Consequently, we have recently used two distinct types of items: instructional and diagnostic. The student receives a series of instructional items, containing statements, on a particular topic. He is then given one or more diagnostic items, containing questions about that topic, to determine the subsequent sequence of materials. These diagnostic items are like test questions, designed to discriminate among students on the basis of the student's understanding of the topic. They are used by the computer to determine the student's need for further review.

Class

In September 1961 System Development Corporation completed the construction of a new educational facility, designed for research and development of integrated educational systems. This facility, called CLASS, reflects the philosophy that automated instruction, though of great significance and potential for education, is but one element in the entire complex of educational functions. To realize their full potential, autoinstructional devices must be applied by educators toward the educational needs that they can most effectively fill, in combination with other instructional methods such as films, educational television, conventional lectures, and textbooks. CLASS will provide an opportunity to explore the important interactions among instructional-method, student, and subject-matter variables.

CLASS also reflects a realization that the instructional process must be considered in the context of the entire educational system. Modern education is big business, and like any large corporation or governmental organization today's school requires many administrative and service functions to support accomplishment of its primary mission. The ultimate success of any educational system depends in large measure upon the efficiency with which these ancillary functions are conducted. Moreover, the various functions cannot proceed independently but require extensive coordination and exchange of relevant information. The recent rejection of the television system introduced in a southern California junior college resulted, at least in part, from a failure to provide for its systematic integration into an existing educational structure. CLASS will permit studies of organizational structure within an educational system and of the interactions that may occur among the components of such a system.

Finally, CLASS will provide advanced technological capabilities, based on high-speed data-processing techniques, which can be applied not only to the instructional process but to all major functions of an educational system. It can be used to simulate many different educational configurations, both for evaluative purposes and for the training of teachers, administrators, and other school personnel in the application of such systems.

Operational flexibility has been a primary consideration in the design of CLASS. The heart of the facility is a large digital computer, the Philco 2000.

The Philco is connected to various display and input mechanisms in CLASS by means of a buffer system designed by System Development Corporation engineers.

Figure 4 shows the major functional areas of the CLASS facility. The two large rooms on the right represent classrooms that can be combined into a single classroom by folding back a sound-attenuating partition. As many as 20 students can be accommodated in the combined area.

Students in the classroom on the right are shown receiving individualized automated instruction under computer control. These students are grouped only for convenience, since they are seeing different sequences of instructional materials and may, in fact, be studying different subject areas. Panels on the sides of each student's desk may be positioned to provide effective isolation from other students.

For individualized automated instruction, CLASS operates in a manner that is functionally similar to the experimental instructional system based on the Bendix computer. Viewing and response devices

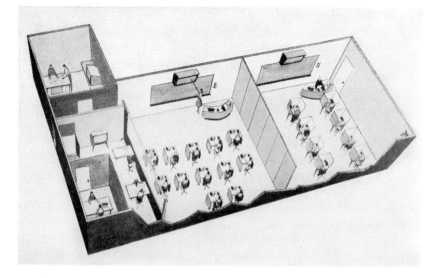

Fig. 4. Overview of CLASS facility. *Classrooms are shown at right, counseling and adminis-trative areas at left.*

Fig. 5. Student viewing device for CLASS.

used in CLASS, however, are considerably simpler and somewhat less automatic. Figure 5 shows the student's viewing device. It contains a 35-mm film strip with as many as 2000 frames of instructional material. Film is held in easily interchanged magazines. Operation of the film transport is accomplished manually by the student, who turns a crank on the side of the viewer.

Item sequence directions are presented to the student by the computer in a digital display on the student response device (Fig. 6). The student responds to multiple-choice questions in the items by pressing appropriate keys on the face of the device. He can then be given knowledge of results in several forms. Colored lights at the top of the response device can be activated to tell the student whether he has answered correctly (green) or incorrectly (red). In addition, a light can be activated at the answer key representing the correct solution. More detailed information can be presented to the student by

Fig. 6. Student response device for CLASS.

directing him to one or more frames on the viewer containing remedial material.

Additional keys on the response device can be used to convey various types of information to the computer or to a teacher. Since the interpretation of each key action can be determined by the computer program, considerable flexibility is possible in the operation of the CLASS system.

Provision has been made in CLASS for human supervision of the instructional process. For purposes of convenience we may call these supervisors "teachers," though their actual roles may differ greatly from those of the teacher in the conventional classroom. At the present time it is impossible to state exactly what the function of the teacher should be in an automated school environment. The determination of this role, in fact, may well be one of our most important research goals during the coming years.

The teacher's station in CLASS (Fig. 7) is intended to provide all information that the teacher might need to monitor the learning situation and to regulate instructional procedures. Each student is represented by a light on the console at the left. This light may be activated by the computer if the student is making too many errors in his autoinstructional lesson or in some other way fails to meet criteria built into the computer's control program. It may also be activated by the student himself by pressing a button on his response device. In either case the teacher is alerted to the student's need for special assistance. The teacher may then use buttons on the console to request computer-generated displays containing more detailed information on the student in question. One action, for example, causes information to be presented through a cathode-ray-tube display, shown on the far right. This display includes the name of the topic presently being studied by the student, the number of errors he has made on that topic, and the number of errors on the entire lesson.

Another action allows the teacher to view the same instructional item being seen at that moment by the student and to determine the response being made by him. This is accomplished through replicas of the student's viewing and response devices, as shown at the center of the teacher's console. Thus the teacher can, for all practical purposes, watch over the student's shoulder without being required to leave his desk.

The classroom at the left of the partition in Fig. 4 is shown being used for group instruction. CLASS is designed to allow 20 students to be taught simultaneously in any combination of individual and

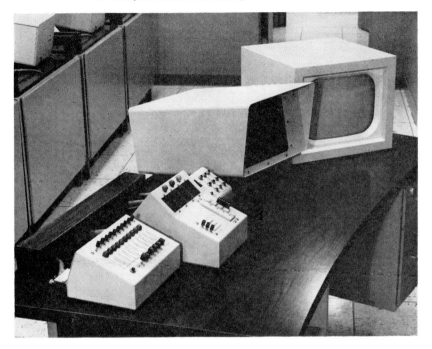

Fig. 7. Teacher's console for CLASS.

group modes of presentation. This maximum is fixed by the available space, not by the computer, which could control instruction for several hundred students simultaneously.

Group education can be accomplished by conventional lecture, film, or television techniques or by automated instruction. In the group mode of automated instruction lesson materials are presented to all students in a common display facility, such as a television screen. These materials contain questions that students attempt to answer through their individual response devices. Either the computer or the teacher may select the sequence of materials based on the performance of the entire group. Computer-generated displays available to the teacher indicate the number of students answering each question correctly and the most frequently selected incorrect answers. Group techniques sacrifice individuality of instruction but require relatively little computer storage and may be quite effective for certain educational requirements.

Teachers in CLASS can select films for presentation on the television screen by telephoning an audiovisual technician in a separate projection room. Once a film has been started, it can be automatically stopped, reversed, and started again by switch actions from the teacher's console.

An observation area to the left of the classrooms permits viewing of the students through one-way glass. When the partition is being used to separate the classroom areas, the far classroom can still be observed by a television camera connected to a monitor in the observation room. Microphones in both classrooms permit sound monitoring and recording.

Another major area of CLASS, shown in the lower left-hand corner of Fig. 4, is the counseling room. In this room a counselor can interview individual students and can call for detailed information about these students on a teletype machine connected to the computer. Printouts may include the student's previous scholastic records and results of aptitude and personality tests as well as his current performance measures. This information will assist the counselor in advising students who are having difficulties in their lessons or who need to revise their class schedules. The counselor may interact closely with teachers to determine student needs and to ensure that students receive the type of instruction that most efficiently meets these needs.

At present many counselors spend a large portion of their time each semester preparing student class assignments for the following semester. Much of this can be done automatically, thereby saving the counselor's time for working with the students. A computer program being planned for the Philco computer will permit automatic preparation and printouts of assignment schedules in CLASS.

The final section of CLASS, shown in the upper left-hand corner of Fig. 4, is an administrative area. This area will be the center for planning, administrative, and logistical functions normally associated with a school system. The computer will record, and make available for display, various types of information such as daily attendance, schedules and other student records, fiscal accounts, and other budgetary data. In addition, the computer will be programmed to perform tasks of registration, bus scheduling, financial accounting, preparation of payrolls, and forecasting of enrollment trends for predictive purposes.

A major function of the administrative section of CLASS will be the training and evaluation of administrative personnel. For this purpose simulation techniques will be used extensively, since the restricted classroom and counseling facilities in CLASS will not provide adequate "live" stimuli for the decision-making activities normally conducted by administrators in an educational system such as a school district. In a single day an administrator can be given a series of simulated messages from other administrators and teachers that will require as many policy and administrative decisions as he would normally face in a month. The computer can select each new simulated message to follow logically from the administrator's earlier responses and, immediately after each response, give the administrator feedback in the form of probable consequence of his actions.

The entire CLASS facility provides a complex simulation laboratory where many different educational configurations may be investigated. Existing educational systems can be simulated for comparison of their operational effectiveness. More important, perhaps, educational facilities and procedures planned for schools of the future can be simulated and their potential contributions evaluated.

Simulation procedures similar to those applied successfully in military environments offer several distinct advantages for educational planning. Imaginative new conceptions for school design may be investigated without the need for costly investments in special-purpose equipment. In some situations it may be desirable to simulate types of equipment that do not yet exist but are still in the conceptual or design phase. The effects of proposed changes in the organization or functions of a school system may be analyzed under carefully controlled conditions, without disrupting the ongoing educational activities of that system.

There seems no doubt that technology will play an increasingly vital role in education during the coming years. Perhaps the most important contribution of facilities such as CLASS can be to help ensure that a systematic integrated approach is taken in the introduction of technological innovations to the schools of tomorrow.

REFERENCES

Coulson, J. E., & Silberman, H. F. Effects of three variables in a teaching machine. *J. educ. Psychol.*, 1960, **51**, 135–143.

Coulson, J. E., Estavan, D. P., Melaragno, R. J., & Silberman, H. F. Effects of branching in a computer-controlled auto-instructional device. *J. appl. Psychol.*, in press.

Evans, J. L., Glaser, R., & Homme, L. E. A preliminary investigation of variation in the properties of verbal learning sequences of the "teaching machine" type. In A. A. Lumsdaine & R. Glaser (Eds.), *Teaching machines and pro-*

grammed learning. Washington, D. C.: National Education Association, 1960. Pp. 446–451.

Silberman, H. F., Melaragno, R. J., & Coulson, J. E. Confirmation and prompting with connected discourse material. *Psychol. Rep.,* 1961, **9,** 235–238.

Silberman, H. F., Melaragno, R. J., Coulson, J. E., & Estavan, D. Fixed sequence versus branching autoinstructional methods. *J. educ. Psychol.,* 1961, **52,** 166–172.

PLATO II: A multiple-student, computer-controlled, automatic teaching device

D. L. BITZER, P. G. BRAUNFELD,
and W. W. LICHTENBERGER

Coordinated Science Laboratory
University of Illinois

PLATO (Programmed Logic for Automatic Teaching Operations) is a research project in the field of teaching machines, currently being conducted at the Coordinated Science Laboratory of the University of Illinois. The main goal of the project is to develop an automatic teaching system sufficiently flexible to permit experimental evaluation of a large variety of ideas on automatic instruction.

This goal is to be realized by constructing a series of machines— each embodying refinements suggested by experience with earlier models. PLATO II—the subject of this chapter—differs from PLATO I [1] primarily in its ability to instruct a number of students concurrently. The teaching logic employed in PLATO II resembles that of PLATO I in most essentials. A résumé of this logic is presented in a later section of this paper.

The research reported in this document was made possible by support extended to the University of Illinois, Coordinated Science Laboratory, jointly by the Department of the Army (Signal Corps and Ordnance Corps), Department of the Navy (Office of Naval Research), and the Department of the Air Force (Office of Scientific Research, Air Research and Development Command) under Signal Corps Contract DA-36-039-SC-85122.

[1] Bitzer, D. L., Braunfeld, P. G., & Lichtenberger, W. W. *PLATO: An automated teaching device.* To be published by the IRE Professional Group on Education.

In PLATO II executive control over the instructional system is exercised by one central computer. Such a teaching system, in which as many functions as possible are centralized in a fast, large-scale computer, has several advantages over one that requires many smaller special-purpose pieces of equipment. These advantages pertain to the power and flexibility inherent in the centralized system:

1. PLATO II makes available to every student the great computational resources of a powerful digital computer. This power can be of distinct advantage in some subject matters. In certain branches of mathematics or physics, for example, the computer can relieve the student of large amounts of necessary, but routine, calculations; or it can quickly plot for the student graphs of his solutions to equations.

2. In PLATO II the teaching logic is determined by programs within the central computer. Therefore, changes can be made in the teaching logic by modifying or rewriting computer programs. No changing of equipment is necessary. This flexibility in teaching logic is particularly important in an experimental program.

3. As the machine teaches, it automatically keeps detailed records of each student's progress through the material. These large amounts of data may later be sorted and suitably processed by the same central computer. The combination of a system teaching large numbers of students concurrently and a digital computer for large-scale data processing should prove a powerful tool in educational research.

Description of Equipment

Figure 1 shows the general organization of equipment in PLATO II. Executive control over the system is exercised by ILLIAC, the University of Illinois' general purpose, medium-speed digital computer. ILLIAC has a high-speed electrostatic memory of 1024 40-bit words and an auxiliary magnetic drum storage of 10,240 words. Its speed is typified by an add time of 75 microseconds and an average multiplication time of 700 microseconds. The use of more modern computers, which are both faster and larger by at least an order of magnitude, should make it possible to use a greatly improved and expanded teaching logic.

Each student communicates to PLATO II by means of his own keyset (cf. Fig. 2). The keyset, resembling a typewriter, has keys for all alphanumeric characters; additional keys for special symbols can easily be added as needed. Thus the student can transmit numerals,

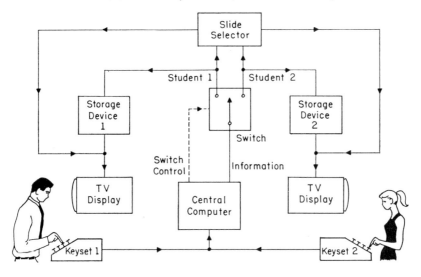

Fig. 1. General organization of PLATO II.

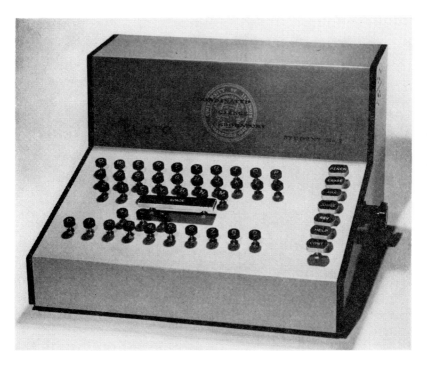

Fig. 2. The PLATO II keyset.

words, sentences, or algebraic expressions to the machine. The student controls the machine's presentation of material by means of special keys, which are described in detail in a later section of this chapter.

The machine communicates to the students by means of closed-circuit television. Each student is provided with his own television screen on which the results of two separate video sources are electronically superimposed. These sources may conveniently be thought of as an "electronic book" and an "electronic blackboard." The electronic book is shared by all students, but, at any given time different students may be using entirely different parts of it. It consists of a set of slides (containing the instructional material), which are continually scanned by a special flying-spot scanner (cf. Fig. 3). On

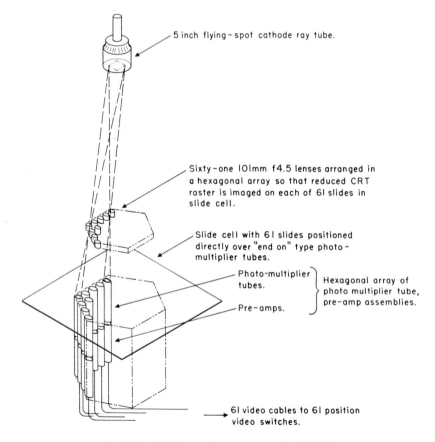

5 inch flying-spot cathode ray tube.

Sixty-one 101mm f4.5 lenses arranged in a hexagonal array so that reduced CRT raster is imaged on each of 61 slides in slide cell.

Slide cell with 61 slides positioned directly over "end on" type photo-multiplier tubes.

Photo-multiplier tubes. } Hexagonal array of photo multiplier tube, pre-amp assemblies.

Pre-amps.

61 video cables to 61 position video switches.

Fig. 3. The 61-slide, simultaneous scanner for PLATO II.

command from ILLIAC, an electronic switch (slide selector) connects the video output from any desired slide to the appropriate student's display. The electronic book currently has a capacity of 61 slides (to be expanded to 122); the slide selector can switch from any slide in the set to any other in about one millisecond.

In addition to the book, each student is provided with his own individual "electronic blackboard" in the form of a storage tube. ILLIAC, by transmitting coordinates of individual points, can write characters, figures, graphs, etc., directly onto any such tube. The tube is then scanned by the television sweep and the video thus derived is mixed with that coming from the "book." Approximately 45 characters per second can be written on the student's screen by this means; $\frac{1}{4}$ second is required to erase the entire contents of the storage tube.

The electronic blackboard is used to display all material which, because it is generated during the lesson, cannot be prestored on slides. For example, when a question is asked on a slide, the electronic blackboard makes it possible for the machine to display the student's answer superimposed on the slide in an appropriate place. Thus the student is able to see and study his answers in their context within the lesson.

Programmed Logic

Whereas the material to be taught is contained on a set of slides, the logical rules governing instruction are determined by programs within ILLIAC. These programs have been written to accommodate a variety of subject matters; for example, the computer program described here has been used for demonstration lessons in mathematics and French verb endings. To change courses on the machine requires only that the slides of the electronic book be changed and a suitable parameter tape be read by the computer; the basic program remains the same.

The PLATO II computer program requires each student to proceed through a fixed "main" sequence of slides and to answer correctly each question posed in the course of this sequence. He may avail himself of supplementary material ("help sequences") for each question of the main sequence that he finds troublesome. Further details of the teaching logic are illustrated in Fig. 4 and discussed below.

Some slides of the main sequence contain only expository material ("text" slides). A text slide is shown in Fig. 5. When a student has

PLATO

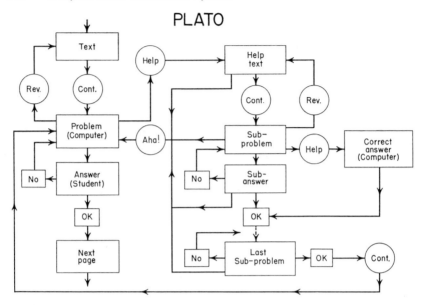

Fig. 4. Diagram of the teaching logic for PLATO II.

3 –

EACH POSITIVE INTEGER IS REP-
RESENTED IN DECIMAL NOTATION BY
COMBINING THE TEN DIGITS:

0, 1, 2, 3, 4, 5, 6, 7, 8, 9.

THUS THE SYMBOL '3,549' IS
INTERPRETED TO MEAN:

$$3 \times 10^3 + 5 \times 10^2 + 4 \times 10 + 9$$

i.e., $3 \times 1000 + 5 \times 100 + 4 \times 10 + 9.$

Fig. 5. Example of a text slide.

finished reading a text slide, he pushes a button on his keyset labeled "continue" and the computer commands the slide selector to display the next slide of the sequence. Just as the "continue" button enables the student to advance through the material, he can return to any previous slide by pushing the "reverse" key.

In addition to text slides, the main sequence contains slides on which one or more questions are posed to the student. Spaces are provided on the slide for the student's answers (cf. Fig. 6). A student must answer each question correctly before he is permitted to continue to the next slide. An attempt to bypass a slide with unanswered questions causes the computer to ring a bell indicating a fault. If, at some later time, the student should return to this slide (via "reverse"), his correct answers will again be displayed in their proper places.

The student types his answer to a question on the keyset. As he depresses each key, ILLIAC plots the corresponding character for display in the appropriate place on the television screen. Upon completing his answer the student pushes the "judge" button, and the com-

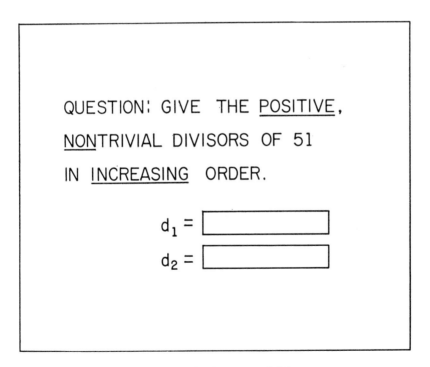

Fig. 6. Example of an "answer" slide.

puter writes either "OK" or "NO" next to his answer (cf. Fig. 7). Methods of judging answers are described below.   If the answer is judged incorrect, the student may submit another answer to the question.   To do this he first erases his old, incorrect, answer by depressing the "erase" key and then types his revised answer on the keyset.   Upon request the computer will judge the new answer.

A student is allowed as many tries as he likes in answering a question.   In trying to answer a question a student is permitted to use the reverse button to review past material.   If he still has difficulty answering a question, he may obtain supplementary material by depressing the "help" button.   This action causes the computer to transfer from the main sequence of slides to the beginning of the appropriate "help" sequence.   A "help" sequence, designed to lead the student to an understanding of the main-sequence problem, is provided for every question in the main sequence.   The "help" sequence may contain a review and reformulation of previous materials pertinent to the ques-

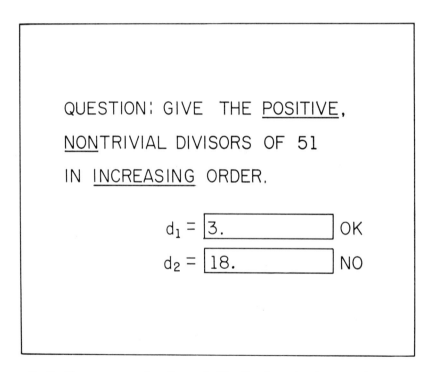

Fig. 7.   The appearance of an "answer" slide after the student has entered answers.

tion as well as suitable hints and suggestions. Often a "help" sequence breaks the main-sequence problem down into a series of simpler problems, each of which the student presumably can work. The rules for proceeding along a "help" sequence are the same as those governing the main sequence: the student moves forward by use of the "continue" button but must answer successfully each question posed in the sequence.

Memory limitations of ILLIAC preclude the use of secondary "help" sequences. Thus, if a student cannot submit a correct answer to a "help" sequence problem and asks for help once more, the machine informs him that no additional aid is available. He is given two alternatives: pushing "reverse" will return him to the problem for further consideration; pushing "help" (i.e., giving up) will cause the machine to provide the correct answer.

At the end of a "help" sequence the "continue" button automatically returns the student to the main sequence slide from which he came. It is expected that he can now answer the main sequence problem and proceed. Otherwise, a renewed request for help will cause the machine to provide the student with the correct answer.

A student who has asked for help may, as he proceeds through a "help" sequence, suddenly realize the answer to the main sequence question. By pushing the "aha" button he will be returned to the main sequence problem and may try his new answer. If it is correct, he is permitted to proceed in the main sequence. Otherwise, a renewed request for help causes the machine to return him to the point in the "help" sequence at which he broke off. Thus a student is not required to go through supplementary material that he does not feel he needs.

Answers may be judged in many ways. For questions having unique, well-defined answers the computer compares the student's answer against the prestored correct answer. For numerical answers tolerances may be specified. In more sophisticated judging routines the computer itself determines the correctness of a student's answer by using it in suitable calculations. This approach is especially useful for questions permitting a variety of correct answers. Though we have not yet implemented this procedure, it appears that the computer should not merely judge an answer but also examine each wrong answer for specific errors, routing the student to special "help" sequences associated with each kind of error.

Finally, in addition to exercising the executive control associated with instruction, the program keeps accurate records of the moves made by each student and the time elapsed at each move. Thus a wealth of precise and reliable data is available concerning each student's progress through a lesson. At a later time the computer can process these data to reveal important information about both the students and the lessons.

The Multiplexing Problem

The multiplexing of several students onto one computer is complicated by the problems of bookkeeping and time sharing. The bookkeeping problem is easily solved. Most of the program is written to handle one student. All data for each student required by the program are kept together in a list. When the computer must turn its attention from one student to another, it saves the current information list and transfers the new information list from storage. This transfer of data lists is necessary because ILLIAC lacks index registers. ILLIAC's memory capacity, in addition, limits the current PLATO II to two students.

Time sharing is more difficult. Students tend to become confused if the computer does not respond immediately to their commands. For example, suppose a given student is typing his answer to a question and does not know whether the computer is available to him. If other students have tied up the central computer, some of the characters in his answer will be lost. Care must be taken, therefore, to avoid situations in which the computer is tied up for long periods.

The problem of time sharing can be alleviated to some extent by the design of the equipment external to the computer. By providing a small amount of control circuitry at each student position, the system can perform some functions for the students in parallel. For example, the computer can tell the control circuit provided for a given student to erase his "blackboard." The computer is then free to do operations for other students while the control circuit completes erasing. When the erase cycle is completed, the control circuit so informs the computer.

Further solution of the time-sharing problem must be obtained by the computer program itself. The computer cannot be tied to a given student for more than a certain maximum time. The reciprocal of this time limit defines a minimum rate at which the computer can accept information. Let us determine this rate for a hypothetical case. A student typing at a peak rate of 60 words per minute will generate one character per 200 milliseconds. The computer must accept information at this rate for n students, or at the rate of one character per

$200/n$ milliseconds. This time is the upper limit that the program can operate without interrogating the keysets. In the computer program for PLATO II (where $n = 2$) the critical time limit is 100 milliseconds. For this program no input operations and only two output operations exceed the critical limit. One of these output operations (erasing a given storage tube) has already been mentioned.

The other operation which exceeds the critical limit is that of plotting more than one character on a storage tube. For example, a student may return to a "page" of the lesson on which he has already entered answers. His storage tube must first be erased, and the old answers must then be plotted on it. When this case arises, the program switches to a special mode of operation for the student in question, called "unfinished business." In "unfinished business" the computer is permitted to plot only one of the characters at a time before scanning all of the other keysets for possible inputs and performing any operations which these inputs may require. The student requiring unfinished business, then, is relegated to a position of lower priority, and the computer completes his unfinished business when it is receiving no inputs. The student's keyset is locked out during this time so that he cannot enter information inadvertently. In case of simultaneous unfinished business students are disposed of, one by one, in the order in which unfinished business was required for each of them. It is thus possible for two students to share ILLIAC and, except when unfinished business is required, never experience delays due to tie-up of the equipment.

Summary

The important features of PLATO II are the following:

1. Each student may proceed through the material in a manner and at a speed of his own choosing, subject only to the condition that he must solve successfully a prescribed sequence of problems. He may submit as many or as few answers to a question and seek as much or little supplementary material as he likes. Probably no one else can know a priori the particular needs of a student, at any point in his progress through the material, as well as the student himself. If the main sequence is written for the best students and "help" sequences for the poorest ones, then each student may use the "help" and "aha" keys to find for himself a suitable path in the spectrum between these two extremes.

2. The machine will accept and display constructed answers as well as the more restrictive answers to multiple-choice questions. The student is told as soon as he has submitted an answer whether it is correct or incorrect. In the latter case the machine can indicate "NO" without revealing the correct solution. Also, since a student cannot proceed before answering a question correctly, the answer to any question may be used in the textual material of subsequent parts of the sequence. Finally, if the student reviews by means of the "reverse" key, his answers to questions on previous slides are again automatically displayed by the machine; the slide sequence now assumes the character of a filled-in work book.

3. The equipment and the programmed logic appear to be sufficiently versatile so that one can change from one subject matter to another by simply replacing slides in the slide selector and giving the computer a new set of parameters. Sequences of material with subject matters varying as widely as number theory and French grammar have been prepared for use with the same computer program.

For the purposes of providing an instrument for research in education the following points seem to be particularly important:

1. The material is presented to every student in a standard, objective fashion.

2. At the end of any lesson the experimenter has at his disposal a complete record of the student's progress through the material. Such records, after suitable processing on the machine, should provide information about each student and also be of use in revising the material taught.

Studies using the PLATO II teaching logic suggest the desirability of one additional feature. With the current logic, as soon as the student gets a problem right—no matter by what means—he is sent on to the next order of business. It now seems clear, however, that in determining whether to proceed the computer should take into account *how* the student came to the correct answer to a question. Three factors seem to be of importance:

How much time was required to solve the problem?
How many wrong answers were submitted?
Was help required?

On the basis of these three factors, the computer should decide whether to go on to the next point in the main sequence or to continue to provide information relating to the current problem.

Preliminary experiments in computer-aided teaching

J. C. R. LICKLIDER

Bolt Beranek and Newman Inc.

As Launor Carter pointed out in his introductory chapter, and as several other speakers have reaffirmed, the potential applicability of computers to education is both broad and deep. We are sensing that computers can fulfill many functions that are essential to the educational process.

To realize some of those functions, we must improve our understanding of instructional programming, engage in sophisticated computer programming, and carry through advanced developments of computer hardware. The gains to be achieved through these efforts are great. To realize other important functions, however, we need only accept and apply what computers offer freely now.

When the distant scene is so very inspiring, one hesitates to divert attention to anything less rapturous near at hand. However, there is a pragmatic element in our philosophy that condones a brief pause to accept a gift, even though it be of modest value. Let me, therefore, devote a part of this discussion to the subject of automated drill. After that, I shall join the march toward the glorious horizon that is dominating our thoughts in this symposium.

This work was supported by the United States Air Force under Contract No. AF 33(616)-8152 and was monitored by the Training Psychology Branch, Behavioral Sciences Division, Aero Space Medical Laboratory, Aeronautical Systems Division, Air Force Systems Command. Dr. Felix Kopstein and Dr. Theodore Cotterman were project monitors.

Paired-Associates Drill Program

Although the teaching procedures called "drill" have unpleasant connotations, there is little doubt that accumulation of facts and elementary behavioral capabilities are prerequisite to advances at conceptual and integrative levels. Drill has a fundamental, propaedeutic function. Moreover, the following facts should be considered:

1. In present educational systems a large fraction of the total time and effort is devoted to drill.

2. It is inefficient to have $n - 1$ children sit idly by while the nth reports that $3 \times 4 = 12$.

3. Neither teachers nor pupils enjoy present kinds of drill enough to oppose its automation.

4. Automation of drill can be accomplished with relatively small investment in instructional programming and computer programming.

5. In drill, as in few other phases of teaching or learning, we can hope to obtain the masses of statistically homogeneous behavior required to reveal the diverse effects and interactions we must know in order to understand the educational process as Dr. Roe, for example, would have us understand it (see chapter by Arnold Roe in this book).

Those considerations led to the development of computer programs that automate a procedure of drill applicable to any instructional material cast in paired-associates form.

The computer itself, a PDP-1 "Programmed Data Processor,"[1] is shown in Fig. 1. It is a small, but versatile, and rather fast machine: 4096 18-bit words of core memory, 5-microsecond memory cycle, an order code of approximately 60 instructions, and a "sequence-break" system for time sharing. At present the input-output equipment are two typewriters, a reader, two tape punches, two digital-analogue converters, one analogue-digital converter, 16 computer-controlled relays, an oscilloscope, and a "light pen." The PDP-1 is excellent for use in teaching-machine research because its time is inexpensive enough to permit unpressured exploration and experimentation and because the sequence-break system facilitates simultaneous operation by several subjects working independently.

[1] Manufactured by the Digital Equipment Corporation, Maynard, Massachusetts.

Fig. 1. The PDP-1 "Programmed Data Processor" System. The control unit, arithmetic unit, and core memory are in the racks at the rear. The input-output circuitry, tape reader, and tape punches are in or on the racks at the left. The main status lights and switches are on the panel to the right of the typewriter in the center of the picture.

Typewriter Version of Paired-Associates Program

In the "typewriter version" all the material—stimulus and response—passes through the typewriter and appears on the typewriter paper. The type sheet for a short demonstration lesson of German-English vocabulary is shown in Fig. 2. (Actual lessons, of course, are longer.)

Typing the "0" key starts the session. The computer types to the student:

> Good afternoon. This will be your German-English Lesson No. 4. If you are ready to start at once, please type "s." If you would like to review the procedure, please type "p."

If the student typed "p" at this point, it would set off a detailed explanation, but (as shown in Fig. 2) the student, by now familiar with the procedure, types "s," and the first word of the lesson is presented at once. (The word is drawn at random from the list of six German words, then typed out in black by the computer.)

```
0

Good afternoon.  This will be
your German-English Lesson No. 4.
If you are ready to start at
once, please type "s."  If you
would like to review the
procedure, please type "p."

s

reichen            to hand·  +
reichen            to pass·  +
       64                 64    good
öffnen             to offer· - ta  n
to open            to open·
     -120               -56    poor
arbeiten           to arbitrate· - ta  y
arbeiten           to look· - ta  n
to work            to work·
     -184               -240    Dummkopf!
kochen             to cook· - ta  y
kochen             to boil·  +
        0               -240    okay
öffnen             to open·  +
       64               -176    hot dog.
rauchen            to smoke·  +
       64               -112    admirable
arbeiten           to work·  +
       64                -48    good
kochen             to boil·  +
       64                 16    very good
machen             to make·  +
       64                 80    Keep it up.
       80

That's it.  You did well.  I'll
be looking forward to the next
lesson.
```

Fig. 2. Type sheet produced by the computer and the student in a brief demonstration lesson. Material typed by the computer appears in black; that typed by the student appears in red, on the original typed sheet.

The word that happens to be selected is *reichen,* which means *to hand* or *to pass,* as in "Please pass me the potatoes." The student knows this and types *to hand,* which appears in red. The computer types "+" for "correct" and, since it wants a second English word, presents *reichen* again. The student types *to pass.* The computer says

"+" again, posts a score of 64 points for the item, indicates that the cumulative score to date is 64, and comments "good."

As it presented *reichen*, the computer removed the corresponding item number from the list of untried items. *Reichen* will therefore not reappear in this lesson. (The criterion could just as well be two or three times correct, but here it is one.)

Now the computer selects another German word. It is *öffnen*. The student thinks he knows it, but he does not. He types *to offer*. The computer says "−" (for "No, that is incorrect") and "ta" (for "Do you want to try again?"). The student types "n" (for "No"). The computer then presents the correct answer, *to open*. The student has to copy that. If he miscopies, the computer "tabs" and requires him to copy it again. Here he copies it correctly. The computer gives him a score of −120 on the item, part for missing once and part for refusing to try again. The cumulative score is now −56. The computer says "poor."

Because *öffnen* was missed, the computer deletes the corresponding item number from the untried table and puts it into the missed table for future reference. It selects the next item by first choosing one of the two tables, untried or missed, and then selecting at random within the table. The choice of table is made with the table probabilities biased to give each item, untried or missed, the same chance of being selected.

The next word turns out to be *arbeiten*. The student displays not only poor mastery of the material but also poor judgment on this item. He answers *to arbitrate*, which is wrong, then tries again with *to look*, which is also wrong, and only after the second failure asks to see the right answer. He copies *to work* and finds that he lost 184 more points and has a cumulative score of −240. The computer says "Dummkopf!" (The rough treatment of the student for misses while he is getting acquainted with the words is deliberate in this version of the program. We shall return to this point.)

Instead of trying to give the English for *arbeiten*, which obviously he did not know, the student should have asked for the answer by typing "///." The computer would have told him the correct answer for a penalty of only 64 points.

Kochen, which comes up next, is missed at first but answered correctly on the second trial. The computer considers that a break-even performance, posts an item score of zero, leaves the cumulative score at −240, and (having adjusted its criteria downward because of the several incorrect responses) says "okay."

Next comes a (second) presentation of *öffnen,* which the student missed on the first attempt. This time the translation is correct. The correctness is reflected in the scores and the comment.

The student gets all the rest of the words right—*rauchen* on first encounter, *arbeiten,* and *kochen* on second (they were missed earlier), and *machen* on first. The computer's comment on the response to *machen* (*to make*) is appropriate to the fact that there have been several good answers in a row but not to the fact that *machen* was the last item. Clearly, although the commentary part of the program is sophisticated enough to take trends and variations of performance into account, there is room for improvement.

At the end of the lesson the computer presents the final score (80) and makes a farewell comment. It is prepared, if the student should offer a reply via the typewriter, to say, "Thank you, the pleasure was all mine," but in this instance the student did not carry courtesy that far.

Even in the brief example just described, it is evident that the scores may be low during the first part of the first lesson with a given set of vocabulary items. Most of the German words are at first unfamiliar to the student. The cumulative score may fall as low as -1000 in a 16- or 20-item test. However, as in the case here, the credits accumulated in the process of giving correct answers to the items near the end of the lesson usually bring the cumulative score up to a positive value. Since all the items must be answered correctly to terminate the lesson, the score is bound to rise at the end. Young students, particularly, like the drama of the contest with the computer and enjoy "coming from behind" to win.

There is a problem—a fairly serious one, actually—if, during a child's first experience with the computer, the score gets too low and the comments too insulting. A good procedure, therefore, is to deactivate score reporting and commenting during the first pass through each early lesson and to tell the pupil only afterward that his score had been low for a time before he began to get the answers right.

As soon as he becomes well acquainted with the procedure, a young student is likely to take over control of the "mode switches," turning scores and comments off when he is doing poorly, and on when he is doing well. Mature students who truly want to learn the material usually settle down to use of the streamlined mode (no score reports, no comments) except for an occasional check of the cumulative score.

There are a few other aspects of procedure with which the students must become familiar—for example, a mode in which, even if there are two or more correct answers (as in the case of *reichen: to hand, to pass*), only one is required, and a simple way of "erasing" errors of typing—but the foregoing is doubtless enough to illustrate the flavor of the technique.

Types of Material for Which the Paired-Comparison Format Is Suitable

Although we have used the paired-associates drill program mainly with language vocabulary—French, Latin, and a little Swedish, as well as German—it is immediately applicable to a number of other materials. We have had some experience in its use in the teaching of spelling, arithmetic, geographical and historical facts, computer order codes, and alphabetical equivalents. Much of the material that students must learn before they can think—much of the raw material for thinking and problem solving—is adaptable to the paired-associates format.

In spelling drill the stimulus items are given in phonetic spelling. In arithmetic the statement of the problem, or the operator together with its operands, is the stimulus and the solution or result is the desired response.

It is not necessary to go in one jump from problem to solution; the alternative answers of each item are considered in fixed sequence by the computer, not at random. If the stimulus is "4 cubed," for example, and the student asks to see a correct answer, the computer will in answer to the first request type "4 × 4 × 4." It will then present "4 cubed" again and give the student a chance to answer or to ask to be shown again. There may be as many steps as desired. A second intermediate answer or bridging response might be "16 × 4."

Should the student be a wiseacre and respond "LXIV," he will be surprised to see the computer type out "+" and give him score credit for a correct answer.

A final comment about the use of the program with diverse materials: the stimulus-response materials (e.g., vocabulary), the comments (e.g., "good," "poor," "You are a moron"), and the signals ("+", "−ta"), salutation, and farewell are all clearly separated from the program itself. The program operates upon whatever materials it is given. Preparation of materials is ordinarily a routine, clerical operation, requiring exercise of judgment only in cases that involve bridging responses or deliberate selection of items. New materials may be introduced into the computer in a few seconds.

Problems and Experiments in Paired-Associates Drill

We come now to the question of use of a teaching machine of the type described.

It is a temptation simply to use it. My son and my daughter like to have half an hour a day each, one for German, the other for French. (Both are studying typewriting extracurricularly to increase their facility.) I, myself, am very happy at last to have a painless opportunity to make what I think is real progress in languages, at which I always have been poor. Two of my colleagues, who are planning to go to Brazil, are currently subverting the tape typist to prepare Portuguese vocabulary instead of the materials I need for experiments. But it would rapidly generate a fiscal crisis if we used the computer only to educate our children and ourselves.

Our serious purposes, of course, are research and development: research on learning and teaching; development of a practical, economical system.

The object of the research is to explore the important variables of the procedure, to optimize the procedure, and perhaps to evaluate it. In pursuing those objects, however, we encounter the difficulties discussed earlier in this conference. The basic difficulty is that teaching and learning are very complex processes. We cannot develop an understanding of 10- or 20-variable processes through one-, two-, and three-variable experiments because many of the interactions are strong. On the other hand, formal many-variable experiments based on classical designs are prohibitively costly and time-consuming. What we are doing, therefore, is

1. to program the mechanism for computer-controlled experiments based upon a "bootstrap hill-climbing" procedure, which, we think, may offer a solution to the problem posed by the unfeasibility of formal many-variable experiments of classical design; and

2. in the interim, to rely upon a mixture of informal experimentation and intuitive observation in an effort to ascertain the variables that are important and to develop three or four effective teaching procedures for experimental comparison.

The observations we have made deal mainly with prompting, response mode, and reinforcement—with Holland's "trivia" and with Briggs' "important variables" (see their chapters in this book).

My feeling about them is that they are important, but only in a propaedeutic sense. I think this is essentially Holland's point. One must manipulate and adjust them in order to achieve an approximately optimum procedure. But one should not spend much effort on experiments that lead to such conclusions as these:

Multiple-choice is as effective as constructed response.
Prompting increases speed of learning and decreases errors.
The strength of reinforcement is inconsequential; it is the information that counts.

Under some circumstances these conclusions are true. Under others they are false. The problem is more nearly to determine the conditions of their truth and falsity than to arrive at the conclusions themselves.

The Criterion of Learning and Teaching Performance

The main criterion of performance used in our observations is rate of acquisition—amount of material mastered per minute. That is the quantity we want to maximize. We understand that "master" is subtle, that a procedure optimized for 10-minute retention may not be best for 10-year retention. That, however, is of necessity a second-order problem. We have not seen any strong inversions between minutes and days or any sizable fund of results for months or years.

In any event, incidence of errors is, for the present purposes, definitely not a main criterion for our purpose, since errors may be, as Crowder stresses (in another portion of this book), a means to the end. Number of trials to mastery is not critical, either, because the duration of a trial varies from procedure to procedure. The important quantity, again, is the amount of material mastered per unit time. It is unfortunate that this is not a universal currency, that a mastered item of German-English vocabulary is not intrinsically comparable to a mastered item of Boolean algebra. This difficulty may be resolved, ultimately, by bringing into the problem the utility, to the learner or to society, of mastery of the learned material, but that is not an approach to be taken in preliminary informal experiments.

Reinforcement

The scores and comments typed by the computer clearly fall under the heading, "reinforcement." Do they reinforce?

First, some indication of the correctness or incorrectness of the student's response is essential. The "$+$" and "$-$" are enough to provide that indication. When we take away the other scores and comments, we still have a procedure effective for many purposes. When we take away the "$+$" and "$-$," too, the result is much confusion and—until the student realizes he should rely exclusively upon prompting requests ("///" for "Show me a correct answer")—little learning.

Beyond that, the answer is neither "yes" nor "no." There is a continuum of circumstances. At one pole the student has no interest in learning the material and prefers entertainment to education. At the other the student has a vital need to learn the material and wants nothing, however amusing, to interfere with his learning it. Perhaps we have not had experience at the extremes of the continuum, but we have had a chance to watch students fairly far from center in each direction.

For the unmotivated young student the scores and comments are essential. Typically, he is pleased by favorable comments, shows irritation at unfavorable ones, talks to (or sometimes about) the computer, and exerts himself to earn score points. If the points are negotiable at 0.03 cent each, he works harder than he does for points without monetary value.

The incentive value of the scores, the comments, and even the money appears to decline somewhat with increasing experience, but it is strong enough and enduring enough to carry the student through to mastery of a practically useful amount of material. The big hope is that before he gets out from under the control of the computer's incentives he will learn enough German words, for example, to let him read interesting German without suffering the pain of dictionary look-up. This hope seems realistic. It is possible for a student to learn dozens of words at a sitting and to master the vocabulary of an introductory course in a week. The learning takes time, of course, but the computer's constant attention and unfailing reinforcement lead the unmotivated student to devote to learning—indeed, to drill—amounts of time he would ordinarily consider suitable for television.

For the highly motivated student to master a given body of material, the scores and comments are, as mentioned earlier, much less important. The important things for him are speed and convenience. This is obvious from a comparison of the paired-associates program on the PDP-1 computer and a closely similar program on a much slower machine, the Royal Precision LGP-30. With the LGP-30, it was found necessary to introduce typewriter spacings, carriage shifts, and ribbon changes into the "dead" intervals (intervals during which the computer was scoring responses and selecting new items) to keep them from seeming too long to the student, but even with such "simulated throat-clearing" the learner's experience is much less absorbing, much less pleasant, than it is with the PDP-1.

Additional evidence is available on the importance of speed and convenience of operation. The greatest advance made in a summer of continual program revision was, in the evaluation of one student, the provision of the "erase" feature. Until it was available, a typing error was not correctable, even though caught before the completion of the answer; after he typed the wrong answer the student had to hit a centered-dot key ("end of answer"), wait for the "−ta," type "n," wait for the stimulus word, and then type the answer again. Streamlining the correction procedure was in one sense trivial but in another sense truly important, for it eliminated the frustrating delay. Along the same line were the substitution of "+" for "Right" and "−ta" for "Wrong. Try Again?" Eliminating 10 computer-typed characters saves a second and saving seconds not only increases the time efficiency of the procedure but also makes the experience more attractive to the student. Eliminating student-typed characters is even more effective. Capital letters and diacritical markings that involve backspacing plus capitalization are evidently more than just a nuisance. A few trials we made with human simulation of a program capable of scoring vocal responses suggested that speech will be important as a response mode, in large part because it is fast and effortless.

The emphasis in the last paragraph upon streamlining of the procedure is not to suggest that reinforcement is unimportant for highly motivated students. The point is that they are reinforced by learning, and the gain in such intrinsic reinforcement achieved by speeding up the procedure (e.g., turning off the comments) outweighs the losses due to decreased exposure time or extrinsic verbal reinforcement.

For students near the center of the continuum we have been discussing, both intrinsic and extrinsic reinforcement are evidently important. Such students often turn off the scores and comments when things are going poorly and turn them on again as soon as they get a few answers correctly in succession. However, even a student who continually changes the score and comment mode switches is appreciative of each advance that accelerates the procedure.

Diminishing Returns from Streamlining: Oscilloscope Version of the Program

The conclusion that human engineering has as much as learning theory to contribute to computer-aided teaching depends, of course, upon the relative human-engineering and learning-theoretic merits of the initial procedure and equipment. In our experience elementary human engineering made a big contribution, increasing performance by at least 50%. However, we appear to be in a region of diminishing returns.

In order to increase further the pace of presentation and reinforcement, we prepared a version of the paired-associates program that uses the computer's cathode-ray oscilloscope as a display screen. The student still answers via the typewriter, which limits the pace, but the display of stimulus items and reinforcers is almost instantaneous. (The oscilloscope display is illustrated in Fig. 3.)

Figure 4 shows the results of four criterion tests on each of 20 Latin-English lessons, with 16 items per lesson. The 20 tests were divided into two sets of 10, equated for item length. I served as subject and studied one set with the aid of the typewriter version of the program; I studied the other set with the aid of the oscilloscope version. The comments were always left on. Item and cumulative scores were always turned off. It seemed to me that the oscilloscope procedure was running the more rapidly, and indeed it was faster. As Fig. 4 shows, however, there was very little difference between the two versions of the program as far as learning performance was concerned.

Part A of Fig. 4 shows the number of words learned per minute as a function of the criterion test. Criterion 1 required that each of the 16 items of a lesson be answered correct'y once, plus the number of times it was missed. Criterion 2 required that criterion 1 be met

KOCHEN

TO COOK

WRONG   TRY AGAIN

KOCHEN

TO BOIL

RIGHT

Fig. 3. Two illustrations of the oscilloscope display during a German-English lesson. Inasmuch as the photograph integrates brightness over the duration of the exposure, whereas the eye does not, the variations in intensity evident in the photograph are not evident in the oscilloscope display seen directly. During the lesson, the German word appears first, of course; the English then appears as the student types it, and the "Wrong, try again" or the "Right" shows up as soon as the student has hit the centered-dot key to indicate that he has completed his response.

twice; criterion 3 required that criterion 1 be met three times; and criterion 4 required that criterion 1 be met four times.

Parts B through E show, for the four criteria, the number of minutes devoted to learning as a function of the number of words per lesson not previously known by the subject. The filled circles and solid lines correspond to typewritten-display tests; the open circles and dashed lines correspond to oscilloscope-display tests. For the sake of simplicity the lines are shown drawn through the origin to leave as many datum points above as below. More sophisticated curve filling does not materially change the conclusion that the displays are not markedly different in effectiveness.

We are not sure that the foregoing finding of diminishing returns is absolute. It may be that the faster pace of the oscilloscope display will be of greater advantage when it is not obscured by the sluggishness

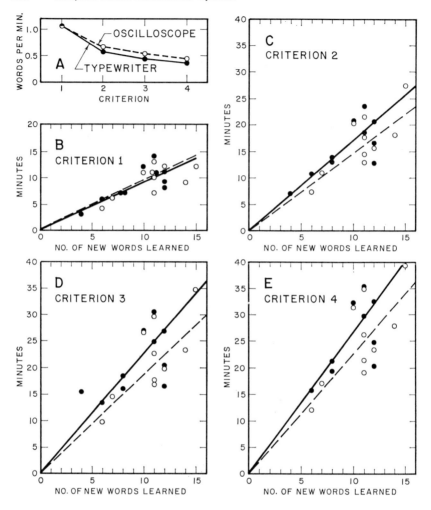

Fig. 4. *Comparison of typewriter and oscilloscope displays. Part A shows the number of words learned per minute as a function of the performance criterion. Parts B through E show, for the four criteria, required learning time as a function of words per lesson not previously known. Filled circles and solid lines show typewriter-display tests; open circles and dashed lines show oscilloscope-display tests.*

of typewriter response. We are working on a multiple-choice response program that will permit the student to indicate his choice by simply pointing to one of three or four words or phrases on the oscilloscope screen. With this program, we can get the item cycle down to a second or two (unless the student has to deliberate), but we will then be squarely up against the problem of "multiple-choice versus constructed-response."

Prompting

The initial version of the paired-associates program provided no way for the subject to see a correct answer except to give an incorrect answer and then to say he did not want to try again. In remedying that defect, we did two things: (1) We introduced the "Show-me-a-correct-answer code," the three slashes mentioned earlier, and (2) we introduced an optional preliminary presentation of the entire vocabulary (e.g., German and English). In informal tests the program with (1) was better than the program without it, and the program with (1) and (2)—with three minutes for the preliminary study—was slightly better still. The value of the preliminary study, however, is questionable. It may improve performance, but it is not inherently attractive. Given the option of using it or not, students usually either read the list through only once or turn immediately to the typewriter.

Implicit Versus Explicit Response

For the students who are poor typists it is frustrating to have to type the entire answer. We therefore conducted a few informal trials, in half of which the computer "trusted" the student. (The other half were with the typewriter version illustrated in Fig. 2.) In the "implicit-response" trials, if the student knew the answer (according to his own criterion), he simply hit the space bar; if he did not know it, he hit the "slash" key. The tests required translation from French to English, English being selected as the response language to minimize uncertainty about spelling. Performance was measured with the aid of paper-and-pencil pre- and posttests. For two poor typists the implicit-response procedure was markedly better than the explicit-response procedure. For good typists the two procedures were approximately equal.

Continuous-Process Drill and "Trapping"

The versions of the drill program thus far described have worked with "lessons," each lesson consisting of some definite number of items

—usually 16. We have also made observations with another version, called the "continuous-process" version, in which there are two sets of items: an immediate set of, say, 16, and a reservoir of several hundred. Until an item is answered correctly, the continuous-process version operates in just the same way as the others. However, when an item is mastered and is eliminated from the immediate set, it is replaced by a new item from the reservoir. This allows the student to work on and on, operating at any one time with a small collection of items in various stages of mastery but never running out of material.

With the continuous-process version, we have observed a phenomenon that we think may be fairly important in automated instruction. We call it "stimulus trapping."

There is, in the most streamlined paired-associates-drill procedure, only one time interval of any considerable length during which the student does not have before him a stimulus requiring response. That is the end of the lesson. At every other time, because the computer reacts so rapidly, there is either (e.g., in a German-English lesson) a German word to which an English equivalent is required, an English word that must be copied, or a "−ta" to which the student must answer "y" or "n." If the student knows the German word, he wants to have the satisfaction of proving it. If he does not know the German word, he wants (at least to some slight extent) to find out what it is. In the other situations the needed response is immediately available and easy to make. As a consequence, almost no one ever stops responding during the course of a lesson.

In our short experience with the continuous-process procedure we have observed that students tend to go on and on, generating piles of typed sheets, until forced by the computer schedule to terminate their work. Apparently, the essential condition for this persistence is that the competing activities be given no opportunity to interject themselves. We do not know yet how strong the stimulus-trapping effect can be made, but we think it is strong enough in the present continuous-process procedure to be of practical value.

Teaching Relations between Symbolic and Graphical Representations

Although we have devoted a major part of our effort to automation of paired-associates drill, it is not by any means our major long-term interest. We consider drill important, and we consider automation of

drill a thing of value within easy reach. Our greater interest, however, lies in using computers to fulfill teaching functions that only
computers can reasonably fulfill. One of these on which we have done
preliminary work is the teaching of relations between symbolic and
graphical representation of mathematical functions.

At present we have a program to facilitate exploration by the student. The student sits at the typewriter and types the coefficients
of an equation—for example, the *a, b,* and *c* in

$$y = a(x - b)^2 + c$$

The computer immediately displays on its oscilloscope screen the corresponding parabola. The student then varies the coefficients in whatever ways he chooses, attempting to develop an understanding of the
relations. In setting up the parabola of Fig. 5A, for example, the

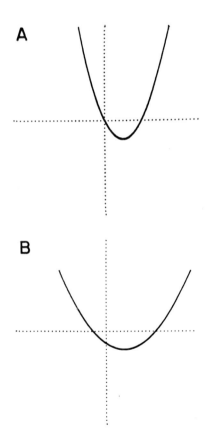

Fig. 5. *Two photographs from the computer oscilloscope screen, showing parabolas
generated by the computer in response to
the student's typed specifications.*

student typed 1/100, 100, and −100 as the values of a, b, and c. Then, for Fig. 5B, he changed a to 1/300. A little time with this program, even in its present rudimentary form, gives a bright student a good intuitive understanding of linear, parabolic, and square-root functions.

We are in the process of preparing the computer programs to display the symbolic equation on the oscilloscope screen (below the graph) and to provide the scales with sliding markers (below the coefficients in the symbolic expression) through which the student can adjust both the coefficients of the equation and the graph. Also, we are programming a mode in which the student will sketch a curve with the light pen on a displayed grid, whereupon the computer will determine and display the best-fitting parabola, together with its equation with the numerical coefficients filled in. The programs will handle cubics, quartics, and quintics as well as straight lines and ordinary parabolas.

This effort will be, for the next several months, a study not so much of a teaching machine as of an automated context for student-controlled exploration and investigation. We think that this area may prove to have almost as much promise as automated teaching. As soon as we have the automated context, however, we shall devote part of the effort to investigation of its use through structured, tutorial procedures.

Other Areas of Investigation

Beyond the two areas described, we are doing preliminary work on (1) computer-aided teaching of structured concepts and (2) the design of a compiler to bring the shaping and use of computer programs closer to the hands of the teacher.

The linear graphs of Fig. 6 are part of a program sequence on such fundamentals of graphical representation as slopes and intercepts. Comparison of Fig. 6A with Fig. 6B illustrates a way in which the computer "points" to an intercept. In the actual kinematic display the circle at $(2, 2)$ in Fig. 6B is a bright point moving rapidly in a circular path. The motion, which is coordinated with display of explanatory textual material, attracts the student's attention.

In most of our current work effort is being made to exploit the computer's capability to select sample problems, to increase their difficulty level when the student's performance indicates he has mastered the material with which he has been working, to go back to fundamentals when troubles of comprehension arise, etc. However,

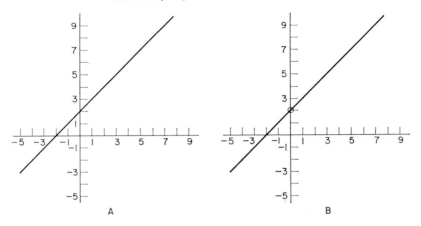

A   B

*Fig. 6. Two photographs from the computer oscilloscope screen during a lesson on funda-
mentals of graphic representation. In B the computer is calling attention to the y intercept. As viewed directly, the circle is a rapidly rotating dot, which attracts the student's
attention.*

these efforts are in progress, as is the work on compilers, and I shall
not describe them in further detail. Suffice it to say that, although
computers will be effective in presenting and scoring programmed
instructional materials of conventional kinds and in bookkeeping, they
promise to be helpful, also—whenever the structure of the subject
material can be described explicitly—in developing local parts of the
instructional program and in controlling conditional progression from
one section of a course to another. They promise to remove at least
some of the routine burden from the instructional (subject-matter)
programmer and to provide important aid in subject-matter-program-
ming research and development.

Economic Aspects of Computer-Aided Teaching

The fundamental practical obstacle to the application of computers
to instruction is cost. Although it may be conceivable in a research
development project to spend $35 per student-hour for a computer, it
is not much more than conceivable—and such a rate is wholly im-
practicable—for tutorial instruction in schools and colleges.

The key to solution of the economic problem, at least in the fore-
seeable future—lies in "time sharing." Part of our work has been

focused on techniques for sharing the time of a fast computer among several or many students. The aim (and clearly feasible prospect) is to have each student operate as though he alone were using a computer of somewhat lesser capability—while, in actuality, the one large, fast computer is devoting a fraction of a millisecond to one student, then a fraction of a millisecond to another. The economic advantage to be gained in this way is great because (1) a large, fast machine costs very much less per elementary operation than a small, slow one, and (2) the student's use of instructional machinery is not uniform on the fine-grained time scale that is important in scheduling a computer's time. (A computer attending to one student spends most of its time idly waiting for an answer.)

The "sequence-break" system of the PDP-1 computer is a joint product of our thinking (mainly E. Fredkin's) and the Digital Equipment Corporation's (mainly B. Gurly's), and we have been greatly appreciative of Digital Equipment Corporation's willingness to develop the system and to incorporate it into their computers. In essence, the system allows us to accomplish economically, with a small amount of hardware and some programming, a function which can now be realized only to a limited extent on very expensive computers but which will almost certainly be widely available a few years from now. The system permits 16 users (or any multiple of 16, given more hardware) to operate in an apparently simultaneous way. (A "user" is actually an input-output device, but there will ordinarily be one input-output device per student.) The sequence of events that converts sequential operation into apparently simultaneous operation may be described as follows:

Let us assume three users for the sake of simplicity. ("Three" is immediately generalizable to n.) The users are associated with "flags" in the computer. The flags are given priorities, 1, 2, 3. Whenever a user initiates an action (e.g., by hitting a typewriter key), the corresponding flag goes up. At the end of each instruction—approximately every 5 or 10 microseconds—the control unit of the computer looks down the row of flags. If any flag(s) is (are) up, the control unit deposits the contents of the active registers of the computer into preassigned memory registers associated with the raised flag of highest priority and "jumps" to a part of the program designated in another such memory register. Thus, if user 2 is in control and user 1 initiates an action, the present state of 2's program is recorded for inspection upon 2's return, and control is given to 1.

The priority system does not keep 3 from interrupting 2, or 2 and 3 from interrupting 1, because high-priority pre-empting holds only during the short period in which the typewriter message is being processed. None of the input-output equipment can recycle rapidly enough to let a high-priority user monopolize the processor's time by repeatedly initiating interruptions.

The details of the sequence-break system are slightly more intricate than the picture just given, but they are not essential to the present discussion. The parallel use of the computer by several students, however, is important, and the potential effect upon cost is rather dramatic.

Because we have at present only two computer typewriters, our demonstrations of time sharing have been limited to two students.[2] The observations, however, may be applied directly to a system for any number. In discussing them we should distinguish between two parts of the time-sharing procedure: (1) computer acceptance of the successive characters that constitute a student's response and (2) computer processing of a whole response, selection of the next material for presentation, and its display.

The first part requires about 50 microseconds per character. If the computer did nothing but accept responses from students who typed continuously at 10 characters per second, therefore, it could handle 500 to 1000 students.

The second part depends upon the complexity and upon the sophistication of the computer programs that process responses, select, and display instructional material, etc. Unfortunately, sophistication of programming has a very important bearing upon speed of processing, selection, and display. In programs prepared with no regard for speed we find delays (caused by inefficient searching and comparing) that would be bothersome if the computer's time were shared among four students. It is easy to increase the speed of such programs by a factor of 5. It will probably be possible to increase the speed by a factor of 25.

Taking a fairly conservative view, we are sure we can operate the typewriter version of the paired-associates drill program with the five typewriters we shall shortly have, and we think we could make it operate with 35 typewriters if we had them. The latter would bring the cost down to a dollar an hour per student for the computer (including enough additional memory to hold the expanded programs),

[2] Swets, J. A., Millman, S. H., Fletcher, W. E., & Green, D. M. Learning to identify nonverbal sounds: An application of a computer as a teaching machine. In preparation.

plus about 50 cents an hour per typewriter. Those figures are based on amortization over four years and include commercial overhead. We mention them because the economic aspect of computer-aided teaching is obviously critical and because it seems important that a system constructed of existing hardware is so close to economic feasibility.

For application in a large school or in a school system it would be desirable (probably essential) to have a computer designed especially for many-user time sharing. The large computer manufacturers have not devoted nearly so much effort to development of such machines as they have to development of single-sequence (or "very-few-sequence") scientific calculators and business data processors. Nevertheless, the general outlines of the design of multiprocessor time-sharing computers have been worked out,[3] and it appears that such computers will be available by the time our educational systems are prepared to exploit them. With computers designed specifically for many-user time sharing, the main economic problem will be posed by input-output equipment; that is by controls and displays for students. For centralized computer systems serving several schools, wire or cable connections will constitute a significant budgetary item. Nevertheless, it seems reasonable to plan on sophisticated computer assistance in the educational process for less than a dollar per student-hour within five or six years.

Conclusions

The main conclusions we derive from our experience thus far with computer-aided teaching are the following:

1. It seems possible, by exploiting the computer's constant capability for quick response and reinforcement, to develop techniques of instruction and intellectual exploration that will "trap" the attention of students and divert their energies from amusements and other less constructive pastimes to education. Deliberate exploitation of both reinforcement and human engineering techniques is essential to this accomplishment.

2. Computers are useful now, or will be in the very near future,

[3] Licklider, J. C. R. The system system. In E. N. Bennett, J. Spiegel, & J. W. Degan (Eds.), *Human factors in technology*. McGraw-Hill, in press.

in research on teaching and learning and in development of instructional programs.

3. The economic feasibility of widespread exploitation of computer-aided teaching in large schools, school systems, government, and industry depends upon the development of time-sharing computer systems and rugged, flexible, inexpensive input-output equipment for student stations.

Computer techniques in instruction

ROBERT L. CHAPMAN and JANETH T. CARPENTER

Thompson Ramo Wooldridge Inc.

The fact that this conference has been organized suggests that a number of us have been thinking along similar lines. Those of us who have been involved in the development of large data-processing systems have seen great advances in the design of computers, associated equipment, and procedures that permit men to operate in conjunction with computers. At the same time, we have been faced with enormous training problems in making these systems operational. We all appear to see in the advances of computer design the opportunity to bring a powerful new capability to bear on our problems of teaching and training. Automation of the instructional process may well revolutionize the field of education.

Efforts are being made at a number of levels today to realize some of the advantages that our technology promises for education. The practical goal we all have in mind in these efforts is to increase both the efficiency and the quality of our training.

Thompson Ramo Wooldridge has been engaged in a project on automated tutoring. I will discuss this project later, but first I would like to discuss the broader picture of the research effort in automated tutoring, to provide some background for the course we chose to follow.

Science versus Technology

Which Comes First?

As an observer looks at the research in automated instruction, he is struck by the fact that two extremely divergent research strategies

240

are being pursued. There seem to be two opposed schools of thought. One of these might be characterized as the "programming's the thing" school. Proponents of this approach argue that the state of our science of learning is too embryonic now for us to be concerned with complex instrumentation. We need to find out the best way to write teaching programs, they argue. Machines really are not necessary; if we use them at all it is just to control the conditions of presentation and to keep the students honest. The heart of improved instruction is in the program, not the machine.

At the other extreme, we have the group we could call the "computers are great" school. Their concern is not with different methods of preparing teaching programs but rather with discovering how to program computers to make them simulate the selection, control, and decision functions which a personal tutor might perform.

A close look should be taken at the arguments for each of these approaches so that a suitable solution can be reached.

The Case for Technology

It is unquestionably within the state of the art to provide highly sophisticated instrumentation for the purpose of instruction. We have such equipment at Thompson Ramo Wooldridge. Although the TRW Modular Information Processing Equipment system was developed for data processing, it has all the features that would enable it to be used as a gigantic teaching machine.

The computer in this system, the polymorphic RW-400 computer, is a flexible arrangement of coordinated computer modules which can be programmed to organize and reorganize itself to fit changing requirements.

A number of consoles are compatible with the computer. One of these is the Display Analysis Console, which can provide the human operator with direct access to the storage and processing capabilities of the system. The D.A.C. has a keyboard that permits two-way communication with the computer. By pressing keyboard buttons labeled in English, the operator can interrogate or request action of the computer. The buttons actuate preprogrammed subroutines that, within milliseconds, cause the computer to reply with displays—two graphic displays and one alphanumeric display.

The Photo Interpretation Console is another component in this system. It is a rear-projection device that constitutes a combination viewer, magnifier, and measuring instrument. The operator can summon any one of a group of photographs and have it appear on his viewing screen side by side with a comparison photograph or map. He can shift and expand both images, have measurements made automatically, and have all of his findings reported immediately to the computer. He can request the computer to take the initiative and question him about specific items displayed on the viewing screen.

What are the implications of this equipment for automated tutoring? It has all the capabilities that the computer enthusiasts are looking for in an automated instructional system. It has power, flexibility, man-machine communication, speed, memory, and decision-making capability.

We had this equipment available in our own company, designed, built, and ready to go. We did not start our investigation of automated tutoring by using this equipment.

Why?

Because it would have required an investment of thousands of dollars to program it and organize it to present a teaching program. Because the kinds of teaching programs available for use in the equipment were not good enough to justify that expense. There are not enough theories or formulations at the present time to justify the use of this powerful equipment.

The Case for Science

In spite of the fact that psychologists have been investigating learning for many years, we still have no satisfactory theory of learning that will permit us to exert precise control over all the variables that exist in a learning situation. (In fact, some people would argue that we have not even identified all the variables.) We have no good idea of what is involved in concept formation, and we do not know how to guarantee that learning will generalize from the training situation to the job situation.

In spite of the gaps in our theories, however, some principles of teaching have evolved over the centuries. It is interesting to note that when a number of great teachers analyzed their methods and wrote down rules for successful teaching they all emphasized more or less the same points. Here is a brief summary of these rules:

Information should be presented in a logical, step-by-step sequence.
Learning should proceed from the known to the unknown.

Instruction should proceed at a student's own pace.

Efforts should be made to insure the student's understanding of each point before he proceeds to the next.

Misunderstandings should be detected and corrected immediately.

New ideas should be made meaningful in terms of the student's own experience.

The student should actively practice what he is learning.

Instruction should be fitted to the comprehension of the learner.

Much of the excitement about the new method of programmed learning stems from the fact that it provides some new ways for implementing these teaching principles. Programmed learning provides a practical means for the *individual* participation of the learner—a condition that is not possible in current group instructional practices. In addition, the careful way in which programmed instruction must be prepared calls for the explicit statement of the goals of the learning sequence, an analysis of the concepts that have to be taught, and a determination of a logical sequence in which the ideas can be presented.

So programmed learning provides a means for putting the teaching principles into practice. However, the way in which most programmed learning sequences are being written has caused many educators some concern. The basic problem is to define the goals of a learning sequence. Most programs at present make use almost exclusively of verbal symbols. What the student learns to do is to manipulate words. Is this the goal of learning? If the student learns to make certain verbalizations in response to verbal cues, will the learning generalize to situations in which the stimuli may involve physical objects and social relationships as well as words?

To improve the generalizability of classroom learning, educators have looked for ways to increase the range of ways of presenting information. They have not only used words spoken in lectures and written in textbooks, but they have provided visualization of ideas by means of chalkboard diagrams, movies, slides, classroom demonstrations, and laboratory exercises. The need for increased visualization of ideas has also been apparent in changes that have occurred in textbooks, in which there has been greater use of photographs, charts, maps, drawings, and so on.

It has not been demonstrated conclusively that a variety of ways of presenting information is essential for efficient learning and generalization. However, the efforts of educators in this direction suggest that they feel it is a very important variable.

Educators are also aware that motivation is a crucial problem. A student who is motivated to learn a subject can manage to learn it in spite of poor learning conditions. But the problem is to motivate the student to want to learn in the first place and, once he has started, to motivate him to continue studying a subject. Good teachers have learned how to stimulate the natural curiosity of students. Reinforcement theory has told us the conditions of frequency and latency of reinforcement that will keep an organism behaving at a high rate. Yet we have not devised ways of incorporating these motivational aids into autotutoring.

Still another problem that our science has left unsolved is that of measurement. In spite of many efforts, we still have no good measuring instruments with which to evaluate the results of our educational efforts. Standardized tests have been developed, and they represent a partial answer.

What does this analysis of the state of our science mean for automated tutoring? It certainly suggests that instrumentation is desirable—if we want to do more than teach students to manipulate written words and if we want to investigate a variety of ways of presenting information. It also suggests that we are not now in a position to determine all the characteristics an automated tutoring device should have. It does suggest that we need instrumentation broad and flexible enough to enable us to pose some questions, collect the data, and determine which characteristics are important and which are not. It suggests that such instrumentation should provide for the controlled presentation of information in the appropriate sense modality, for controlling the conditions of reinforcement, for measuring the effects of what we are doing, and for responsiveness to the learning needs of the individual student. It suggests that simple mechanical teaching machines or programmed textbooks will not enable us to ask the necessary questions or collect the data we need. It suggests the need for a device with broader capabilities.

Science and Technology Revisited

It seemed to us, after making this survey of science and technology, that in a way both schools of thought are right. We do need to devote a great deal of attention to programming methodology. But at the same time, to investigate the broader questions of programming that must be investigated, some instrumentation is needed to permit efficient presentation, reinforcement, decision making, and data collection to enable us to get the answers.

The solution seemed straightforward: design a special-purpose computerized machine to do these things. And this is what we did. The result was a device which we have named the TRW Mentor (see Fig. 1).

The Mentor is a flexibly programmed, self-contained, computerized presentation-and-response device. Its main functional characteristics are flexibility and control of the presentation of information (and of reinforcement) and responsiveness to the needs of individual students.

The device itself contains the necessary logic for scoring, deciding, selecting, and controlling (see Fig. 2). Student responses are automatically scored; decisions are made by the machine on the basis

Fig. 1. The TRW Mentor automatic tutoring device.

Fig. 2. The scoring, deciding, selecting, and controlling logic of the TRW Mentor.

of the scores; the machine selects the subsequent presentation on the basis of the decision and controls the conditions of the presentation.

Automatic scoring capability includes single-item tests, multiple-item tests, or a complete test battery. Both the response choice and the time taken to respond are recorded permanently on punched tape. A priori scoring formulas can be used in accumulating performance measures.

Presentations can be synchronized visual and auditory stimuli or either of these alone. Figure 3 shows the basic presentation alternatives. Visual stimuli can be still frames or motion pictures, drawings, animation, text, charts and graphs—intermixed in any desired order. Auditory stimuli can be speech, music, tones, or any other sound. Presentations can be time-controlled by the machine program or can be paced by the student.

The educator who writes a teaching program for the Mentor specifies what is to be presented to the learner and under what conditions. In addition to linear sequences, he can program review of subject material (Figs. 4 and 5), repetition of items, variation of both content and style of instruction (Fig. 6), branching as a result of single responses

VISUAL MODE   AUDITORY MODE

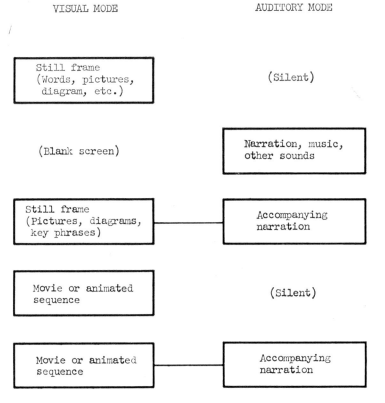

Fig. 3. The presentation alternatives available in programming the Mentor.

Fig. 4. Programming of optional review.

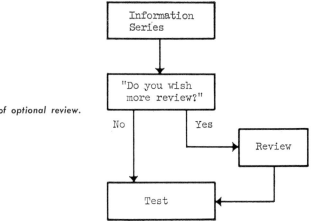

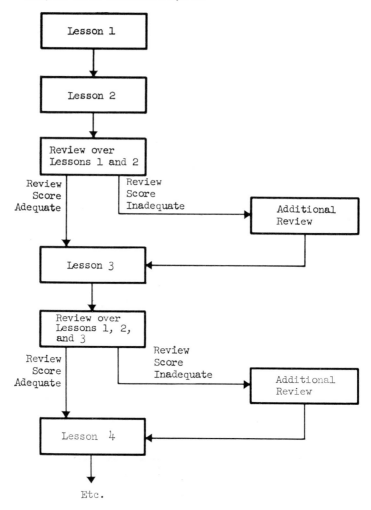

Fig. 5. Programming of periodic review.

or a series of responses (Figs. 7 and 8), and skipping ahead to more challenging topics for faster learners (Fig. 9). The resultant program thus can be highly responsive to the needs of individual learners.

The finished program inputs to the machine are two reels—one of film and one of magnetic tape. The film capacity is 17,000 frames in color or 25,000 frames in black and white.

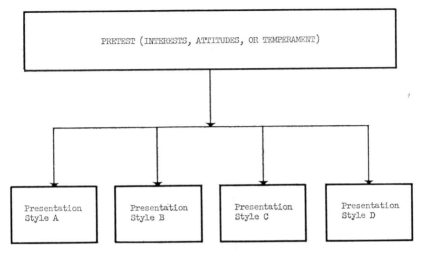

Fig. 6. *Variation of programming style based on student characteristics.*

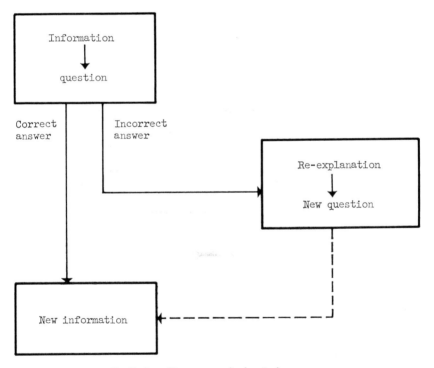

Fig. 7. *Branching as a result of a single response.*

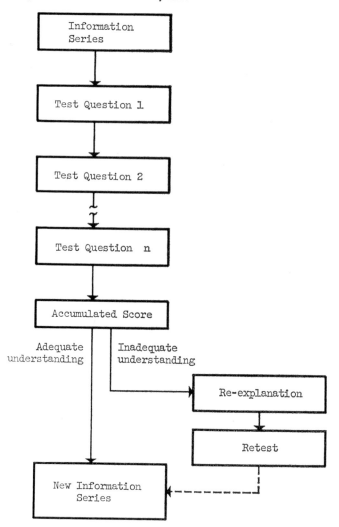

Fig. 8. Branching as a result of a multiple-items test.

A Research Strategy

Given the capability of the equipment we have just described, what is an appropriate research strategy to pursue to achieve our goal of more efficient training procedures?

Obviously a long-term research program is needed to enable us to test hypotheses, redesign the instrumentation, and develop the training programs. Tests of the effectiveness of any particular configuration should not be made on a one-shot basis. They should be made over a sufficient period of time and with enough students to enable us to have some confidence in our answers.

Such a program costs money. And this is a real problem.

When we discuss the requirements of a research program with other people, they usually agree on the basic reasonableness of our approach. But when questions of cost come up, the concensus seems to be that the instrumentation should cost very little. To do the necessary research to determine the requirements for instrumentation, you must presuppose the answers in order to design a simple machine that will not cost much. This is an anomalous position, yet it seems to be the prevailing attitude.

So one of the first tasks in a research strategy seems to be to attempt to change some attitudes about costs.

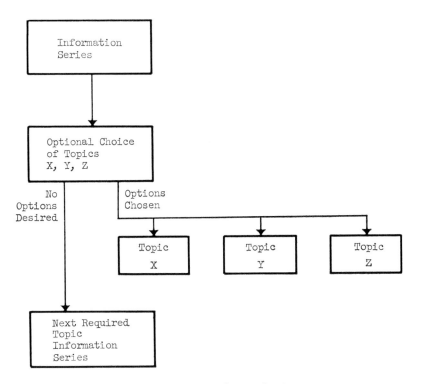

Fig. 9. Programming of optional topics.

The development of an efficient automatic instructional device that cuts training time and reduces training failures would certainly cut training costs in the long run. We need to be concerned with relative, rather than absolute, costs. The relative cost compares the value of the results with the expense of obtaining them. The savings in training costs that could be achieved by the development of efficient procedures are tremendous compared with the expense of developing them.

Once we solve the problem of support, a number of major psychological issues need to be resolved to achieve the greatest automatic tutor effectiveness. A few of these issues are the following:

1. The problem of concept formation. What is the best sequence of ideas and the best means of presenting and developing understanding of concepts? Is it better to start with a whole concept, give the student an overview of where he is going, then break the concept down into its elements and teach each of them separately? Or is it better to start with the elements or parts and build up to the whole?

Does the student learn by manipulating symbols (i.e., words) or is it necessary to help him to invest the symbols with meaning by presenting information in different ways and allowing him to respond to it in different ways?

Is learning facilitated by presenting a student with conclusions and examples and then letting him apply the conclusions to new examples? Or is learning facilitated more by supplying real-life examples of phenomena and letting the student draw the conclusions?

2. The problem of presentation modality. What is the appropriate modality of presentation for different concepts? Are some ideas better learned visually, some auditorily, and some by combinations? Or does it depend on the individual?

3. The problem of individual differences. Is one programming method best for all students, regardless of their abilities, prior knowledge, interests, and preferences? What about different subject matters —are the same programming techniques equally applicable for all kinds of material?

4. The problem of automated tutoring in the educational context. How can machine teaching be used most efficiently in combination with other educational methods—lectures, discussions, homework, laboratories, special projects? What is the most efficient "teaching mix"?

5. The problem of appropriate reinforcement. Are there other effective reinforcers besides knowledge of results? What extrinsic positive reinforcers can be used? Is there any place for negative reinforcement?

6. The problem of interest value of automated tutoring programs. How do you interest a student in a subject? How do you gain his attention and hold it once you have it?

Once we begin to get the answers to some of these questions, it should be feasible to re-evaluate equipment requirements and specify what functional characteristics an ideal automatic tutor should have.

PART III

Computer
Technology
in Automated
Teaching

Automatic computers and teaching machines

HARRY D. HUSKEY

University of California, Berkeley

Interest in teaching machines is very fashionable at the moment, and there is much speculation about their role in education. This is reminiscent of the situation in other fields of endeavor in which people have theoretically extrapolated far ahead of the hard-facts support. For example, before the first electronic computer was put into operation 15 years ago it was obvious how to build a general-purpose stored-program automatic computer. However, for a number of years the delivery time of such computers was always 18 months from whenever you asked. On another level, many years ago Norbert Wiener talked of the social implications of automation, yet it is only in the last year that labor unions have been paying much attention to this problem.

Public interest in new technological developments tends to follow an *underdamped* curve as shown by the solid line in Fig. 1. Because of excessive public enthusiasm in the initial stages, there may be a period when the development is essentially ignored. I feel that the interest in teaching machines has this same underdamped behavior. Therefore, I believe that although a revolution in teaching methods is certain to come we should be cautious in making statements implying the imminent total revamping of the educational system. We should try to operate on a critically damped curve (shown by dashes in Fig. 1).

In an earlier chapter Dr. Carter mentioned that of the seven basic teaching activities (development of thinking, imparting subject matter, developing creativity, developing skills, teaching socialization, encouraging physical development, and child care) probably only one

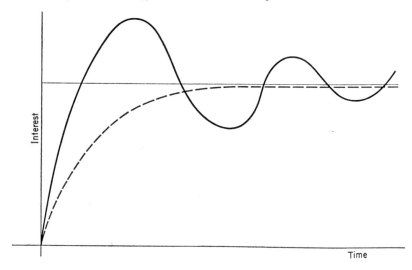

Fig. 1. Underdamped and critically damped response.

can be provided almost entirely by teaching machines. Therefore, in presenting the economics of teaching machines, it must be considered that neither the teacher nor the other facilities of the classroom are replaced. Thus, whatever the cost of teaching machines, it must be added to the current cost of classroom instruction. Its value must be measured in terms of improvement of the end product rather than in terms of substitution for the current process.

Those who are working with computer-controlled teaching machines should not be overly concerned about the need for large inexpensive memories or buffers. There is current work in several laboratories in this country dealing with computer components that are microinches in size and with processes that may permit as many as 10^{12} elements per square inch and perhaps 10^5 layers in a cubic inch. (Note that in 1960 all the books that were printed in the United States had a total of about 10^{14} characters in them.) In terms of more immediately available components, such as thin film devices, the price per bit of computer memory is going to come down by an order of magnitude.

There are problems in designing devices with 10^{10} or more components, but considerable effort is being expended here to explore the possibilities of "self-organization" or of "principles of inductive design."

Therefore, in my opinion the problem with respect to teaching machines is not the requirement for larger memories but the need for much more serious research on the use to which the memories (even small ones) are to be put.

It is not difficult to write control programs for computer-controlled teaching machines. Whenever the researchers in the field can establish a rigorous precise language for describing their procedures, translators can easily be developed to translate these procedures into operating programs for any computer of their choice. At Berkeley work is proceeding on DIALGOL, a language and a translating system designed to help produce new compilers with a minimum of effort. DIALGOL is a dialect of ALGOL,[1] which is an algorithmic language for scientific computation.

The rest of this chapter describes the features of a proposed language suitable for communicating procedures among humans, among machines, or between humans and machines.

Computers and Teaching Machines

The state of a machine-student system, including the components of the reaction of the student to the last stimulus, can be represented by a finite vector whose components are real numbers. This vector can include as much of the past history as desired. In many cases the procedures can be scaled so that the components of the vector are integers. This last case is treated here, and it will be obvious to the reader that the extension to vectors with real components is trivial.

Thus the current status of a machine-student system is given by a vector called the *state vector*. The system operates in the time domain in discrete steps represented by the presentation of information to the student and the acceptance of a response from him. On the basis of the past history and the current response, new material (a frame) is selected from a *library* for presentation to the student. This presentation may include fortifying items as well as new material and questions.

The selection of material can be efficiently described in terms of table-look-up procedures or in terms of functional operations. Thus, using the past history and the current stimulus response, an index, I, may be computed. The item in the library corresponding to I would be the material to be displayed next to the student. In functional notation this would be "Library[I]."

The succession of states through which the machine-student system

[1] Nauer, P. (Ed.) Report on the algorithmic language ALGOL 60. *Commun. Assoc. Computing Machinery*, 1960, **3**, 299–314.

passes has a partial ordering relation of the following character: each state has a unique successor, and each state has one or more predecessors. This is true in either bypass or scrambled programs. The succession of states may be called the *schedule, program chart,* or *flow chart.* In this presentation the term *program chart* is used, since the term "schedule" implies more than is desired about timing of the activity and the term "flow chart" does not sufficiently emphasize the sequential nature of the set of states through which the model passes.

The program chart must specify how each component of the next state vector is derived from the current state vector and the input vector. These specifications are given by *statements.* In some cases the statements develop results by the use of formulas (assignment statements). In other situations the results depend upon the evaluation of functions or the execution of procedures (procedure statements). In still others, and particularly in the over-all program, the order of events must be specified (sequence statements).

Assignment statements may involve arithmetic or logical expressions. These expressions may contain constants, variables, or labels. Ultimately these quantities must be written in terms of specific symbols.

In the next section the syntax and semantics of the proposed language are presented. To make it easy to talk about the language, a very simple meta-language is introduced. Sets of objects need to be defined; for example "letters." The symbols ⟨ and ⟩ around a name, as ⟨name⟩, denote a class of objects called by the identifier "name." A definition symbol " :: = " is used, and the vertical line " | " is a meta-linguistic symbol for "or." Let us consider, for example, the following:

⟨letter⟩ :: = ⟨small letter⟩ | ⟨capital letter⟩
⟨small letter⟩ :: = a|b|c|d|e|f|g|h|i|j|k|l|m|n|o|p|q|r|s|t|u|v|w|x|y|z
⟨capital letter⟩ :: =
    A|B|C|D|E|F|G|H|I|J|K|L|M|N|O|P|Q|R|S|T|U|V|W|X|Y|Z

The materials just presented mean that the classes of objects called *letter* consist of objects in either of two classes called *small letter* or *capital letter.* Furthermore, the class *small letter* consists of precisely the symbols a,b,c, etc. Thus the meta-linguistic symbols translate as

Symbol	Meaning
⟨...⟩	the class ...
:: =	consists of
|	or

Symbols

⟨symbols⟩ ::= ⟨letter⟩ | ⟨digit⟩ | ⟨bracket⟩ | ⟨punctuation⟩ | ⟨operator⟩
⟨letter⟩ ::= A | B | C...X | Y | Z | a | b | c...x | y | z
⟨digit⟩ ::= 0 | 1 | 2 | 3 | 4 | 5 | 6 | 7 | 8 | 9
⟨logical value⟩ ::= **TRUE** | **FALSE**
⟨bracket⟩ ::= (|) | { | } | [|]
⟨punctuation⟩ ::= . | , | ; |
⟨operator⟩ ::= ⟨arithmetic operator⟩ | ⟨logical operator⟩ |
                              ⟨sequential operator⟩
⟨arithmetic operator⟩ ::= + | − | * | / | = | →
⟨logical operator⟩ ::= ⌐ | ∧ | ∨ | = | →
⟨sequential operator⟩ ::= **GO TO** | **DO** | **IF** | **THEN** | **ELSE** | **FOR**
⟨relation⟩ ::= ⟨arithmetic relation⟩ | ⟨logical relation⟩
⟨arithmetic relation⟩ ::= < | ≤ | = | ≠ | ≥ | >
⟨logical relation⟩ ::= ⊃ | ≡ | ≢ | ⊂

Most of the symbols have their conventional meanings. The asterisk, *, denotes multiplication. The arithmetic and logical operators "=" and "→" are used in assignment statements and are read as "replaces." The first three logical operators are called NOT, AND, and OR. Their values, as well as the value of the logical relations, are given in Table 1. The sequential operators are used to specify the sequential dependence of components of the state vector as well as to specify the sequential aspects of the structure of the model as a whole.

Identifiers

⟨character⟩ ::= ⟨letter⟩ | ⟨digit⟩ | #
⟨identifier⟩ ::= ⟨letter⟩ | ⟨identifier⟩⟨character⟩ |
                              ⟨character⟩⟨identifier⟩

The symbol "#" is used to denote a space or a blank; thus JOHN SMITH can be written JOHN#SMITH. Note that the definition of identifiers is recursive. An alternate definition could be: the class called *identifier* consists of all sequences of symbols that can be made from the symbols of the class letter, the class digit, and the space symbol, such that at least one character is a letter. In order to decide if "25joHN#smITH" is an identifier according to the recursive definition, it is necessary to start with one of the *letters* and see if the *chain* of symbols can be reached by suffixing or prefixing elements of the class character.

TABLE 1   VALUES OF LOGICAL EXPRESSIONS

Boolean Expression	Operation	Values TRUE = 1, FALSE = 0			
a		0	1	0	1
b		0	0	1	1
$\neg a$	NOT	1	0	1	0
$a \vee b$	OR	0	1	1	1
$a \wedge b$	AND	0	0	0	1
$a \supset b$	IMPLIES	1	0	1	1
$a \subset b$	IS IMPLIED BY	1	1	0	1
$a \equiv b$	IS EQUIVALENT TO	1	0	0	1
$a \not\equiv b$	IS NOT EQUIVALENT TO	0	1	1	0

The foregoing definition is syntactic; that is, by use of the definition it can be determined whether a chain of symbols is an identifier. On the other hand, it says nothing about the meaning of identifiers. For example, there is no way to tell if JOHN SMITH and JOHNSMITH are equivalent (names of the same object).

Semantics. For practical purposes, two identifiers are said to be equivalent if their first 15 characters are respectively identical. The limit 15 is arbitrary, but it has been found by experience to make it possible to refer to the components of most systems using the appropriate English terms.

Simple Variables

Syntax

⟨simple variable⟩ ::= ⟨identifier⟩ | ⟨integer⟩ | **TRUE** | **FALSE**
⟨integer⟩ ::= ⟨digit⟩ | ⟨integer⟩⟨digit⟩

It is not yet possible to define variables. Therefore, a subclass called *simple variable* consisting of identifiers, integers, or logical values is defined. An integer is a concatenation of digits. The class *variable* consists of simple variables or of subscripted variables. If *integer expressions* had been defined, then subscripted variables could be defined as

⟨subscripted variable⟩ : : = ⟨identifier⟩[⟨integer expression⟩]
    ⟨variable⟩   : : = ⟨simple variable⟩|⟨subscripted variable⟩

As indicated in the introductory material, multidimensional arrays are not considered. Subscripted variables correspond to components of a vector.

Semantics. Variables may be two types, integral and logical. An integer expression is precisely defined below and will be seen to be the integer type (i.e., to have integer value). The symbols [and] enclose the subscript (instead of using below-the-line techniques) as a concession to typewriters and computer input-output devices.

Expressions

To facilitate the discussion of expressions, it will be convenient to classify operators as indicated in Table 2.

TABLE 2   CLASSIFICATION OF OPERATORS

	Operators			
Type	Unitary	Additive	Multi-plicative	Relational
Integer	$+ -$	$+ -$	$*/$	$< \le = \ne \ge >$
Logical	$\neg$	$\vee$	$\wedge$	$\supset \equiv \not\equiv \subset$

The unitary operators occur in such expressions as $+a$, $-b$, or $\neg$HOME (read "not home"). The other operations are binary. The result of a binary operation (not relational) is of the same type as the operands. All binary relations are of **logical** type.

Terms and Expressions

Let v, t, and e be generic representations for members of the respective classes variables, terms, and expressions; that is, v means any variable, and an expression such as v + v means the sum of any two

are used to "call" procedures. After execution of the procedure the process continues with the statement which follows the **DO** statement.

Examples of sequence statements are

> **GO TO** Home
> **DO** Payroll
> **DO** Procedure (Operation Code)

Conditional Statements

⟨conditional statement⟩ :: = **IF**⟨logical expression⟩**THEN**⟨statement⟩|
  IF⟨logical expression⟩**THEN**⟨statement⟩**ELSE**⟨statement⟩|
    ⟨relation expression⟩: ⟨statement⟩|
  ⟨relation expression⟩: ⟨statement⟩**ELSE**⟨statement⟩

The logical expression is any expression of **logical** type (whose value is either **TRUE** or **FALSE**). If the expression is true, then the statement is executed; if not, the statement is skipped. In the case of **ELSE** the statement preceding the **ELSE** is executed if the condition is **TRUE** and the statement subsequent to the **ELSE** is skipped (and conversely if the condition is **FALSE**).

Examples.

> **IF** sick **THEN GO TO** Hospital
> a < b[i + j]: i + 1 → i **ELSE** i − 1 → i

Procedure Statements

⟨procedure statement⟩ :: = ⟨label⟩: {⟨compound statement⟩}
  ⟨compound statement⟩ :: = ⟨statement⟩|
    ⟨compound statement⟩ ⟨punctuation⟩⟨statement⟩

A complex of statements may be enclosed by the begin-end symbols { and } and given a label and may then be used as a unit in the higher level program. The procedure is called into action by a **DO** statement.

Examples.

> SIN X: {(statements which compute the sine of X)}
> ADD: {a + b → c}

For Statements

Let AE stand for an arithmetic expression; then

⟨for statement⟩ :: =
    FOR⟨identifier⟩ = ⟨AE⟩(⟨AE⟩)⟨AE⟩**DO**⟨statement⟩ |
        ⟨identifier⟩ = ⟨AE⟩(⟨AE⟩)⟨AE⟩{⟨compound statement⟩}

Thus the words **FOR** and **DO** may be omitted if the statements are enclosed in the begin-end symbols { and }. A sorting procedure can be written as

SORT: { **FOR** j = 1(1)n **DO**
        i = j(1)n{a[i] < a[j]:
            {a[i] → T, a[j] → a[i], T → a[j]}}}.

Declaration Statements

⟨declaration⟩ :: = ⟨type⟩⟨identifier⟩⟨alternate name⟩⟨sub_tructure⟩
                ⟨dimension⟩⟨value list⟩
    ⟨type⟩ :: = **INTEGER** | **LOGICAL** | ⟨empty⟩
    ⟨alternate name⟩ :: = ⟨empty⟩ | : ⟨identifier⟩
    ⟨substructure⟩ :: = ⟨empty⟩ | : {⟨sublist⟩}
        ⟨sublist⟩ :: = ⟨subitem⟩ | ⟨sublist⟩, ⟨subitem⟩
            ⟨subitem⟩ :: = ⟨identifier⟩(⟨integer⟩ : ⟨integer⟩)
    ⟨dimension⟩ :: = ⟨empty⟩ | (⟨integer⟩)
    ⟨value list⟩ :: = ⟨empty⟩ | ⟨value⟩ | ⟨value list⟩, ⟨value⟩
        ⟨value⟩ :: = = ⟨integer⟩ | = **FALSE** | = **TRUE**

The declaration statements make it possible to specify whether a variable is the **integer** or **logical** type and to provide for the possibility of abbreviated names. They also make it possible to pack information to conserve space in the object computer and to provide for vectors and for the definition of the initial values of variables. Most of the components of a declaration statement may be missing (empty). If a variable is not declared, it is assumed to be integral. (For example, if the variable ABC is not declared, the effect is the same as if the statement "**INTEGER** ABC" appeared.) Unless a variable is an integer, the declaration statement must appear prior to the appearance of the variable in any other kind of statement.

The Program Chart

⟨program chart⟩ : : = ⟨label⟩:⟨compound statement⟩

Syntactically, the program chart is a labeled set of statements. Generally, it will consist of some declaration statements followed by statements that make up the body of the program.

Example

A computer program for controlling a teaching machine is given in Tables 5 and 6 in order to illustrate the use of the foregoing language. The program (Table 6) is universal in that it can process many program tables relating to different subject matter (Table 5). The program table has four main entries. The first is the frame number which is presented to the student at this step. The second entry ranks the button responses that the student pushes. In the example illustrated button number four corresponds to the correct answer. Depending upon the response, there are three possible frames (next frame serial number) which may be presented next. For each frame it is possible to specify three (out of, say, 25) appropriate remarks that may be used to praise or to reprove the student.

The program chart is given in Table 6. The program starts with 12 declaration statements which define the vectors involved in the program and the substructure of two items called ANSWER and NEXT. It is assumed that the complete program involves 500 frames. Thus the items shown in Table 5 are declared to be vectors with 500 components each. For illustration purposes, the remarks specifications are stored in separate words (REMARK1, REMARK2, and REMARK3), whereas the ANSWER RANK and the NEXT FRAME SERIAL

TABLE 5   PROGRAM TABLE, TYPICAL ENTRY

Serial No.	Frame No.	Answer Rank				Next Frame Serial No.			Remarks		
300	512	3	2	5	1	4	326	295	265	5	13	7

TABLE 6   PROGRAM CHART FOR COMPUTER-CONTROLLED
TEACHING PROGRAM

NEXT BUFFER(3),
REMARK(25),
FRAME(500),
ANSWER RANK(500),
NEXT FRAME(500),
REMARK(500),
REMARK2(500),
REMARK3(500),
NEXT BUFFER(3),
ANSWER BUFFER(5),
ANSWER: {ANSWER1(1:4), ANSWER2(5:8), ANSWER3(9:12),
   ANSWER4(13:16), ANSWER5(17:20)},
NEXT: {NEXT1(1:10), NEXT2(11:20), NEXT3(21:30)}.
START: $1 \rightarrow$ i, $1 \rightarrow$ jPAST, $0 \rightarrow$ m, **GO TO** PRESENT.
CONTINUE: NEXT BUFFER [k] $\rightarrow$ i, j $\rightarrow$ jPAST, **IF** m $\neq 0$ **THEN**
   PRESENT REMARK [m].
PRESENT: PRESENT FRAME [i].
 RESPONSE $\rightarrow$ j, ANSWER RANK [i] $\rightarrow$ ANSWER, **DO** SPREAD
   ANSWER;
 NEXT FRAME [i] $\rightarrow$ NEXT, **DO** SPREAD NEXT;
 GO TO CHOICE [ANSWER BUFFER [j]].
   CHOICE [1]: $1 \rightarrow$ k, REMARK1 [i] $\rightarrow$ m, **GO TO** CONTINUE.
   CHOICE [2]: REMARK2 [i] $\rightarrow$ m, $3 \rightarrow$ k, jPAST $< 3:2 \rightarrow$ k **ELSE** $3 \rightarrow$ k;
     GO TO CONTINUE.
   CHOICE [3]: $0 \rightarrow$ m, **IF** jPAST < 4 **THEN** $2 \rightarrow$ k **ELSE** $3 \rightarrow$ k; **GO TO**
     CONTINUE.
   CHOICE [4]: $0 \rightarrow$ m, $3 \rightarrow$ k; **GO TO** CONTINUE.
   CHOICE [5]: REMARK3 [i] $\rightarrow$ m, $3 \rightarrow$ k; **GO TO** CONTINUE.
SPREAD ANSWER: {ANSWER1 $\rightarrow$ ANSWER BUFFER [1], ANSWER2 $\rightarrow$
   ANSWER BUFFER [2], ANSWER3 $\rightarrow$ ANSWER
   BUFFER [3], ANSWER4 $\rightarrow$ ANSWER BUFFER [4],
   ANSWER5 $\rightarrow$ ANSWER BUFFER [5]}.
SPREAD NEXT: {NEXT1 $\rightarrow$ NEXT BUFFER [1], NEXT2 $\rightarrow$ NEXT
   BUFFER [2], NEXT3 $\rightarrow$ NEXT BUFFER [3]}.

NUMBERS are "packed" into words. These items are transferred, respectively, from the vectors into items called ANSWER and NEXT. Then subroutines or procedures called SPREAD ANSWER and SPREAD NEXT (see bottom of Table 6) "spread" the parts into separate computer words, so that they may be readily accessed, using the indexing features.

TABLE 7   SYNTAX SUMMARY

1.1. ⟨letter⟩ ::= a|b|c|...|y|z|A|B|C|...|Y|Z

1.2. ⟨digit⟩ ::= 0|1|2|3|4|5|6|7|8|9

  ⟨logical value⟩ ::= **TRUE**|**FALSE**

1.3. ⟨punctuation⟩ ::= ,|;|.

1.4. ⟨brackets⟩ ::= (|)|[|]|{|}|"

1.5. ⟨arithmetic operator⟩ ::= +|−|*|/|=|→

1.6. ⟨logical operator⟩ ::= ⌐|∨|∧|=|→

1.7. ⟨relation⟩ ::= <|≤|=|≠|≥|>|⊃|⊂|≡|≢|

  ⟨sequential operator⟩ ::= **GO TO**|**DO**|**IF**|**THEN**

2.1. ⟨identifier⟩ ::= ⟨letter⟩|⟨identifier⟩⟨character⟩|⟨character⟩⟨identifier⟩

  ⟨character⟩ ::= ⟨letter⟩|⟨digit⟩|⟨blank⟩

2.2. ⟨integer⟩ ::= ⟨digit⟩|⟨integer⟩⟨digit⟩

3.1. ⟨variable⟩ ::= ⟨identifier⟩|⟨integer⟩|⟨logical value⟩|

  ⟨identifier⟩[⟨integer expression⟩]

3.2. ⟨expression⟩ ::= ⟨term⟩|⟨expression⟩⟨A⟩⟨term⟩|⟨U⟩⟨term⟩|

  ⟨expression⟩⟨R⟩⟨expression⟩

3.3. ⟨term⟩ ::= ⟨variable⟩|⟨term⟩⟨M⟩⟨term⟩|(⟨expression⟩)

3.4. ⟨A⟩ ::= +|−|∨

3.5. ⟨M⟩ ::= *|/|∧

3.6. ⟨U⟩ ::= +|−|⌐

3.7. ⟨R⟩ ::= ⟨relation⟩

  ⟨relation expression⟩ ::= ⟨expression⟩⟨R⟩⟨expression⟩

4.1. ⟨statement⟩ ::= ⟨assignment statement⟩|⟨sequence statement⟩|

  ⟨conditional statement⟩|⟨**FOR** statement⟩|

  ⟨procedure statement⟩|{⟨compound statement⟩}|

  ⟨label⟩:⟨statement⟩|⟨empty⟩|⟨declaration⟩

4.2. ⟨assignment statement⟩ ::= ⟨expression⟩ → ⟨variable⟩

4.3. ⟨sequence statement⟩ ::= **GO TO**⟨label⟩|**DO**⟨label⟩

4.4. ⟨conditional statement⟩ ::= **IF**⟨logical expression⟩**THEN**⟨statement⟩|⟨relation expression⟩:⟨statement⟩|**IF**⟨logical expression⟩**THEN**⟨statement⟩**ELSE**⟨statement⟩|⟨relation expression⟩: ⟨statement⟩**ELSE**⟨statement⟩

4.5. ⟨**FOR** statement⟩ ::= **FOR** ⟨identifier⟩=⟨AE⟩(⟨AE⟩)⟨AE⟩**DO** ⟨statement⟩

4.6. ⟨AE⟩ ::= ⟨arithmetic expression⟩

4.7. ⟨procedure statement⟩ ::= ⟨label⟩:{⟨compound statement⟩}

4.8. ⟨compound statement⟩ ::= ⟨statement⟩|⟨compound statement⟩ ⟨punctuation⟩⟨statement⟩

4.9. ⟨label⟩ ::= ⟨identifier⟩|⟨integer⟩|⟨identifier⟩[⟨integer expression⟩]

4.10. ⟨declaration⟩ ::= ⟨type⟩⟨identifier⟩⟨alternate name⟩⟨substructure⟩ ⟨dimension⟩⟨value list⟩

4.11. ⟨type⟩ ::= ⟨empty⟩|**INTEGER**|**LOGICAL**

4.12. ⟨alternate name⟩ ::= ⟨empty⟩|:⟨identifier⟩

TABLE 7 *(Continued)*

4.13.	⟨substructure⟩ ::= ⟨empty⟩ | :{⟨sublist⟩}
4.14.	⟨sublist⟩ ::= ⟨subitem⟩ | ⟨sublist⟩,⟨subitem⟩
4.15.	⟨subitem⟩ ::= ⟨identifier⟩(⟨integer⟩:⟨integer⟩)
4.16.	⟨dimension⟩ ::= ⟨empty⟩ | (⟨integer⟩)
4.17.	⟨value⟩ ::= ⟨empty⟩ | = ⟨integer⟩ | = ⟨logical value⟩
4.18.	⟨value list⟩ ::= ⟨value⟩ | ⟨value list⟩,⟨value⟩
5.1.	⟨program⟩ ::= ⟨label⟩:⟨compound statement⟩

The entry to the program is labeled START. The statements after START initialize some of the parameters, and then the cycle begins with CONTINUE. There are three incompletely defined statements in the program: PRESENT REMARK, PRESENT FRAME, and RESPONSE. These depend upon the actual teaching machine—that is, upon whether it shows slides, film, or presents the material in some other way and upon the means of recording the student's response. The presenting of remarks may involve lighting indicator lamps, typing information, or using some other type of presentation.

After the frame is presented, the student makes a response (which in the current example is a choice of one of five buttons). This response is recorded as j. There is a "switch" written as **"GO TO** CHOICE [ANSWER BUFFER[j]]" which, depending upon the rank of the answers and the actual button pushed, switches the program into one of five programs labeled CHOICE[1] to CHOICE[5].

For the frame illustrated in Table 5, the fourth button is the correct answer, and the program would go to CHOICE(1). An encouraging remark would be displayed and, as determined by k, frame serial number 326 would be presented next.

The branching in the illustrated program depends in some cases upon the answer to the preceding question. Clearly, the choice programs could be made to depend upon as much of the past history as desired.

Table 7 summarizes the syntactical definitions contained in the body of this paper.

Summary

A language suitable for describing computer programs for controlling teaching machines has been defined and examples illustrating its use have been given. The language is closely related to the algorithmic language ALGOL. Most of the features of this language are operational in a system called NELIAC,[2] which runs on the following computers:

Sperry-Rand M460	IBM 704
Datatron 220	IBM 709
CDC 1604	IBM 7090

Compiling speed on the IBM 704 is more than 1000 704 commands per minute for large problems (it is faster for smaller problems), and the efficiency of the object program compares favorably with other compiler-produced programs. The language described in this paper is sufficiently rich so that, with the addition of a few procedures primarily handling input and output, the compiler for the language can be written in the language itself. With such compiling speeds, the usual technique is to compile-and-run. Corrections are done in source language, and this is sufficiently close to readable English so that the program is its own documentation.

[2] Huskey, H. D., Halstead, M. H., & McArthur, R. NELIAC—A dialect of ALGOL. *Commun. Assoc. Computing Machinery,* 1960, **3**(8), 463–468.

sc
sc

sl
gc
to
re
of
ch
th
ho
th
ph
be
co
ac
sul
ab
hir

a c
my
pro
sol
rec
He
of
will
nur
afte
befc
his
ing
gets
so t
will
T
cal
thes
T
into

Systems considerations in
real-time computer usage

HERBERT M. TEAGER

Massachusetts Institute of Technology

Real-time computer usage, by definition, provides computer solutions at a rate and reaction time appropriate to the particular job being undertaken. This usage can cover a multitude of possible time scales, ranging from hours or weeks, for a very slowly changing process (such as an on-line computer for space probe navigation), to small fractions of a second in other physical processes.

Major considerations in a human-computer coupled system include (1) the class of problems to be solved (and thus the amount of computation needed); (2) the psychological issue of selecting a form of input-output and language that can minimize human reaction time by making it simple to express desires and evaluate results accurately; (3) the selection of appropriate time scales for machine reaction and computation times in order to match and enhance human thought; and (4) the total cost of the system and its cost per computation (i.e., the system capacity and the cost per unit capacity) as compared with other systems.

The first of these issues is clear in the present context: in automated instruction we wish to couple a computer and a human in an intellectual process with time scales on the order of human problem solving and reaction times. Since the last three problems, including the over-

This research took place under the auspices of the M.I.T. Computation Center and M.I.T. Research Laboratory of Electronics. It was supported in part by contract NONR 1811(69) of the Office of Naval Research and by a grant G19910 supplied by the National Science Foundation.

273

even for a language such as ALGOL. The translation problem is independent of the mode of computer usage, but it does assume additional importance in a real-time situation because it interposes the delays of a translation and constant reformulation on the part of the user.

A further problem arises from the constraints of keyboards and punched cards. These constraints cause almost all machine languages, algebraic and otherwise, to be one-dimensional in character and almost completely symbolic. There is an immediate difficulty in attempting to communicate some problems (say, the analysis of an electronic network) in symbolic form rather than a pictorial two-dimensional form; certainly, the consistent use of circuit diagrams and sketches, etc., in published literature tends to indicate that such forms have definite psychological value in stating a problem succinctly. Keyboards, in addition, generally have a relatively small character set compared with the range of symbolisms that might be desired.

Having translated a problem into a symbolic form, a person must concentrate on the transliterations of symbols and then face the painstaking process of operating a keyboard, stroke by stroke, looking constantly for errors. During this procedure he is concentrating most heavily upon avoiding keystroke errors, and all thoughts of his original problem, or even of the program he is copying, have been forgotten.

After the decks are punched the user must wait his turn in a queue for his problem to be run. It is normally a matter of a day or so before the first results come back—generally in the form of a bitter complaint that some convention of the programming language has been misused; and so the process goes until eventually the user receives a printed page or a ream of printed pages in whose columns the insight that he wanted is buried. To uncover the desired information he may resort to hand plots and trials with new data.

From a systems viewpoint, what can be done if this process is now to be carried out in real time?

Of primary importance is the development of graphical input and output facilities that can remove the user from the restrictions of keyboards, limited character sets, and one-dimensional languages. This is not so farfetched as it may sound. The problem of reading the known block printing of *one* person, entered sequentially, is not nearly so difficult as recognizing an unknown handwriting in an unknown orientation. In real-time usage, moreover, uncertainty need not be equivalent to an incorrect recognition, since uncertainty can be communicated to the user for immediate clarification.

This same general concept of bringing errors and inconsistencies immediately to the user's attention and allowing him to make corrections in an appropriate language should materially reduce the frustrations and delays of present-day error correction. It can have a further benefit of saving computer time if the computer program can wait for corrections (and process something else) rather than continuing.

Independent-user consoles and programs for typewritten and graphical input and output languages are being developed at M.I.T. These facilities give every evidence of meeting their design objectives. Graphical-plotted outputs and, to a lesser extent, displays, are also being developed to complete the psychological match between computer and user.

The psychological problem of matching computer reaction time to the user's reaction time forces a solution to the problem of *priorities* among many "simultaneous" users. A user (who after all is entitled to only a fraction of the running time of a computer) probably should not be led to expect that he has the full capacity of the machine at his beck and call. It is possible that he may ask for a computer process that might take hours to terminate or that cannot be terminated at all. He should not request such processes, but, if he inadvertently does, no one else should be delayed because of the request. The user should know what fraction of the machine capacity is his in order to know when to terminate or modify his approach in solving a problem.

Having reserved a place at the computer console, the user should not encounter delays (apart from those for which he is directly responsible) that are not consistent with his fraction of the computer running time.

The user should have reference either to his own previous programs or to general programs without keeping decks of cards or other permanent records in hand. For this purpose, a backup memory (such as a disk file) would have to be organized as an information retrieval system. It is difficult at present to state general requirements for size and organization of this library.

It is generally impossible to predict (for most work of the class being considered) the amount of machine time that will be needed to solve a problem at one sitting. The only reasonable solution, apparently, is to run programs in sequence for fixed periods of time, rather than letting them run to completion in one period. Such time periods might be on the order of a few seconds for a typical large, fast system but would have the effect of scaling all programs, both short and long, almost equally in time. The choice of the time interval would be dictated by the number of users and the fraction of machine time used for nonproductive computation. It would be desirable to aim at a figure of, perhaps, 95% efficiency, where efficiency is defined as the fraction of machine time spent in useful computation.

It is assumed that input-output from all user consoles would normally occur via time-shared "channels," concurrently with all other running programs, and thus the user would have even less chance to feel neglected.

The placing of time limits on the running of programs imposes other constraints upon the total system. If programs are not to be run to completion in one pass, then memories must be expanded (at a proportionate or greater cost), programs shortened (so that all programs can fit in memory concurrently), or some scheme devised for cycling the programs in and out of memory via temporary storage such as tape or disk. Luckily, multiprogrammable hardwares such as "channels" do exist, and the machine cost for cycling need not be large if there is room for at least three programs in memory at the same time —one running, a second on its way in or out, and a smaller third program controlling the scheduling and input-output.

Three additional features of the machine are required at this point. Computers must have a means of protection for nonactive programs, a means of automatically relocating a program at a different memory location than it had during its last cycle, and a system of time clocks, capable of "interrupting" and "trapping" the running program, for setting and observing time intervals.

Scheduling and memory allocation in a system having these features becomes simply a question of interposing short (in terms of memory size) programs among large ones in the cycle. Efficient time sharing with minimum computation can often be provided by such a simple strategy as sorting the program lengths in order, arranging the long programs in decreasing order of length, and interposing the short programs in increasing order. Difficulties exist, however, in achieving this. The major problem concerns the distribution of program sizes. Most programming systems are written with a belief in a Parkinsonian type of law; that is, programs should expand to fill all the available space. This has led in turn to unnecessarily large (all-memory) multipass programming systems. To make such programs, and others to come, usable in a time-shared system, they must be tailored to meet a very reasonable general constraint; they must never occupy more contiguous memory at a given time than is likely to be needed over one time cycle.

The remaining hardware questions pertain to the distance between computer and input-output equipment, the cost and complexity of user input-output equipment (i.e., consoles), and the cost and complexity of buffering equipment.

It appears from our studies that it makes no essential difference to the user where he works, so long as the facilities available provide the right service. There does not appear to be any difficulty in connecting the user to a machine over low-data-rate telephone lines for type-written and handwritten inputs. The single exception to this might be in the provision of graphical cathode-ray tube displays with rapidly changing information, which requires a large fraction of machine time (or additional expensive hardware) just to "maintain" a display. There does not, however, seem to be any real advantage to the user in having this particular form of graphical output. For example, a cheap, high-speed, mechanical digital plotter can operate over tele-phone lines; such a plotter, in addition to providing the same end objective of a graphical output, provides a large-scale "hard copy" for further study.

Thus it would appear that relatively cheap and simple consoles, buffers, and connecting lines are highly adequate. High data rates and voluminous outputs are generally an indication of a poor match between user and machine and a source of delay for the digestion of information.

This discussion would not be complete without some mention of re-liability. With the introduction of solid-state machines, catastrophic failures of main frame hardware are likely to be very uncommon, and the cost of added insurance in the form of many identical small ma-chines is now unwarranted. Troubles are far more likely to occur in electromechanical units, such as backup memory and input-output devices, and mere duplication is not the answer to these problems.

Real-time computer usage, with carefully conceived hardware and software and with the attendant techniques of time sharing, holds the greatest promise for further advancement in computer-aided thought.

Summary

Personal real-time computer usage implies time sharing and multi-programming in addition to an understanding of the psychological problems faced by the user. If a human is to collaborate effectively with a machine, all sources of difficulty leading him to make errors or to slow his comprehension of the man-machine relationship must be eliminated. Such difficulties will otherwise discourage the user or dull the tool.

Major innovations in programming languages, such as graphical languages, and equipment in the form of input-output consoles are needed. Problems also exist in the programming systems, peripheral hardware, and internal workings of the computer itself. These problems are posed, and indicated directions of solution are considered.

To summarize, real-time time-shared computer usage is now feasible and practical. To make it effective and efficient, much thought must be given to psychological, mechanical, and programming considerations. Slavish adaptation of standards that were developed for essentially different usages will only delay the day of more fruitful human-machine cooperation.

Interactions between future computer developments and automated teaching methods

G. ESTRIN

University of California, Los Angeles

We stand in the middle of a technological revolution that has forged an apparently powerful weapon: a new level of combination of elements with rapidly controllable stable states (i.e., memory cells) and threshold detection devices that can be interconnected to produce any desired Boolean function of the inputs (i.e., combinatorial circuits) to achieve a new state of the system. The elements have existed for a long time; what is new is our ability to define and construct complex systems, containing large numbers of elements, that can perform sequences of storage and combinations at high speeds. With such systems it is possible to solve complex problems by sophisticated procedures.

For every problem solved, however, others are created. These new obstacles arise from our present inability to formulate good conceptual models of our operational systems; from our ignorance of the effect of many tiny deviations between the idealized operations assumed in our models and the actual operations of machines in our systems; from limitations in the machines themselves; and from mismatch between the machines and the humans using them.

Great creative effort is required if we are to overcome our lack of

The work reported in this chapter was supported in part by the Office of Naval Research under contract No. 233(52) and reproduction in whole or in part is permitted for any purpose of the United States Government.

understanding of the complex systems we have developed. Paradoxically, this effort must draw upon our human resources at a time when we need to concentrate on the more basic problems of life, including survival in the atomic age. In consideration of the increasing need for educated humans capable of dealing with all these problems, it is clear why the potentialities of automated instruction are being probed.

However, we should not expect to find immediate help from present methods of automated instruction; rather, we may initially expect further sapping of creative talents in order to define effective instructional methods and measures of their effectiveness. Fortunately, one factor may operate in our favor: a conjecture, supported by Roe's experiment,[1] states that any method of programmed teaching results in improvement over unprogrammed methods even when one cannot differentiate between the effectiveness of the different types of programming. This conjecture seems reasonable, but before it is accepted we must be certain that our performance criteria measure actual transfer of knowledge rather than some artifact of the teaching and testing situations.

Goals in Automated Teaching Research

A number of significant tasks may be described for automated teaching research. These tasks, although neither exhaustive nor mutually exclusive, provide a background for a subsequent discussion of developments in computer technology.

Transmission of Defined Bodies of Knowledge

This category includes what may be called well-bounded sets of information. One example might involve drill in mental or manipulative skills in which both the elements and the well-defined structural characteristics of a body of knowledge are to be transmitted. If a human teacher were attempting to teach vocabulary, he would undoubtedly seek to use context at a level at which a machine could not compete. However, the human and machine teachers are not mutually exclusive, and the machine may aid the teaching process using

[1] Roe, A. *Automated teaching methods using linear programs.* University of California at Los Angeles: Department of Engineering, December 1960. (Report No. 60-105)

highly constrained methods for which it is efficient. Examples of such well-bounded training problems are contained in the programs of Uttal and his group at IBM (Stenotype and German language courses), Licklider's vocabulary training, and Senders' flight-trainer tracking skills. In these programs (described in other chapters of this book) there would be little argument about a measure of performance.

Transmission of Poorly Known or Unbounded Bodies of Knowledge

This category includes concept formation and transmission of working methods that are tested by problem solving. The set of problems used as a measure of teaching effectiveness is always subject to criticism, and one-to-one correspondence between the information transmitted and that fed back is lost. Perlis' experiments in teaching programming, the applications of Crowder's and Skinner's methods, and the training in graphical communication by Licklider's group fall more in this category, as do most programmed teaching efforts.

Test of Models of Human Behavior or of Approaches to Automated Teaching Based on Such Models

Classically controlled multiparameter behavioral experiments attempt to test hypotheses, compare programming methods, or use the programs themselves as probes of behavioral patterns. A great need exists for an experimental tool that can be modified with very small cost in effort and time so that experimentation using several approaches is not discouraged. It is with relation to this flexibility that the role of special purpose teaching aids and general purpose installations must be considered.

Improvement of Man-Machine Symbiosis

If computers are to be used economically in automated teaching, appropriate man-machine interaction, or symbiosis, is required. This fact is implicitly recognized in the design of the System Development Corporation "CLASS" and the Illinois "PLATO II," described elsewhere in this book.

In the communication of information from man to machine detailed notation must be used to prevent ambiguity. This same detailed notation, however, causes inefficient processing of information transmitted from machine to man. Teager, Uttal, Licklider, and Chapman, and in a general way Perlis and others working on information processing languages, have creatively engineered powerful means of communication by which excessive notation is eliminated.

A further example of man-machine symbiosis is provided by John Senders' observation of the significant improvement in a trainer performance test when the trainee was given sufficient information and time to learn the trainer characteristics.

The next section of this chapter describes forthcoming advances in computer systems that offer potential aid to the effectiveness of teaching methods. A reciprocal effect is also probable. Automated teaching must influence the problem-solving capabilities of all future automata, since computational tools can fully succeed only if methods of communication between man and machine are vastly improved.

Modern Computer Developments

By far the most dramatic advances in computer technology have come in the introduction of new components. Almost daily, new applications of solid-state phenomena to switching and storage are announced. We may inquire as to the effects of these innovations on automated teaching.

The speed of switching and storage elements has been increased to the point where the limitations in performance of complexes of these elements arise from the linear circuit elements, interconnections, and distances associated with simultaneous excitation or observation of an ensemble. For some time it has been possible to change the state of individual elements in 10^{-9} second, but ensembles in advanced systems lose two orders of magnitude in performance relative to that number. This difficulty is being overcome by the use of microminiaturization and of techniques to produce more complex circuit elements. Although initial development in this work has not maintained the performance of individual simpler elements, they are evolving constantly higher performance.

How are these developments related to the objectives of automated teaching? It has been pointed out that higher performance of individual elements permits more sophisticated processes to be effected in a given time. Much of the motivation for recent computer developments has come from our defense and space efforts and has thus resulted in computer complexes requiring very little power or weight and capable of operation over large environmental extremes. These particular characteristics may become significant in the first "moon classroom," but by far the more significant factor for our objectives is the reduced cost resulting from mass-production techniques. The initial investment that permits production lines to produce large volumes of partly controlled, partly categorized semiconductor devices is very large; such funding would not ordinarily be available unless the market were guaranteed. Workers developing automated teaching systems and devices should utilize elements that are in large-volume use, with resulting quality and cost benefits. At the same time, they should remain alert to the more glamorous components announced in the press, advertisements, and technical literature.

The memory cells and combinatorial elements that formerly used electron beams in high vacuum now use either the control of flow of electronic charge in solid-state semiconductors or the control of the orientation of precessing bound electrons in solid-state magnetic materials. These elements take the form of two-terminal unidirectional diodes; three-terminal (or more) amplifying switch transistors; multi-wired ferrite toroids; and magnetic path closures through elementary areas of ferromagnetic metal surfaces on moving media in the form of tapes, cylinders, and disks. The storage elements at the output of systems are still primarily in marks, holes in paper, and opaque areas of photographically processed media. Research and development laboratories are making remarkable progress in the use of other solid-state phenomena such as superconductivity and electroluminescence and in the development of techniques of control of semiconductor, ferromagnetic, conducting, and insulating properties of thin films. These efforts, if successful, will permit the automatic production of components and full systems in, conceptually, the same manner as the simple elements themselves.

The detailed properties of the elements are of concern to those deeply involved in the research and technology of computer components. Those concerned with computer *systems* generally face these elements after they are combined with conductors, insulators, resistors, connectors, motors, positioning devices, and power sources to define complexes with prescribed input and output information-processing characteristics. These complexes may be simple printed circuit cards containing groups of memory cells or combinatorial elements; structured configurations such as counters, adders, or multipliers; large specialized memory complexes in which individual elements or groups may be randomly accessed; memory complexes in which the elements periodically pass an observing station; or conceptually infinite tape memories in which the information is sufficiently preordered so that it can be programmed to appear at an observation point at a desired time in a complex information-processing activity.

Improved methods for interconnecting the foregoing complexes have made it possible for the modern giant general-purpose and special-purpose computer installations to be produced at an amazing rate. Moreover, the use of computers in automating the system design procedures has considerably reduced the differential between the production cost of many-of-a-kind computer systems and that of reasonably conventional few-of-a-kind computer systems.

The crucial motivating influence in the trend to large general-purpose computer installations is still the resulting decrease in cost per computation. This lower cost per computation is achieved by the lower cost per element, the ability to use techniques permitting higher speeds of operation, the use of multiple processors and storage complexes sharing common parts of the system, and the use of the large computer itself for compilation of groups of programs for more efficient handling. The trend toward still lower cost per computation has also resulted in procedures that come even closer to the problems faced by this symposium: that is, methods by which the large installation is continuously given a supply of independent problems. Machine system efficiency may be maximized, by one criterion at least, if every component processes information all the time (assuming that most of the machine time is spent in effective computational manipulations). This goal may be approached if one has the following conditions: many distributed sources of problems and related data; mechanisms capable of scanning those sources and delivering the problem statements and data to simultaneously operating memories in the central computer, under control of supervisory programs capable of feeding pieces of independent programs to high-speed internal processors in some suboptimal procedures; and mechanisms for delivering answers to the distributed outputs of the system, thereby making room for new problem inputs.

Work is currently in progress on computer complexes having the characteristics just described. The simultaneous sets of operations in the system are called "multiprocessing." Automatic time sharing of common pieces of the system for different problems is called "multi-programming." Sequential scanning that gathers and distributes procedures and data is called "multiplexing." The rate at which new problems can enter the computer complex is partly determined by the length of time required for humans to digest answers and formulate questions and, therefore, depends on the types of output displays available, the strength of languages developed for communicating new questions to the machines, the time required to communicate with distant sources, and the prior training of the humans interacting with the system.

This computer complex must deal with many of the basic problems faced by an automated classroom. The linking of man and machine is the weakest part of the system itself. The invention of display devices that can give essential structural information in a set of numbers representing a problem solution and of efficient languages that are not restricted by excessive detail is far behind the component and internal system development. Some systems contain sophisticated display and input devices, but these are very costly and their cost is multiplied because they are needed at the distributed outposts of the system.

In contrast to the high-cost devices for communication between computer and man are the mass-produced systems invented for the improvement of information transfer from man to man. The latter include the television set, moving picture and slide projectors for visual display, the tape and disk recorder-reproducers for aural display, and the typewriter keyboard and facsimile systems for input. Some automated teaching systems seek to improve communications by using a computer program to control the sequencing of a very large set of man-to-man information transfer devices. Others use the computer system to generate sequencing programs that can be applied within the constraints of special-purpose teaching devices.

Computer control of human-to-human displays is conceptually desirable, but it does not complete the loop of human interaction with machines. We must still remain alert to the many efforts to conceive automata that are capable of higher level activities such as pattern recognition, perception, generalization, and self-organization. Attempts to produce such automata, capable of imitating animal behavior (which we admire greatly but poorly understand), have naturally absorbed a tremendous amount of intellectual energy: these attempts will produce, at the very least, exciting by-products in both automatic devices and formulation and filtering of behavioral and biological models. It is quite likely, however, that sophisticated cognitive devices attempting to match man and machine will not be available in the near future. This does not mean that we should discontinue the effort to develop cognitive devices. It does mean that we must possibly face a longer term program for the training and development of a mechanism whose adaptive capabilities are well established, that is, the human being.

We are rushing headlong into an age in which control of nature and of our society will be largely dependent on our ability to interact with information-processing machines. Recognition of this fact should make us consider the introduction of training for effective interaction with machines at the earliest levels of education. Our society has grown enormously through development of speech, reading, writing, art, music, and a technology permitting mass distribution of information. In general, manipulative skills such as keyboard manipulation have served a "middleman" function, independent of feedback. If the development of these manipulative skills can be made an added educational objective of the 12 to 20 years of education devoted to an individual in our society, we may be able to establish a far greater guarantee of success in reaping benefits from information-processing systems. This is not to say that we should diminish the development of the obviously powerful human skills that can be used creatively in the absence of a transistor or an electric light. It does suggest that we seek to develop manipulative skills in a machine environment containing time lags and displays characteristic of our information-processing systems and that these methods be incorporated in the set of educational objectives. If such an educational objective is achieved, while concurrently the purely human values are raised, it will be possible to develop and implement automated teaching procedures and more powerful use of information-processing systems.

Index